Anne Kursinski's
RIDING AND JUMPING CLINIC

Anne Kursinski's RIDING AND JUMPING CLINIC

A STEP-BY-STEP COURSE FOR WINNING IN THE HUNTER AND JUMPER RINGS

Anne Kursinski with
Miranda Lorraine

TRAFALGAR SQUARE
North Pomfret, Vermont

First published in paperback in 2011 by
Trafalgar Square Books
North Pomfret, Vermont 05053

Original hardcover edition published in 1995 by Doubleday
A division of Bantam Doubleday Dell Publishing Group, Inc., New York, NY

ISBN: 978-1-57076-496-7
Library of Congress Control Number: 2011934728
BOOK DESIGN BY CLAIRE VACCARO

COVER DESIGN BY RM DIDIER

Printed in the United States of America

10 9 8 7 6 5 4 3 2

Contents

PART IV ✻ ADVANCED JUMPING

PART V ✻ HORSEMANSHIP

PART VI ✻ SHOW PREPARATION

PART VII ✱ COURSES

PART VIII ✱ GOALS

Preface to the Paperback Edition

I am extremely pleased. My book is going into its second edition! When I first wrote this book in the early 1990's, I had no idea it would be so well received. I simply put into words my philosophy and the system I believe in. A system I developed and refined from life experience and time spent with fine mentors, both human and horse. My hope was to give back and teach future riders and horses.

Today I continue to have people tell me how much they learn from reading and rereading this book. It has helped them win competitions or overcome particular problems with their horses. Some have told me they keep it by their beds, others in their tack trunks. Several colleges use it as a textbook for their equine studies classes. I am always thankful for this positive feedback.

In 1995, when *Riding and Jumping Clinic* was published, I had been on three U.S. Olympic Teams, a Pan American Team, several World Cup Finals and two U.S. World Equestrian Teams. Since the book has been in print, I won another Olympic Silver Medal in Atlanta in 1996, competed in my third World Equestrian Games, and went to my fifth Olympic Games in Hong

Kong 2008 as the alternate rider where the U.S. won the Gold Medal. I have had a wonderful career with amazing horses, owners, and adventures!

Throughout my career, all my horses and students have used the exercises in this book. My passion for excellence, discipline, attention to detail, and great horsemanship I continue to share with riders and trainers. My philosophy of learning correct basics, understanding how to communicate with your horse, and always being your best, are timeless concepts. With consistent practice and application I have seen horses and riders change dramatically.

I am still riding, training and competing. I love riding horses! There is nothing like watching and feeling horses learn, develop, and change—physically, mentally and emotionally. I get tremendous pleasure from producing great horses. I found "Avenue Blue" as a green four-year-old in Germany and brought him along to be a circuit champion in Wellington, Florida and Grand Hunter Champion at Lake Placid. Of course, my most famous partnership has been with Eros. We started together in 1992 when he was a five-year-old from Australia. In 1996 we won an Olympic Silver Medal together in Atlanta. For years we won international Grand Prixs and Nations Cups. Eros is retired on my farm in New Jersey now at the age of 24. He has been an amazing teacher and lifelong friend!

I truly enjoy teaching riding. I give several clinics throughout the year. Riders come and work with me at my farm Market Street when I am home. Having taught for quite a long time, occasionally I have riders tell me they worked with me years ago and still can hear my voice ringing in their ears! I hope what they hear is mostly good!

This summer I had a new experience, traveling to Europe with the U.S. Young Riders Team. This is exciting and new for our U.S. show jumping young riders to get experience on Nations Cup teams while under 21 years old. These kids are the future of our sport. I enjoy sharing my training and competing experience with these riders in an international setting.

I intend to continue teaching the art of riding, training, and horsemanship to future generations. For me, there are no short cuts. To be a true winner, there are no substitutes for hard work and dedication. They have served me well.

I am extremely thankful to all of the horses in my life. I would not have accomplished so much without them. The horses have been my greatest teachers!

Anne Kursinski
2011

FOREWORD

Anne Kursinski and I have lives that seem to intertwine. We've known each other for almost two decades and we're actually almost related. My family's closest friend in Connecticut married Anne's uncle in Pennsylvania, where on many weekends I stopped en route to and from Charlottesville, Virginia, while attending the University of Virginia. Of course Anne wasn't around at that time, but common ground was established.

Anne first came to my attention and impressed me while I was judging on the West Coast. She was not a stylist in the conventional sense of the word at that time; she grew into that. What I particularly noticed was her "hungry" attitude. She was aggressive and positive and didn't care that she did not come from the cookie-cutting mold. With her bold approach and great "eye" for a distance, I knew, even way back then, that this girl would probably go on to Olympic and professional status. Jimmy Williams, her mentor and teacher, knew it too, I'm sure.

In the very early eighties there was quite a distance between California and the Northeast of the

United States, not only in mileage but also in the level of top-class show jumping. Anne was itching to see the world, spread her wings, and go for the "Big Time." Kathy Kusner, Melanie Smith, and I all encouraged her. It was the right time for her to leave the nest, hard as it would be to separate herself from family, friends, and especially Jimmy. Coincidentally, just at that time I was in a position to offer Anne both a home base at my New Jersey farm, Hunterdon, and a ride on one of the fanciest grand prix jumpers in the United States. A friend and former client of mine, Tom Everhart, owned the horse and had sent it from Rodney Jenkins to Conrad Homfeld. Now this fabulous gray, Third Man, was available *again*. His new jockey would be Anne Kursinski, and a great partnership it would turn out to be.

From that moment on Anne and I have worked together side by side. I have never taught Anne; she has learned what she has from me mostly by association, a powerful teaching tool. By incorporating my ideology into her already very strong system, Anne has ended up just the way I hoped she would: an Olympic star, a professional, and a most popular, capable teacher and trainer. And what is most important to me is the way she does it all. With class!

Anne, with Miranda Lorraine, has a lot to tell us and to show us in her RIDING AND JUMPING CLINIC. To teach really well one must be able not only to explain but also to demonstrate. A picture is worth a thousand words. And with Anne's succinct style, in both teaching and riding, she is able to convey through the medium of this book exactly what she wants the reader, her student, to learn.

Being a product of practical jumping horsemanship, classical jumping horsemanship, and dressage, Anne Kursinski really has had it all. Very few people in the hunter/jumper industry can boast such a comprehensive background. There is no question that her system and ideology work for the hunter, jumper, and equitation horse and rider. But the wonderful thing is that she has stuck by the most important element of all: simplicity. Because Anne's techniques are so natural and correct she is able to convey all to us in a most direct, simple way. To teach something, be it elementary or advanced, in a simple way is what good teaching is all about.

Nowadays most riding enthusiasts appreciate the value of the exercise approach to the sport. Anne utilizes this modern concept to the fullest. She has described and shown us in detail many, many invaluable exercises both on the flat and over jumps, the springboard toward a good show-ring performance. Now if you concentrate on the work at hand, this very instructive book will do its job.

George H. Morris
Pittstown, New Jersey

INTRODUCTION

*A*s an international-level rider who is also a teacher, I spend a lot of time watching other riders; my regular students at home, those who come to clinics that I give around the United States and abroad, and my fellow competitors at shows in this country and around the world. To further both my students' education and my own, I'm always looking for the elements that make a particular rider successful—and those that get in the way of success.

What I've found consistently is that the one key ingredient for success is a thorough grounding in the basics of riding. Natural talent, no matter how great, can't make up for a lack of basic knowledge and skills—but solid basics, combined with real desire and commitment, can make any rider a good rider. As I tell my students, if you want to improve and you're willing to put in the time, patience, and effort to master the basic skills one by one, you can go as far as you want to go.

That's where this book comes in. Step by step, in pictures as well as words, it gives you the program I've developed to teach the basics that are essential to quality riding in every branch of the sport. Whether you are a seasoned competitor or a beginner, naturally gifted or simply eager to learn, by following the program I've laid out here you will steadily, week by week, increase both the quality of your riding performance and the pleasure you derive from the time you spend with your horse.

That's a fairly bold claim, but one I feel confident in making because the program I'm going to give you is a tested one. It's the same program that carried me to two gold medals at the 1983 Pan American Games and a silver medal at the 1988 Olympics. It's also the program I have used for many years with riders who have sought my help — from novice amateurs to United States Equestrian Team members, from hunter-jumper riders to three-day-event competitors, and to dressage enthusiasts.

Putting this program together has been a gradual process. At every step in my own development as a rider, I've watched and listened to the best and the brightest horsemen I could find, analyzing what they did and sifting out ideas and techniques that I've felt would enhance my own performance. (That, by the way, is a practice I recommend to you — because, while I'm sure my program can help you, I would never say that my way is the only way, or that what I do cannot be improved upon. In fact, I'm still watching and listening — I can always learn something that will make me a better rider and horseman.)

My equestrian education has come from a base as broad as the spectrum of interests that my students today pursue. Looking back at all the riders and all the ideas that have influenced me, I owe special thanks to three teachers. First, I am eternally grateful to Jimmy Williams, a California hunter-jumper legend and my first trainer, who frequently embroidered lessons at the Flintridge Riding Club with unconventional but effective ideas from his movie stunt-riding days. He taught me how to think like a horse and to understand "feeling" (a very basic concept to my program, and one that I'll explain shortly). Along with all he taught me himself, Jimmy introduced me to dressage rider Hilda Gurney, an Olympic bronze medalist who led me to know and understand classical dressage theories and showed me how to apply them in training and competing a horse from first level to Grand Prix. Hunter-jumper coach and rider George Morris gave me encouragement, refined and focused my education as a rider and a horseman, introduced me to giving clinics, and enabled me to become competitive on the international jumper circuit.

Wonderful and invaluable as these three mentors have been for me, the many different horses I've had as partners — from babies to Olympic stars — have taught me more than any person could. I got into this sport because of a love of the animal — the horse. He is beautiful and often elegant, athletic and fast, honest and kind. Why does he do all of the crazy things we humans ask of him, and do them so willingly? I have learned that your horse will teach you almost all you need to know, if you will only *listen* to him and allow him to educate you.

THE BASICS
BEHIND THE BASICS

One point that all three of my mentors made increasingly clear to me, and that I want to make equally clear to you, is that there are no magic tricks to good riding. The way a professional makes riding look easy comes from hard work—not secrets or sorcery, but years of disciplined practice. So I do not promise that advancement will be yours overnight if you follow my program. Even with the help of more photographs than most riding books present, some of the techniques I'll describe will require a good deal of patience and perseverance to master. But I *do* promise that, if you stick with the program, advancement will come.

From what I've said so far, you've probably already gathered that your attitude is all-important to your success in my program. Four qualities In particular must underlie all your efforts: positive thinking, honesty, patience, and "feeling."

1. Think Positively

Positive thinking gives you a head start in any endeavor, athletic or otherwise. Part of the positive thinking you'll need in my program involves your attitude toward it: I want you to trust what I say. You may be wondering how much you'll be able to learn from reading a book instead of having me right there to answer your questions—but the fact is that, even if you were one of the students who comes to me every week, instead of answering your questions as they come up I'd tell you to hold them and let the program work for you. If you approach these exercises trusting that what I tell you to do will work if you follow my directions conscientiously, you'll find that all the pieces will fall into place.

Another part of positive thinking involves your attitude toward your own performance. If you decide ahead of time that your horse is going to spook at a funny-looking jump, he probably will—because you rode yourself into the problem by telling yourself and him that lie was going to. If, on the other hand, you decide that he'll have no need to spook if you ride him confidently to the jump (but you also have a plan for dealing successfully with a problem if it happens), he probably won't spook—or at least won't do it anywhere near as badly. Set reasonable goals, expect yourself to meet them, and most of the time you will. And when you assess your progress, compare the performance you've just completed with your own earlier performance, not with anybody else's.

One more hint about expectations: I found early on that whenever I ride with the idea that I have weeks, or even months, to get a particular point across to my horse or myself, I get it across quickly. But if I put myself in a pressure cooker—"I have to accomplish this in the next five minutes!"—I actually *lose* ground. Know where you're going in the long term, but break that overall goal down into small, manageable increments (dependably riding round circles, for example), and appreciate yourself when you accomplish one. There's nothing like recognizing that you've achieved one goal to give yourself a head start on the next one.

2. Be Honest

Although you might not expect it to, honesty goes hand in hand with positive thinking. You need to be honest with yourself, right from the start, about your own and your horse's current level of education and fitness, and about the time, effort, and money you are able to invest in your riding. Don't ignore shortcomings; identify them as factors you can recognize and deal with—and recognize good qualities, too. (A horse's good mind and heart can cancel out a lot of minuses in movement and looks.)

Assess yourself as well as your horse. Consider your own fitness, for example. As a rider, you're an athlete; to ride your best, you have to be in the best physical condition you can be. How fit you are—how trim, how supple, and how strong—affects the length of time you can ride effectively. Don't push yourself beyond what you can do—exhaustion leads to frustration and bad temper. Instead, do an exercise for five minutes and then walk for five, using the break to think about what you just did and what you need to do differently when you try again. And use some of your out-of-the-saddle time for exercise—regular walking, swimming, or bicycling, for example—to build strength and suppleness and trim any extra weight you may be carrying. (If you've been thinking of how heavy and stiff your horse is, think again—*you* may well be the one who's heavy and stiff.)

Be aware, too, of the personality you bring to the sport. Are you the laid-back type, passive, even "wimpy"? Or are you a Type A, aggressive about achievement and wanting to see improvement *now*? Recognizing the kind of person you are will give you a handle on using that personality to your advantage. If you know you have a temper, recognize that you're going to have to keep it in check; if you find yourself wanting to beat up on your horse, remember that, in some way, you are the one who's making him ineffective. You won't progress until you find out how you're impeding yourself and fix it. You are responsible for you!

Structure your riding time to fit your natural timetable and your horse's schedule. If you know you're a morning person, for example, try to find a way that you can ride early in the day, when you're at your best. Remember that your horse is even more a creature of habit than you; if he's expecting dinner at 4 P.M., don't arrive at his stall with bridle and saddle at three fifty-five. (If that's the only time you can ride, arrange to have him given part of his meal a couple of hours ahead of time, so that you aren't asking him to work on an empty stomach.)

3. Be Patient

Patience can be a hard quality to maintain, but it's vital to training, and it's easiest to preserve if it's supported by understanding. Recognize the difference between your role and your horse's. You're the brains of the partnership. His capacity for learning is quite small; like a child, he needs your patient repetition to absorb what you want to teach him. You must learn to think the way he does—enough, at least, to present what you want him to learn in a way that lets him learn it. Take your time.

Recognize, too, that you and your horse each have tolerance levels, physical and mental, beyond which—no matter how much you want to keep going—fatigue and frustration set in and productivity stops. As you advance in the program, you'll expand your capacity for work, and his, but the limits will never disappear entirely. Get to know the signs that tell you one of you is reaching a limit, and stop before you get there.

If something you're trying to accomplish isn't going well, remember something Jimmy Williams used to say: "A smart person changes his mind; a fool never does." Be smart enough to stop and really think about what's happening and what you may need to change in what you're doing—even if that means getting off your horse and finishing for the day. One thing that's always useful if you're having trouble with an exercise (and a good way to wind up a difficult session on a positive note) is going back to the previous exercise. Your horse will benefit from the refresher, and so will you.

Repeated instances of "not getting through" may mean that you're doing something wrong and not realizing it—if your basic position is incorrect, for example, you may be giving your horse a very different message from the one you think you're sending. Seek out a professional trainer to watch you work and tell you where the block is. One or two sessions with a knowledgeable observer should be enough to get you back on track.

If, along with "not getting through," you find yourself increasingly struggling to control your temper or overcome feelings of frustration or failure, the expert who will probably do you the most good is a sports psychologist. (A nearby university with a strong sports program, or the trainer of a local professional sports team, may be able to give you a reference.) Bring a tape recorder along to your appointment; ask questions, and review the session on tape after you get home. Approach the advice you get with a "try it" attitude. If it works right away, great; if it doesn't, give it some more time; in a few days you may see its usefulness more clearly. Not every point that a sports psychologist makes, or that I mention in this book, will click immediately, but eventually it will. Most of us get more out of what we hear or read the second or third time around.

4. Develop "Feeling"

When I talk about "feeling," I'm talking about a very special quality—and one that is the basis of every real success you'll ever have as a rider. At the most fundamental level, "feeling" is being constantly aware of your horse, of everything he's telling you—because he's talking to you all the time—and of everything you're saying back to him.

The first time somebody put you on a horse in a riding ring, you probably didn't hear a thing your horse was saying—because your mind was so full of what *you* were doing and feeling and hearing from your instructor. Some riders, unfortunately, never get past that point; a gifted few bypass it entirely and are aware of the conversation from the first time they sit on a horse.

Fortunately, "feeling" is something you can learn. The first thing to learn—and something I'll be reminding you of continually—is awareness that there is a conversation going on. Once you know it's happening, you'll want to listen to it, and eventually you'll become a skilled participant.

The language of the conversation, of course, derives from your and your horse's actions and reactions. The first times you try to converse in any language, there are some stutters, some garbled words, and some odd constructions; with practice, though, you absorb the grammar and syntax and pronunciation and rhythm. In riding, too, some humbling and stumbling are inevitable; you move awkwardly and self-consciously. But the simple fact that you know you are trying to talk to your horse (and listen to him) with your body will help you focus on the "feeling"; eventually the comprehension and the fluency you want will develop. You'll be *communicating* with your horse.

Some people are born with more "feeling" than others, but anyone who really wants to can develop it. And to be the best rider you can be, "feeling" is crucial; with it, you and your horse will be on the same wavelength. As Jimmy Williams used to put it (and I can't think of a more valuable thought to pass on to you): "The sign of a great rider is a happy horse." With "feeling," you'll have the key to a happy horse.

I.

BASIC
FLAT WORK

CHAPTER ONE

WHY FLAT WORK?

To me, flat work is something you do for your horse and yourself. For him, flat work provides the same benefits that an aerobics class does for you: it develops athletic ability and suppleness, making him better able to stretch, bend, lengthen, and shorten. It also makes him more responsive to your aids. For you, flat work presents an opportunity to develop "feeling": to become more aware of what your horse is doing and how you influence him, which will enable you to control him better.

The skills you'll develop in flat work—straightness, lengthening and shortening, turning—will be useful over fences as well. Remember, though, that my program is a structured one, so resolve to master flat work now, before you go on to jumping, because if you can't accomplish a movement on the flat, you won't be able to do it over fences, where every shortcoming you have becomes magnified, and where speed and continual changes in balance will complicate your efforts.

A "FEELING" PREVIEW

Before you head for the tack room, I'd like you to start working on developing feeling with a very simple exercise from the ground. *Watch* your horse move at the walk, trot, and canter—as a friend longes him, or as he is just loose in the field. Put one of your hands in the other and squeeze with the rhythm of the gait as you watch what your horse does with his back, his neck, and his head at each gait.

Keep watching and squeezing to imprint his rhythm and his motion in your mind; that's the motion you're going to want to work in harmony with, like a skater or a dancer with a partner. At first, you're simply going to want to be aware of that movement and "go with the flow." As your balance improves, you'll be able to progress from just following his movement to influencing it—to "leading."

ASSEMBLING YOUR EQUIPMENT

The key words in selecting clothing and equipment for you and your horse are *safe, simple,* and *effective.*

Your clothing should complement your efforts, not restrict them or burden you.

1. *Always* wear an approved hunt cap. I use one with the safety harness properly fastened. (Accidents wouldn't happen if we knew ahead of time they were going to. Since we don't, we have to be prepared.)
2. Choose a shirt, jacket, and pants that fit well, without billowing (which could cause a spook) or binding. I prefer breeches, but jeans and well-fitting chaps will do.
3. Gloves provide a better grip than bare skin and protect hands from blisters and cuts.
4. Boots should have heels and ribbed rubber soles. Again, I prefer polished riding boots (to go with the breeches), but polished paddock boots are fine with chaps.

Select workmanlike tack and make its condition your responsibility. (In too many clinics, I've found riders who don't realize their stirrup leathers or girths are so cracked, or the stitching around the buckles is so rotted, that they're about to break.) And remember that if you regularly school in very mild tack you can move up just a notch when you show (though don't make show day the first time your horse has had that new bit in his mouth!) and obtain extra control without being severe.

1. Use a plain snaffle and no martingale for schooling, if possible. If you school in minimal equipment, you'll learn to apply your aids both more subtly and more effectively.

Fig. 1 I prefer a drop cavesson for schooling because it helps to keep the horse's mouth closed and his mind on his job. It gives me the feeling that I have a good connection to his mouth. A regular hunter cavesson or a figure eight is fine, too.

2. For showing, you can move up to a slow-twist snaffle, or a stronger bit, and add a martingale, if necessary.

Choose a jumping saddle that's comfortable for you and your horse. Use the following checks for fit (you'll need a friend's help with a few of them):

1. Place the saddle farther forward on his back than normal, with the pommel just behind the peak of the withers. Then move it back by firmly pressing the pommel down and back until his conformation stops the progress.

2. Standing at the girth, look at the relationship of pommel to cantle; the cantle

Fig. 1

should be an inch or two higher than the pommel. If the cantle is even with or lower than the pommel, the tree of the saddle is probably too narrow in front for the horse. (If the horse has high, narrow withers and a very downhill topline, move to Step 4. If there's adequate clearance, you may just need extra flocking inside the rear panels.)

3. From the same spot, look for the deepest point on the saddle. It should be in the center; farther back, it will cause soreness.

4. With the girth done up and someone in the saddle, check for clearance under the pommel; you should be able to insert at least two but no more than three fingers in the gullet. More, and the tree is too narrow; less, and it's too wide.

5. Move to the rear of your horse and try to look forward under the saddle; if you can't see all the way to the front, the tree is either too narrow or too wide.

6. Stand by the shoulder and look at how the panels fit the sides of his withers and his shoulders. They should lie close, with no gaps just below the withers and no jutting out.

7. To check whether the saddle fits you, sit in the deepest part just behind the pommel. Place your hand behind your seat; there should be about two inches between you and the cantle. If there's less, the saddle is too small; if much more, it's probably too big.

Fig. 2

Fig. 2   8. With your leg correctly positioned (more about that in a moment), your knee shouldn't extend much, if at all, beyond the flap of the saddle.

9. Make sure your stirrup irons leave a little space between your foot and the outside branch—I see a lot of riders using irons they could easily get stuck in. My feet are average width, and I use size 5½-inch irons.

When all your equipment is safe and fits you and your horse properly, you'll be ready to feel what flat work has to teach you. You'll develop a sense of straightness, of balance, and of lengthening and shortening. Above all, you'll come to know your horse and yourself better—before you go on to jumping.

CHAPTER TWO

MOUNTING

While you may normally use a mounting block or get a leg up, you should learn to mount unassisted for two very practical reasons. First, in both adult and junior equitation classes, you may be required to mount from the ground. Second, someday you may *need* to be able to mount without help—out on a cross-country ride, or in any number of other situations. It may be a little challenging at first, but with practice you'll become supple enough to manage without much trouble. By all means lengthen the stirrup leather to mount a very big horse.

Fig. 3

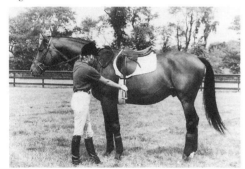

Fig. 4

Fig. 3 Put both reins into your left hand, the left rein lying normally and the right one lying flat over it. Your reins should be short enough to give a light contact with the mouth: not so short that you risk pulling your horse backward as you mount, but not so long that he can walk off.

Fig. 4 Stand alongside his shoulder (always facing toward the rear so as not to be kicked). Use your left hand, on the reins, to keep him still and your right hand to hold the left stirrup perpendicular to his side.

Fig. 5 As you put your left foot into the stirrup, push your toe into the girth—so that you don't poke him in the ribs. When your foot is securely in the iron, move your right hand up to the cantle of the saddle. Grab the mane with your left hand so that you don't pull on his mouth.

Fig. 6 Then push off with your right foot and pull yourself up with your right arm; at the same time, step down in the left stirrup and straighten your knee. Bring yourself up in one smooth motion, swinging your right leg up and over the back of your horse, clearing the cantle. Keep your left hand resting on his neck or in

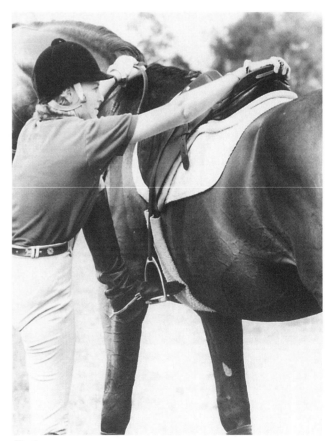

Fig. 5

Fig. 6

Fig. 7

the mane throughout. As you swing your right leg down, feel for the right stirrup and lower your seat *gently* into the saddle— don't just flop onto his back like a sack of potatoes.

DISMOUNTING

To dismount, first take both feet out of your stirrup irons. As when you mounted, have your reins short enough to give yourself a light contact with your horse's mouth.

Fig. 7   Put both reins in your left hand and—again in one fluid motion—swing your right leg back and up to clear the cantle of the saddle. At the same time, shift your right hand to the pommel and hop straight down. Your left hand on the mane and right on the pommel will help balance and guide you down.

POSITION AT THE HALT

Your position is a key ingredient of the "feeling" relationship between you and your horse. The more of you there is in contact with him, the greater the influence you'll have over him. Think about the positions of a dressage rider and a jockey and you'll see what I mean. With a deep seat and long, long legs, the dressage rider controls every part of the horse's body throughout a test. The jockey, almost perched on top of the horse, controls direction and urges speed but can do little else (nor does he need to).

The position I'm going to show you is the safest and most effective one I know. It will work for you no matter what your own conformation.

Seat

Fig. 8 The easiest place for your horse to
carry you is in the deepest part of the saddle,
which should be right behind the pommel.
Sitting here, you'll be able to feel and follow the
motion of your horse.

Fig. 9 Take your feet out of the stirrups, let
your legs hang, and your seat will automatically
find the right spot. Your knees will drop down,
your legs will be as long as they can, and your
position will be classically correct.

In this picture, you see a little room between
my back and the cantle. The skirt is just long
enough to carry my thigh and knee.

Fig. 8

Fig. 9

I am sitting evenly on both seat bones and
have pushed my knees down, as well as my heels,
to lengthen my legs.

Take your legs off and the position should
stay the same; if you're in that deep spot, you
won't need leg to stay on—just balance.

Without stirrups, you'll find it easier to be
sure that you're sitting evenly over both seat
bones. If you aren't even, you'll feel precarious; if
you are, you'll feel centered and secure.

Exhale to relax your muscles; feel your legs
getting longer as you do. Think "down and
around"—you want to wrap your legs around your
horse so that you're sitting in and around him,
not just on top of him.

Legs

(see Fig. 9) With your foot hanging loose out of the stirrup, the iron should hit your anklebone. At this height, you should be able to keep weight in your heel comfortably.

The length may feel a little long at first, but you'll find it becoming comfortable if you persevere. The more advanced you become on the flat, the longer your leg will become—and the longer the stirrup that will be comfortable for you.

Fig. 10 The stirrup leather is parallel to the girth and my weight is in my heel so my leg is *under* me—not behind or in front of me. My knee, leg, and ankle are relaxed and resting against my horse's side.

With the stirrup leather parallel to the girth and your weight in your heel, place the iron on the ball of your foot, the inside

Fig. 10

branch against the inside of your foot. (Riding with just your toe in the iron makes the stirrup too easy to lose; riding with it all the way "home"—back on your instep—robs you of flexibility.) Put just enough weight on the stirrup itself to "carry" it, no more or you'll force your leg away from your horse's side. If you push down too hard in the irons, your legs and ankles become stiff and rigid.

Fig. 11 Now sink weight into your heel. The heel should be your deepest point—deeper than your toe, because it acts as an anchor, stretching down your Achilles tendon. If you let it get higher, your leg will swing around. As you deepen your heel, you'll feel your calf muscle automatically becoming stronger and tighter.

My leg is truly *around* my horse; it's secure, but without driving him crazy.

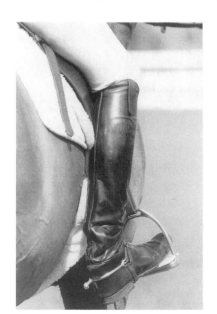

Fig. 11

Your ankle acts as a shock absorber. Push down into your heel—but not so far that your ankle looks almost broken, as some equitation riders do. The ankle needs to be flexible. Think of your ankle, your knee, and all your joints as being "oily," ready to adjust to absorb concussion and let you move in rhythm with your horse.

Turn your toes out slightly. This position helps with flexibility and gives you contact with the inside and back of your calf. (Toes turned in would encourage you to pinch with your knees and take your lower leg off.)

Fig. 12 To get an idea of the amount of pressure your calf should exert at any time when you're not closing it for a specific purpose, rest your hand on your thigh. Just the weight of the hand keeps it on the leg; that's the pressure you want—no more. If you grip harder without any particular reason, you'll push yourself up out of the saddle and send your horse a signal that will confuse him. Feel your horse breathing, and let your calf pressure breathe with him, in and out; he should accept the contact.

If you're stiff, your lower leg will come away from his side—which will make him nervous, because he won't know when that leg is going to grab him.

Just as bad, clamping him tightly will drive him crazy. Your position is a conversation, remember. All you need to tell him now is "I'm here, friend."

Think "push down" in your knee as well as in your heel—oily joints!—to help your leg stay down and around your horse. Remember, the more of you there is in contact with him, the more influence you have. Pushing down with the knee will also help you to keep the knee from gripping. Your contact should be just *below* the knee, in the top of your calf; your boots should develop a worn spot there.

Fig. 12

Upper Body

"Tall in the saddle" was perhaps the greatest compliment one character ever paid another in the old cowboy movies in which my trainer Jimmy Williams worked as a stunt rider. It's a phrase worth remembering—because it's how you should be sitting, too. Just as you want your leg long, you want your body straight and stretching up to influence your horse as much as possible; picture yourself "growing" every time you sit in the saddle.

Fig. 13 Here I'm sitting as I stand, allowing my muscle memory to hold my bones in place. I'm "centered" with my horse—not hanging on, just sitting there.

Fig. 13

1. Stretch up through your middle, so that your body is straight. Imagine that you're suspended by a string tied to the top of your head, like a puppet; every part of your upper body hangs there, straight but relaxed. Exhale and you'll feel your muscles letting go of tenseness; keep breathing normally and you'll help them stay relaxed.

2. To get rid of any stiffness in your back, push your stomach forward just a little; that makes your back a little concave but supples your back muscles and counters any tendency toward a sloppy roached back.

3. Breathe naturally. If you're holding your breath, you're stiff, and vice versa.

4. Your shoulders, elbows, and wrists must be supple and elastic (more oily joints!) so that you can follow the movement of your horse's head and neck (and not hit him in the mouth or otherwise restrict his movement). The ideal is a straight line from your elbow to his mouth, letting your arm function as a continuation of the rein.

5. Your elbow should be just in front of your hipbone. If it's behind your upper body, your reins are too long; if your arm is straight—no bend at the elbow—the reins are too short.

Fig. 14

Fig. 14 A good example of too short reins: my elbow is straight and stiff—and too far ahead of my hipbone.

Fig. 15 6. Keep your fingers firmly *closed* around the reins to keep the connection with your horse's mouth consistent. Open fingers make the feeling inconsistent since you're grabbing intermittently instead of maintaining a constant presence—and as you open and close your fingers, your elbows and shoulders become stiff. Your thumbs belong on top of the reins, and your hands at about a 45-degree angle (the same angle as your horse's shoulder), with just enough roundness in your wrists to be supple. If you weren't wearing gloves, you'd just barely see the side of the nail on your index finger.

Fig. 15

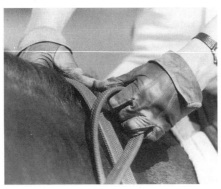

Fig. 16

Fig. 16 7. Your hands should be over and just in front of the withers (if they're over the pommel, your reins are too long), and close enough that you could stretch your thumb tips sideways and touch one to the other—about five inches apart, the same width as the average horse's mouth. This gives you a sort of rectangle of control, with the reins as the long sides, the bit and your hands as the short sides.

Check your hands by simply touching your thumbs together.

8. Carry your head right above your shoulders, with chin up, and eyes always looking where you want to go. Your horse will go there automatically. If you have to check what your horse is doing, glance down without tipping your head and look up again.

9. Your head weighs about twenty pounds, so the minute you drop your chin, you unbalance yourself: shifting your center of gravity forward, roaching your back, and sending your horse onto his forehand.

POSITION IN MOTION

What I've just described is the classical position, the one you'll sit in most of the time. As you ride, you may have to do something very different for a moment, like turning your toe way out to use a spur, but you'll always come back to this position, which will feel increasingly relaxed and natural as you practice it.

Now, how do you accommodate your position to your horse's motion? Largely by "feeling" and *following*.

1. For your legs, the key word is "breathe." You'll increase and decrease pressure to send him messages, but most of the time your legs just breathe with his sides.

2. Your seat follows his back, almost as if you were on a swing, your hips supple and moving, your joints elastic and shock-absorbing. You're part of his movement, neither "sack-of-potatoes" loose nor stiff and resistant. (Remember what you saw when you watched his movement from the ground? He is graceful and elastic, like a dancer. That's the movement you want to be part of.)

3. For the sake of balance, your center of gravity moves with your horse's—and in general, the faster he's going, the farther forward his center of gravity is.

Fig. 17   Thus, your upper body should be right on the vertical at the halt, so that you and your horse are in perfect harmony. At the walk you need to be a degree or so ahead of the vertical, so that your centers of gravity remain aligned.

Fig. 17

Fig. 18   You can see I'm about thirty degrees ahead at the posting trot.

Fig. 18

Fig. 19

Fig. 20

Fig. 21

Fig. 22

Fig. 19   In the canter I'm fairly close to the vertical again (where you don't want to send him on his forehand, so that he has to speed up to stay balanced) . . .

Fig. 20   . . . but more forward as the canter speed increases. However, as you lift your weight off your horse's back, keep your seat close to the saddle so that your center of gravity remains close to his.

Your elbows open and close, letting your hands move forward and back with the motion of your horse's head and neck, so that your contact stays constant and your body moves *with* his.

Fig. 21, 22   In these two pictures you see that my arms change position in relation to the movement of his head and neck and to his balance; the rest of my position stays the same. In the first, the phase of the stride where his neck is up and back, my hands are in their normal position; a moment later, in the downward phase of the stride, they follow his head and neck forward. (In both phases, the contact and the straight line from elbow to mouth remain the same.)

If you find yourself bouncing, at any gait, there's stiffness somewhere in your joints—and where you're stiff, you're blocking out whatever message your horse is sending to you. Remind yourself to breathe, relax, follow, and "feel."

CHAPTER THREE

USING YOUR AIDS
WITH FEELING

When you're riding, the relationship between yourself and your horse should be one of "best friends" who respect each other, want the best for each other, and do everything they can to work together. Like a pair of figure skaters, you should act as one, with lightness and harmony—which is only possible when you understand each other.

Every time you ride, you talk and your horse talks. In some cases a real conversation goes on, while in others horse and rider talk past each other. The more feeling you achieve as a rider—the more you make yourself aware of and open to your horse's messages—the more there will be a real exchange of information, and the happier the two of you will be.

Your horse is constantly trying to talk to you with his eyes, ears, and body language, telling you he's happy or unhappy, relaxed or tense, confident or confused. A naturally gifted rider is instinctively aware of this communication, but any rider can learn awareness.

What such learning requires is commitment: a resolve to concentrate on everything your horse does. With practice, you'll master the ABC's of communication. Your awareness of your horse's body language—and of how to respond—will become a natural part of riding.

Besides being aware of what your horse is telling you, you need to be conscious of everything you're communicating to him (and in what tone: just as in human conversation, it should be pleasant and middle-volume unless you have a really serious reason to yell). If you're telling him to turn left with a direct rein but maintaining strong contact on the right at the same time, for example, you're going to confuse him. (Put a finger in each corner of your mouth and pull back on both at the same time that you try to turn *your* head left and you'll see what I mean!) If you're not getting the reactions you're looking for, check back over everything you're doing, and you'll probably find the fault there. If you can't identify it yourself, ask an expert to help you out. And be especially careful if you feel your temper heating up. If you can't control your own feelings, you can't control your horse.

THE LANGUAGE OF THE CONVERSATION

The basic language in which you speak to your horse is a range of pressures. An increase of pressure tells him he's doing something incorrect or something you want him to change; a decrease of the same pressure tells him he's got it right now. Of course, if you *don't* decrease the pressure when he does what you want, all he can figure is that he's still not right. So you must always be clear, consistent (the same degree of pressure to ask for the same change every time), and timely with what you tell him. And listen to his responses; if he's getting quick or laying his ears back, it might be because he doesn't want to work as hard as you're telling him to—but it also might be because your mixed messages are driving him crazy. Look for what *you* might be doing wrong first; don't assume it's always his fault.

At the most basic level, your seat and legs are your driving aids, and your seat and reins are your retarding aids. Your horse's "engine" is in the rear—his propulsion comes from his powerful hindquarters—so you always ride him from back to front. In general, your legs control what he does with his body from the saddle on back; your hands control the forehand. Your seat acts as a mediator between your hands and legs, modifying or accentuating what they tell him.

1. To get a feel for leg and seat pressure, once again place your hand on your thigh. That's your basic "I'm here" message. Now leave your hand where it is but gradually straighten your elbow until . . .

Fig. 23 2. . . . as I'm doing here, you bring your arm up to the vertical and press down with force (the degree you'd use to push your seat into the saddle). At every "level" along the way, hold the pressure for a moment to absorb the feeling into your body-language "vocabulary." You'll *see* almost no difference, but you'll *feel* one.

3. Come back to the "resting" pressure and absorb that for a moment more; then transfer that feeling to the contact between your calves and your horse's sides.

4. When you want to go forward, you'll simply increase the pressure in both calves.

5. To move over, you'll increase pressure in just one calf.

6. In your hands, as in your legs, you want to *feel*, not hang. Have a friend grasp your hand and increase pressure from fingers just closed . . .

7. . . . to what he imagines thirty pounds would feel like and back again. As with your hand on your thigh, you'll hardly see a change,

Fig. 23

but you'll feel the difference. In most cases, the pressure you put on your horse's mouth should just equal the pressure he puts on your hands; increase only to tell him you want a change. Make the increase equal to the change you want, and decrease as soon as you get a response.

TRANSITIONS

Now that you have your basic position down and some understanding of the aids, the next area we're going to work on is transitions from one gait to another, which will allow you to put the basic aids into practice.

Halt to Walk to Halt

Fig. 24 1. At the halt, make sure your seat is in the saddle and your heels are down before you ask for anything new. Every time you return to the halt, use the opportunity of a moment when you're not asking for anything else to check your position: Are your seat, heels, and hands where they should be? Are your eyes looking straight ahead? Go all through your body-position checklist, asking yourself, "Am I in the right place?"

2. To prepare to go forward, make sure that your legs are against your horse's sides and "breathing" with them (the hand-resting-on-thigh pressure), and that your eyes are looking where you are about to go.

3. To move into the walk, increase the pressure against his sides slightly. As soon as he steps forward, lighten again, maintaining just enough pressure to keep him moving forward at a relaxed walk (which translates into about 4 miles per hour). Let your hands follow the forward-back motion of his head to maintain your quiet "handshake" on the reins.

Fig. 25 I've closed my legs to tell my horse, "Walk." He's obedient and happy in his expression, but his switching tail and the tight look over his ribs show that I've had to use some strength.

Fig. 26 As he continues, I'm letting him carry me, maintaining my correct position—sitting up, light hands, long legs, eyes straight ahead—and going *with* him.

Fig. 24

Fig. 25

Fig. 26

4. To come back to the halt, first stop any driving aid you may have been using with your legs. Then increase the feel on the reins the same amount that you increased leg pressure to get the walk (just closing your fingers more firmly should apply sufficient backward contact). As your horse slows and begins to stop, decrease your hand pressure to tell him he's doing the right thing. Repeat the increasing and lightening until he halts (you should need just a couple of squeeze-releases for this simple transition).

Fig. 27 Here, as I begin to increase contact, I keep my heels down and my seat in the saddle so that I don't allow him to change my position. In preparation for the halt, I deepen my seat and he lightens his forehand and shifts his weight back.

Fig. 28 We have a balanced halt: our centers of gravity coincide, and I've maintained a straight line from elbow to mouth.

Fig. 27

Fig. 28

Walk to Trot to Walk

Fig. 29 1. Return to the walk and then apply slightly stronger leg pressure to move into an active, working trot (about 8 mph), the same way you'd press a little harder on a car's gas pedal to go 30 mph than to go 20. To begin the walk-trot transition, I just closed my legs and kept my rein contact light. Now, as I feel the trot rhythm begin, I shift my upper body forward a few degrees and increase my rein contact just enough to say, "No faster."

Fig. 29

2. Let the movement of your horse's inside hind leg—his biggest pushing mechanism—thrust you out of the saddle to begin posting. (His outside shoulder picks up and comes forward at the same moment; if you can't feel the thrust through your seat at first, watch the outside shoulder—and try to be aware of what's happening underneath your seat, so that you can eventually rely on feel alone, posting automatically on the correct "diagonal.")

3. Think "forward-down," not "up-down," as you post. Come out of the saddle just enough to clear the pommel, then touch again in a two-beat rhythm. (After all, you want to follow the motion—your horse is moving forward, not up. His center of gravity is moving forward too, so you'll naturally close your hip angle a bit and incline your upper body forward to about 3o degrees to stay over it.) Each time your seat lifts out of the saddle, feel your weight traveling down through your "oily" knees and ankles to your heels.

Fig. 30

Fig. 30   Our balance, harmony, and equilibrium are about perfect here; I'm *with* my horse, not interfering in any way. As my seat touches the saddle, my upper body stays 3o degrees forward. My hands follow the mouth—they don't go up and down—and I maintain the straight line from elbow to bit.

4. Riders who practically stand up in their stirrups aren't feeling and following the motion; they're usually *above* the horse, not *with* him, on some rhythm of their own.

Fig. 31   When my body is *on* the vertical, I'm *behind* the motion of the trot and my center of gravity is not lined up with my horse's. My hands are pulling me up. My horse and I look stiff rather than supple.

5. Keep your hands relaxed and quiet, following the slight head motion (less pronounced than at the walk) with "oily" joints.

6. If your hands go up and down as you post, your shoulders and elbows are rigid

Fig. 31

(perhaps because your upper body is too vertical). If they're relaxed, the motion will travel through them rather than stopping there.

7. Once your horse is in the trot, he should stay there without your nagging him, so relax your driving leg aid to the normal hand-on-thigh pressure. If he slows, close your leg more firmly again to remind him of what you want. When he responds correctly, lighten again to tell him you're pleased.

8. To come back to the walk, check first that you have relaxed your leg pressure. Then open your hip angle to bring your center of gravity back toward the vertical, which telegraphs him that you want him to change something.

9. Then tell him what: take more feel of his mouth (you'll already have a little more leverage as a result of your straightening) to tell him to bring back his center of gravity and return to the walk. As you did in the walk-halt transition, squeeze and soften but maintain the contact—no loop in the reins. The feel of elastic contact is the same as the one you need to pick up and set down a full bucket of water without spilling a drop. If you jerk the bucket, you'll spill the water; if you're limp, you'll never lift it at all.

10. When your horse steps into the walk, maintain a comfortable contact and allow your arms to follow his head and neck movement ("oily" elbows!). This, by the way, is the same relaxed feeling you should have in your hips as he walks—supple, sitting in and around him, following the motion as you would the motion of a swing as its own momentum carries it forward and back.

Fig. 32

Fig. 32 The beginning of the transition. We're still in the trot; I am beginning to sit "in" and open my hip angle to bring both our centers of gravity back. I've raised my hands slightly to help him stay up as he changes his balance.

Fig. 33 As he steps into the walk rhythm, I bring my upper body back to the vertical. I still have a good contact, resisting his mouth, and I've put more weight into my heel to give me strength so he cannot pull me down and forward.

Fig. 33

11. I like the sitting trot to be a little slower (about 6 mph) and shorter-strided than the posting trot. Your upper body should look much the same as it does in the walk: just a degree or two in front of the vertical, to stay with your horse's center of gravity. Relax your hips, relax the muscles in your seat, and let your legs hang down around him naturally. Staying soft and elastic will enable you to absorb the shock of the trot motion.

Fig. 34

Fig. 34 If you couldn't see my horse's legs, you might imagine from my position that we were walking rather than trotting. At the sitting trot, my seat and legs are down and around him, with my heel the deepest part. My back is relaxed, my hips absorb the trot rhythm, and my contact is elastic.

Tensing your seat muscles makes them hard, so that you bounce instead of sit the trot; gripping with your knees will pop you up out of the saddle.

Walk to Canter

1. Start by asking for the canter with *one* very basic aid: increase the pressure of your outside leg just behind the girth (left leg for the right lead, right leg for the left lead), leaving your inside leg quietly at the girth. You don't need to throw your upper body around or jump up and down in the saddle.

Fig. 35

Fig. 35 To ask for the left-lead canter, my right-leg aid is all I need. I'm already prepared: sitting in the center of my horse, not leaning forward or over his left shoulder; my eyes are up because I can depend on "feeling" to pick up the lead—I don't need to look. My left leg stays at the girth, not in front of it, and I maintain my seat *in* the saddle.

2. Someone watching you from the middle of the ring should see nothing different at this point; your upper body should stay the same.

Fig. 36

3. If your horse doesn't respond, increase your leg pressure—and, if you must, add a kick or a tap of your stick behind your outside leg.

4. As your horse steps into the canter, you'll feel more swing and see his head nodding more than in the trot, so you'll need to follow more with both your hips and your arms and hands.

Fig. 36 Because my horse is pulling down a bit, I keep my heels down, my seat firmly in the saddle, and my body on the vertical.

Fig. 37

Fig. 37 A moment later he's responded, rebalancing himself, so my arms and body are going more with him. Once again, my *horse* is carrying me in the canter.

5. A feeling that you're going to bounce means you need to relax your hips, knees, and seat muscles. As you do, you'll feel your weight drop into the saddle.

6. Try to feel the lead you're on through your seat bones. The inside hind leg comes forward slightly more than the outside, with a greater thrust. If you're a novice, you may need to see which shoulder goes forward more to know which lead you're on—but by staying aware and correlating what you see with what you feel, you should gradually begin to distinguish leads by feel alone.

On the left lead, both the left fore and left hind are forward of the right legs. You'll feel your horse's left hind leg up under your seat. If you looked over the shoulder you'd see the left fore reaching more than the right.

Canter to Trot

1. Sit up a little more (the canter movement will have naturally closed your hip angle a little) and come back to the vertical—but not behind it—and increase your feel of the mouth. Your horse is built with most of his weight from the saddle forward, so in downward transitions he'll tend to fall on his nose and pull you out of the saddle, stiffening his back and making you less effective, so that he doesn't have to take you into his rebalancing equation.

2. You need to go against this natural defense mechanism of his. As he heads forward or even down, think of maintaining your secure position by deepening your heels, sitting *down* in the saddle, and lifting him with your hands and the leverage that comes from your deep position. Bend your elbows a little and tighten your arms; keep your hip angle open, your seat in the saddle, and your weight down to bring him back.

Fig. 38

Fig. 38   I'm beginning to ask for the trot, keeping my seat and my heel firmly down. Because I don't want my horse to fall into the transition, I'm bending my elbow to lift his forehand. Meanwhile my eyes continue to be *up*, not looking at him.

Fig. 39   He's beginning to shift his weight back and lighten his forehand, so the feel in my arm and rein is slightly less. My eyes and body position stay the same.

Fig. 39

Fig. 40   As I feel the trot rhythm develop, I relax and go with it. His head and neck are lighter, so I've been able to soften my feel, lower my hands, and simply follow the mouth.

3. If he doesn't respond, increase the pressure in your hands (but keep making the pressure squeeze-release, so that you don't give him something to lean on). Continue repeating until he slows. (To go from the canter to the walk, apply the same aids but with proportionately greater pressure.)

Fig. 40

4. If you feel him pulling you out of position, fix yourself in the saddle, deepening your heels and lifting him more with stronger pressure in your hands.

Canter to Halt

Fig. 41 I start with a nicely balanced canter.

Fig. 41

Fig. 42 As I ask for the transition, I maintain my position and add a little more seat and leg pressure to bring his hindquarters farther under and so help him to balance.

Fig. 42

Fig. 43 He pulls down and I simply resist him with both hands working together. I don't compromise my position; I'm firmly anchored in my saddle. My eyes are up throughout.

Fig. 43

Fig. 44 My perseverance is rewarded. He shifts his balance back and up. As he halts, I lighten my aids but my position stays the same.

Fig. 44

COMBINING AIDS — THE BASIC HALF-HALT

So far, you've used transitions to find out how much leg you needed to move up into a particular gait, and how much hand you've needed to come down. Now, for the first time, you're going to be sending your horse a message by means of combined aids, with a half-halt in its simplest form. (Later in the program we'll go on to a more sophisticated version.)

As its name says, this aid asks for half of a halt. You'll put pressure on your horse's mouth, but as you feel him slowing in response you'll relax and allow him to continue. You'll use the half-halt when you want to slow him in preparation for a transition, to make the transition clean (for example, to take him from canter to walk without any trot strides on the way), or to put him back together when you feel him getting quick or heavy. Put another way, you'll use it to "test your brakes," to answer questions like "Is my horse listening to me? If I wanted a full halt right now, could I get it?"

You'll apply this simplified half-halt with your hands and arms alone, keeping your seat and legs where they are.

1. If, for example, you're in the canter and you feel your horse getting heavy, apply pressure on his mouth — the same amount you feel him putting on you — with a slight lifting motion, and keep enough leg that he doesn't break back to the trot.

2. If he doesn't respond, lighten the feel in your hands just for a moment . . .

3. . . . and then reapply, making sure you are lifting and not pulling down. Continue until you feel his forehand lightening; then soften your pressure on his mouth and let him continue forward.

Fig. 45 Here I'm beginning my half-halt: I'm firmer with my arms and even deeper with my seat and heel.

Fig. 46 As he "comes back" to me, I'm rewarding him by lightening my feel on the reins. (I've also fallen a little forward and lightened my seat — something I'll need to correct in the next stride.)

Fig. 45

Fig. 46

Many riders can go from canter to halt more accurately than from canter to walk, where they always end up with some trot steps in between. If you think "canter-halt" even though you want canter-walk, so that you almost halt and then allow your horse to walk, you'll get a smoother transition.

You may have to be a bit strong with your horse the first few times you use the half-halt to demand a clean transition, especially if he's been getting away with sloppy transitions, but decrease from "rough" to "firm but definite" as soon as you can.

Canter to Walk with Half-Halts

Fig. 47 In this canter, my position is good; although my horse is slightly overflexed and leaning down on my hands, I haven't let him disturb me. My elbows are bent to help lift him.

Fig. 47

Fig. 48 To make the transition, I sit *in*—heels down, elbows bent—and take a firmer feel of the mouth with my hands *and* arms.

Fig. 48

Fig. 49 As he responds to my half-halt and steps into a relaxed walk rhythm, I soften my "backward" aids. He and I are balanced correctly and I'm allowing him to carry me. Now that I don't need maximum leverage, my legs are relaxed and my heels are not as deep as they were.

Fig. 49

Walk to Canter with a Half-Halt

1. For a walk-canter transition (another place where your horse is likely to want to give you trot steps in between), feel his mouth just before you apply your leg. That gets his attention and prevents him from running forward.

2. Then, as you close your leg, keep thinking the four-beat rhythm of the walk until you feel his inside hind lift into the canter. If you think "one-two-three-four," your seat bones will be more likely to keep following the motion (and encouraging him to stay in that rhythm) until he picks up the new gait. If you don't, if you're just holding yourself in limbo waiting for the new rhythm, you make it easier for him to pick up the trot instead of building impulsion in the walk.

CONCLUSION

While all the aids I've described in these transitions are straightforward and simple, the ability to coordinate them with *feeling*—smoothly and effectively—takes time to develop. So give yourself plenty of practice; you'll find your efforts are richly rewarded.

CHAPTER FOUR

BENDING

Contradictory though it may sound, bending your horse is a major tool for keeping him straight. The contradiction becomes easier to understand when you stop to think that, for a horse, "straight" means having the hind feet track directly behind the front feet—through a turn or around a circle as well as down a straight line. To be straight, he *has* to bend—not just turn his head and neck to the side, but arc his whole body, head to tail. And doing that requires seat and leg aids, not just hands.

To see what I mean about needing all the aids, try bending your horse with your hands alone:

1. On the long side of your arena, in the walk, use just your hand to bend his head and neck to the inside for a few steps.

2. Then straighten him and bend him to the outside. Although his head and neck curve to one side and then the other, the rest of his body stays straight.

Bending successfully requires you to send your horse *from your inside leg to your outside rein.* You've probably heard instructors use that expression many times, but up to now you may not have understood its meaning. Here's why it's so important: when you have your horse going from your inside leg to your outside rein, your inside leg is at the girth, asking him to bend in his ribs by pushing his rib cage to the outside of the track. As he shifts his weight out a little, he should naturally bend his head and neck slightly to the inside, in the direction of the pressure (the way you look around when somebody taps you on the shoulder). At the same time, he becomes more active with his inside hind leg, stepping deeper under his body to balance himself better. That results in his carrying more of his weight over his hindquarters, where his "engine" is.

Fig. 50   You can test this basic "leg-on" bending reaction for yourself from the ground. Position your horse parallel to a wall or fence, so that he can't walk away. Stand beside him (taking care that he doesn't kick or strike at you). Without touching his mouth, tickle him or lightly pinch the flesh on his shoulder just in front of the girth. You'll see him bend his neck around as if to bite at a fly. Reward him by stroking that area.

When he understands what you want, move your tickle back behind the girth where your leg would normally be. As you see here, he bends his head and neck around; it's a reflex reaction. (You may need to keep a hand on the reins to stop him from moving away; if so, be sure your feel is loose enough—as mine is—that you don't jerk his mouth as he turns his head.)

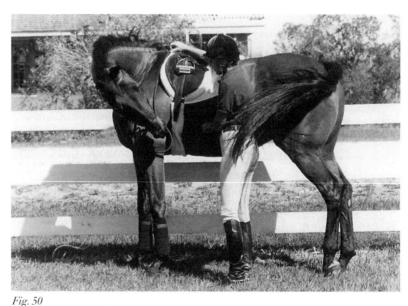

Fig. 50

When a horse bends around inside-leg pressure, he puts a slight head-to-tail curve in his body, with the curve in his neck "filling out" the outside rein. As well as bringing his inside hind leg deeper under his body to balance himself, he also takes a contact on the outside rein, lightens up on the inside rein, and frees his inside shoulder.

Taking that contact on the outside rein is important—because it makes your horse "straight," or, more precisely, it makes him conform to the track. All horses naturally favor one side (just as most people are left- or right-handed) and tend to be crooked, in most cases to travel with their haunches to the inside and their shoulders to the outside (a position in which it's impossible to perform athletically, smoothly, elastically, and quickly). But if your horse is bent around your leg, your outside rein against his neck keeps his shoulders from falling out, and your inside leg tells him to keep his haunches under him so that they track directly behind the forelegs, not to the inside of them.

Develop your horse's responsiveness to the inside leg in both directions. Most horses, like most people, are naturally more supple in one direction than the other; to make him as capable a performer as possible, you want him equally supple in both.

Turn on the Forehand

The turn on the forehand, which breaks down bending into its most basic elements, is an exercise to confirm both your understanding and your horse's of just how he should move away from your leg. In this movement, the hind legs turn around the forelegs, in response to pressure from just one leg aid, while the forelegs pivot around one spot. When done slowly, from a halt, the turn on the forehand allows you to "stop the action" and really feel your horse's responsiveness to your leg as well as your own ability to apply just the right amount of leg for the result you want. It also teaches, very effectively, coordination of hand and leg aids. If you apply too little of one or not enough of the other, your horse will tell you right away, by responding incorrectly; but because the movement is performed slowly, you'll have plenty of time to find the right balance.

1. In the halt, make sure you're sitting perfectly straight in the saddle, with your weight evenly distributed over both seat bones and the reins having even contact on both sides of your horse's mouth. His head and neck should be straight.

2. Ask for a turn on the forehand to the left by pressing your left leg just behind the girth. Maintain enough contact on the mouth to keep him from going forward, but no more—you don't want him backing up. Let your right leg rest quietly against his side, making him think "forward" just a little—only enough to counteract any urge to back.

3. As soon as you get a step to the right, release the pressure for a moment and let him stop. Going one step at a time will give you a chance to think about how much pressure gives you how much response—and will also keep your horse from running sideways and evading the exercise.

4. Ideally, the first time you close your left leg, your horse should simply step away from the pressure by reaching his left hind under his body and slightly across his right hind.

5. The next time you squeeze, he should step directly sideways with his right hind.

6. If he doesn't listen when you apply your leg, try using a "cluck" with your leg. If he

still doesn't respond, turn your toe out and prick him with your spur—tap, tap, tap—until he steps away from your leg. (Don't just dig your spur in and leave it there; your leg must be *alive,* closing to get movement and relaxing as your horse responds, so that there's feeling in the turn, telling him "Yes, this is correct," or "No, that's wrong.")

If he continues to ignore your spur, reach back behind your leg and tap him with your stick. When you ask for the next step, go back to leg pressure alone first, and escalate only if he's still not listening.

7. Each time your horse takes a step, pause for a second to monitor what you're doing. Then squeeze again. You should be able to maintain a nice rhythm, one step at a time, just like the walk. Slow him if he starts to rush; liven him up with a little more pressure, a wake-up spur, or a tap with your stick if he moves too slowly.

8. As you're experimenting with how much leg pressure you need to keep him moving, you'll also find out how much feel on the mouth you need to keep him in one spot. Backing is a worse mistake than going forward, because it means your horse isn't *thinking* "forward"—which he should be doing unless directed otherwise. (Be very aware of keeping his neck straight. If you feel him begin to bulge through his outside shoulder, keep your outside rein against his neck to make sure he stays perfectly straight.)

Fig. 51 I'm going to do a half turn on the forehand to the left, away from my left leg. To give myself a reference point, I'm starting next to a fence line. Before asking for the first step, I make sure my position is effective: I'm sitting evenly on both seat bones in the deepest part of the saddle; my reins are short, so I'm ready if my horse tries to walk forward to resist; and, of course, my eyes are up.

Fig. 51

Fig. 52 As he begins to yield from my left leg, my right leg remains quietly on his side to keep him thinking forward, not back; my outside (right) rein is keeping his neck straight, not allowing his forehand to step to the right. He is responding to the pressure of my left leg, not to a pull on his head to the left.

Fig. 52

Fig. 53

Fig. 53 We continue very straight—with no bending whatsoever—and very centered. My eyes are up and I'm not leaning one way or the other. My elbows are even and relaxed—I'm not pulling more on one rein than the other—and my right leg rests quietly on his side.

Fig. 54 Here we are just finishing the turn. One more step and we will be parallel to the fence. I have resisted him with my arms and back so he cannot step forward. The aids are nearly invisible, in that the reins are light and he is quietly yielding to my leg. My position is still pretty good—long leg, deep heel, straight upper body—except that I'm glancing down; I should be looking up and ahead.

Fig. 54

Turn on the Haunches

To help you gain control of both ends of your horse—so that you can not only feel what his shoulders and his haunches are doing but also influence both ends—next you'll add an elementary turn on the haunches to your vocabulary. In this movement, the haunches stay in one spot while the forehand moves around them.

1. For a turn on the haunches to the left, start with a balanced halt. Then move both hands a little to the left, maintaining your normal five-inch distance between them. The shift lays your outside (in this case, right) rein against the horse's neck, encouraging him to move away from the pressure; the inside rein opens up a little space into which he can move. *Don't cross the neck with your outside hand;* your right rein *always* stays on the right side of the neck, your left on the left. And don't pull back on your horse's mouth; just maintain enough contact that he won't think you want him to go forward. He should be slightly bent in the direction he is going.

2. As you move your hands to the inside, lay your outside leg behind the girth to prevent the haunches from swinging right as they might otherwise do. Leave your inside leg at the girth (where, as before, it's simply asking him to keep thinking "forward" so that he doesn't move backward).

3. Mostly in reaction to the feel of the outside rein against his neck (with your supporting outside leg), your horse should move his shoulders around to the left rhythmically, in balance, and make a tiny circle with his hind feet.

4. If he hurries during this training phase, ask for only one step at a time and stop in between to analyze his response. Are your aids clear enough that you're getting through, or

Fig. 55   *Fig. 56*   *Fig. 57*   *Fig. 58*

is there "static on the line"? Check your straightness, make sure you're not pulling back or giving any other mixed signals, and try again.

Fig. 55 I have just taken one step to the left. I'm sitting in the center of my horse, not leaning into the turn, and my eyes are up. My left leg is in a correct, quiet position. My left rein, slightly off the neck, acts as a leading rein, bending him in the direction of the turn.

Fig. 56 Halfway through the turn, he is nicely between my hands and legs. I am sitting deep in the saddle so that he thinks forward. My light contact with his mouth stops him from stepping out of the turn.

Fig. 57 At this moment, my outside (right) leg is active, preventing the haunches from swinging out (to the right). I am very centered. If I leaned left or right, ahead or back, I would disturb his balance.

Fig. 58 I'm "swinging" his outside (right) shoulder to the left with both reins to the inside. Still sitting in the center of him, I'm keeping a straight horse—my hands are close together, my eyes are up. My right leg is active to help support the right rein against the neck; my left leg is passively "there," encouraging a slight left bend.

Leg-Yield

After learning how to influence both the shoulders and the haunches, move on to leg-yielding, which will further develop your communication skills and your horse's suppleness and responsiveness. In leg-yielding, you move him both forward and sideways, his body bent slightly but evenly around your active leg—no leading with either the shoulders or the haunches, and no shambling forward. (For riding a dressage test you would want the shoulders leading slightly, but in training I prefer to try to keep them very even with the haunches—otherwise it's easy to overdo the angle.)

1. At the walk, ride into the short end of your work space and turn down the "quarter" line, an imaginary line parallel to the long side of your work area, leaving about fifteen feet between you and the rail—which is now on your left, let's say. As you advance down this quarter line, you'll be moving your horse both forward and sideways, keeping his body parallel to the long side, until you reach the rail.

2. Make sure your horse's body *is* parallel to the rail as you start, and as you work keep checking his position in relation to the fence line to be sure he *stays* parallel and doesn't angle one end or the other in the direction of travel. Straightness—keeping his shoulders and haunches in line—is an important part of this work. As with your earlier bending work, you'll probably need some experimenting to find the hand-to-leg ratio that keeps him straight and produces the smooth forward-and-sideways movement you're looking for.

3. Move both hands just far enough toward the inside of the ring to bring the outside rein against your horse's neck; you're going to be bending him around your inside leg, but *very slightly.* The tendency of most riders in leg-yielding is to *overbend* to the inside, causing the horse to fall on his outside shoulder, while the tendency of most horses in any bending work is to lead with the shoulders and avoid putting the haunches to work. To counteract both these tendencies, think "straight" even as you move your hands in. Your outside rein controls the degree of bending; if you *see* any bend in the neck, you're probably hanging on the inside rein.

4. To begin leg-yielding to the left, apply your right leg slightly behind the girth (where it will also help keep the haunches in line) each time you feel his inside hind touch the ground, with the same squeeze-release-squeeze pattern in rhythm with his step that you used in the turn on the forehand.

5. Maintain your left leg at the girth (slightly ahead of your right leg) to keep him moving forward without clashing your leg aids.

6. He should respond by stepping farther under as well as forward with his right hind foot, crossing the left hind . . .

7. . . . and then sideways with the left hind . . .

8. . . . and farther under . . .

9. . . . and sideways until you reach the fence line.

Fig. 59   As my horse's inside hind leg touches the ground, I press him sideways and he steps leftward with his left fore. Both my position and his are very straight. My left leg rests quietly on his side, not away from it.

Fig. 60   As he moves left, I'm keeping

Fig. 59

him bent very slightly right—and parallel to the rail. As he crosses his legs over, he bends a little in his ribs and fills out the left rein with his neck. Notice that my right leg is back, my left at the girth.

Fig. 61   His neck is straight because my arms and hands are quietly in a correct position—not pulling or crossing over the withers. Nor am I dropping a shoulder or a hip or

Fig. 60

Fig. 61

my eyes. I'm riding with "feeling"; I "go with him," trying to do just enough to keep him straight and no more—like balancing a broom in the palm of my hand.

10. If you feel your horse trying to race sideways toward the rail, send him more forward by lessening the pressure in your right leg and closing your left leg and rein against him a little.

11. If he hurries forward, increase your right-leg pressure, make sure your left isn't strongly against him, and feel his mouth a little more until he slows.

12. Keep checking for straightness. If you find your horse's shoulders getting way ahead of his haunches, carry your hands more to the inside. As you do, think about the *feeling* you had when you brought your outside rein against the neck in your turns on the haunches (like thinking "halt" when you want to half-halt, focusing on the feeling of a simpler related movement will help you achieve the more complicated one.)

13. If you sense that your horse's haunches are lagging, use the *feel* of a turn on the forehand to help you maintain the shoulders' position while you apply more leg to move the haunches over.

In many cases, students can't feel this kind of loss of alignment on their own at first. So having a friend observe you and tell you if you're no longer straight is helpful. And if you aren't straight, focusing on the *feeling* of the appropriate turn exercise will help you straighten and stay straight. When a rider I'm working with doesn't notice that her horse is leading with his shoulders, I tell her, "Stop. Look at your horse in relationship to the fence line. Now do a quarter of a turn on the haunches." Right away, she moves both hands to the inside, bringing her horse's shoulders directly in front of the haunches again. "Now *that's* the feel you should have in motion to control the shoulders in the leg-yield," I tell her.

Likewise, if I see her horse is leading with his haunches, I have her stop and do a quarter turn on the forehand, focusing on the *feeling* of his haunches moving over but his shoulders staying straight. Once she knows how leg-yielding while staying straight should feel, achieving it becomes much easier.

Stride Length

Now that you have the basic tools for controlling speed and straightness, the next step to master is basic lengthening and shortening of your horse's stride length. I'm *not* talking about extension and collection here, but simply about developing your ability to get (and to *know* you're getting) a long*er* stride and a short*er* stride—covering more ground or less ground with each of his footfalls. For this work, you may find it useful to have a helper on the ground to confirm and correct your impressions about how you're affecting the horse's stride.

This work will help you begin to develop a "clock" in your head—a sense of timing and rhythm, which you'll need to produce the consistency of pace so necessary in the dressage ring, on a hunter course, and going cross-country in combined training. Along with your basic gaits, such as your 4-mph walk and your 8-mph working trot, you'll work toward developing, say, a smooth, consistent 6-mph lengthened walk, a 10-mph lengthened trot, and a shortened walk that's rhythmic but with such very small steps that it's almost a halt.

To continue emphasizing the importance of "forward," begin with lengthening.

1. In the working walk, increase the feel in your legs with a "squeeze-soften-squeeze" sequence that almost asks for a trot, then softens, and squeezes again, in rhythm with your horse's steps.

2. Let your hips swing forward to follow the walk, as they should naturally do, while you close your legs and feel your horse gaining more ground by taking longer strides.

3. Yet your hands don't allow him to trot, nor do your legs push quite that hard.

4. As he stretches and nods his neck, watch this motion and allow your elbows to open and close, so that you follow with your arms but don't drop the con-

tact. Don't smother him so that he can't lengthen, but don't let him trot. (Think of him as an accordion, expanding and contracting.)

Fig. 62 Here I'm encouraging my horse to lengthen by giving in my arms and pushing with my seat and legs. I've slightly dropped the contact.

Fig. 63 My legs are at the girth, saying, "Forward . . . straight," and I'm totally following with my shoulders and elbows. My arms are a continuation of the reins; I have a straight line from my elbow to his mouth. I don't need to lean forward to follow his mouth. Notice how my closed fingers allow him to stretch fully.

Now that you've pushed your horse into a longer stride (make sure your helper on the ground confirms that you have), teach him to shorten his stride by using your retarding aids more than your driving aids.

1. With both hands, take more contact in rhythm with the stride, as if you're going to stop . . .

2. . . . but keep your legs squeezing and softening to tell him, "No, don't stop. Stay active—take a shorter step but don't stop, a shorter step but don't stop, almost stop but don't stop, almost stop but don't stop." Keep the movement rhythmic, so you get regular short steps, not choppy ones.

Fig. 64 Here I shorten my horse's strides by resisting with my arms and my back, while my seat and legs tell him to continue forward. I keep a straight line from my elbow to his mouth. His frame shortens along with his short strides, but he isn't overflexed.

Fig. 62

Fig. 63

Fig. 64

3. Keep alternating the length of steps you ask for—short, short, short, then working (regular), working, then long, long, long, and back again, in the walk and then in the trot and canter so that you feel the different lengths and rhythms and develop your horse's understanding of your aids.

Fig. 65 4. In the posting trot, the moment to close your leg or increase your feel of the mouth, is when your seat touches the saddle. That's the time when you can influence what your horse does with his inside hind leg. Applying pressure then will encourage him to stretch it forward into the print of the front foot and even beyond.

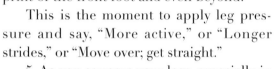
Fig. 65

This is the moment to apply leg pressure and say, "More active," or "Longer strides," or "Move over; get straight."

5. As you squeeze your legs, especially in the trot and canter, be sure your contact with his mouth is elastic, so that he *can* stretch into the longer stride. Remember that he can only lengthen his stride as far as his nose is poking out.

6. If he's overflexed or very short in the neck, he may throw his front leg forward, but his stride will still be short because he *has* to touch the ground at a point beneath where his nose is.

Fig. 66 7. When you shorten, the moment to increase your feel of the mouth is when your seat brushes the saddle in the "down" phase of the trot stride—when your horse's inside hind has reached forward and is meeting the ground.

This is the moment when I say, "Shorten your stride and lighten your fore-hand."

Fig. 66

8. Then relax a little, and repeat the aid, taking with the same degree of pressure, at the same point in the next stride.

9. Shortening the canter will take a little more work because things will be happening faster. You'll probably need to take a little more feel because there's more power going into your hands at each stride . . .

10. . . . but keep enough leg that your horse doesn't drop into the trot.

In both lengthening and shortening, you and your helper on the ground should each see your horse's shape changing.

1. As he lengthens . . .

2. . . . his neck extends, his nose pokes out, and his whole frame gets longer.

3. Your helper should see the hind feet overstepping the tracks of the front . . .

4. . . . and you should feel a little more thrust from behind (some people compare it to tooth-paste being squeezed from a tube) and hear a longer time between footfalls.

Fig. 67 My horse's nose is in front of the verti-cal, and he's really stretching his whole body. I'm following this stretching motion with my arms and shoulders. My hips and seat follow his back.

5. As your horse shortens stride, his frame shortens too.

Fig. 67

6. His steps should become shorter without becoming mincing—there should still be plenty of activity coming from the hindquarters.

To develop your sense of your horse's pace and your own ability to produce consis-tency, do some experimenting. In a normal working canter, count the number of strides you get down the long side of your ring. Do it several times, and try to keep the number the same every time. Next, shorten his canter as much as you can; again, count the number of strides you get through several trips down the long side, aiming for consistency. Then do the same exercise with lengthening.

Listen to your horse's strides. In each pace try to make them as consistent as a metronome. With practice, as you get to know how his lengthened and shortened gaits feel and what balance of leg and hand aids produce them, you'll be able to choose and then maintain whatever rhythm you want.

Fig. 68 Here my horse is producing a shorter stride overall than in the previous photo. His neck is up and rounder, and his hind legs are *Fig. 68*
under him a bit more. I am sitting closer to the vertical, my elbows are bent, and my hands are slightly higher. These are two perfect examples of the same moment in the stride, one long stride and one short.

CHAPTER FIVE

INFLUENCING
LATERAL MOVEMENT

You've already experienced the fact that bending your horse comes more from the influence of your seat and legs than from your hands. His motion is created from behind and travels forward; your legs urge him to produce pace, rhythm, and impulsion, and your hands "receive" that impulsion and keep it constant as they go forward and back in rhythm with his head and neck movement.

In asking for lateral movement, your hands work together as a unit, as they did in the turn on the haunches. They contain and organize your horse's energy but never pull back on the mouth, never drag the head in or down. Think of what you want to do as "resisting forward."

The elements of control you'll work on in the following figures are the same ones you'll rely on for all your turns—wide or narrow, on hunter and jumper courses, or around dressage rings.

Riding a Circle

Before you begin riding a circle (or any of the figures in the rest of this section on basic flat work), visualize how the figure should look. If you're going to ride a circle, visualize a round shape—not an oval egg—that brings you back to the track at the precise place where you left it. Once you know where you're going, you can begin.

Fig. 69 1. Keeping them at the five-inch-apart distance, shift both your hands slightly to what will be the inside of the circle (without increasing pressure). Your inside direct rein tells your horse to turn onto the track of the circle, while the outside rein comes against his neck to support his outside shoulder. Moving both hands together keeps your contact on both sides of his mouth equal and prevents your pulling his head in too much.

The movement of my hands is slight, just enough that the inside rein becomes a direct rein slightly off the neck.

Fig. 70 2. When your horse is correctly bent, you should just see the corner of his inside eye. The bend will bring your inside rein slightly away from his neck and the outside rein against it, so that the neck "fills out" the outside rein.

Fig. 69

Here the inside (right) rein is off my horse's neck, my inside leg is asking him to bend and step into the left rein, and he's slightly bent throughout his body. At the same time, my outside rein, together with my outside leg, is doing no more than support the outside of the horse.

3. Rhythmically squeeze your inside leg against the girth in time with the forward

Fig. 70

step of your horse's inside hind. The pressure, slightly greater than you'd use to send him forward in the gait, tells him to *bend* around the leg, not to fall in, and puts him onto the outside rein. You're asking him to bend, nose to tail, just enough to conform to the track of the circle he's on.

4. Your outside leg belongs a little behind the girth to keep the haunches from swinging out. Use only as much pressure against him as he's using against you. If there's no pressure from him, keep your leg passively resting on his side, ready at any moment to become active.

You're applying your aids correctly when your horse stays on the track you want, giving you the size circle you visualized *and* the feeling that he's going where you want him to.

1. If your horse falls off the circle to the outside, you need more outside leg behind the girth and outside rein pressure against the neck. Move both hands more to the inside (but not across the crest).

Fig. 71 My outside aids (rein and leg) are supporting my horse's right shoulder and right hind leg to be certain we stay on our track.

2. Make sure you're not hanging on the inside rein, which

Fig. 71

would make your horse's neck bulge out still more.

3. If he leans in, you need more inside *leg* to keep him from falling in—*not* more inside rein.

4. If he speeds up, apply a half-halt, taking his mouth a little more strongly with both reins, in rhythm with his inside hind leg, until you feel him slow. Then continue as before.

5. If he slows down, add leg—but either speeding up or slowing down, remember that you are responsible for the rhythm of the gait and the length of stride. Choose 4 mph, or 6, or 8, but stay consistent.

Riding Half-Circles

Riding half-circles gives you practice in applying your bending aids in both directions and your horse practice in keeping his balance in both directions. In this exercise you'll come off the rail, follow a circular track until you reach a point just opposite your starting point, and then return to the rail on a diagonal track.

1. As you come off the rail onto the curving path, bend your horse around your inside leg at the girth. Keep your outside leg quietly against his side a little back from the girth to prevent the haunches from swinging out.

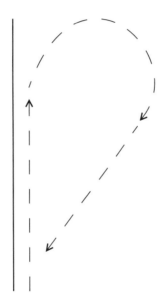

Half circle to the right

2. When you complete the half-circle, you straighten him to begin the diagonal path back . . .

3. . . . and then gradually shift to your new inside aids as you approach the rail again. With your new inside leg at the girth and your old inside leg moved back to the outside-leg position . . .

4. . . . put him on your new outside rein with your new inside leg.

Fig. 72

Fig. 73

Fig. 74

Fig. 75

Fig. 76

Fig. 72 As I begin the half-circle to the left, I'm looking left. I have him bent evenly from nose to tail, his neck neither way in nor way out.

Fig. 73 He's bent only as much as my circle. My inside hand and rein are off the neck, maintaining a light contact with a direct rein. My inside leg at the girth is asking him to bend left, and he's responding through his entire body.

Fig. 74 Now I'm starting to focus on the diagonal line. My inside leg is asking the horse to hold his bend and stay on the outside rein. My inside rein is following the mouth.

Fig. 75 A moment later we complete the half-circle and are traveling straight on the diagonal line, heading back to our imaginary rail. Both reins, both of my legs, and both eyes make him straight. Nearing the rail, I use my right leg at the girth to make him take the new outside (left) rein and bend right. My left leg is slightly behind the girth to guard his haunches, and my hands are slightly right.

Fig. 76 Regaining the track, I straighten with just a suggestion of a right bend from head to tail—not head pulled in or haunches way in or out. My right leg is at the girth, my left leg slightly behind the girth.

5. After you complete several half-circles, try a variation: half-circle in reverse. Come off the track on a diagonal . . .

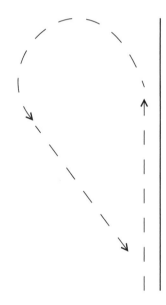

Half circle to the left

6. . . . and then ride a half-circle back to the rail.

Once you're comfortable riding individual circles and half-circles, put several of them together to give the two of you practice riding accurately and balancing through a series of turns, such as you might meet in competition. For example: half-circle, long side, diagonal, half-circle, diagonal, side, half-circle in reverse, diagonal, side, circle. Make up different variations of your own.

Riding Figure Eights and Serpentines

To develop your lateral control still further, practice figures that take you smoothly from one bend to another.

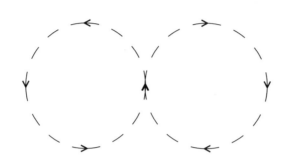

Figure eight

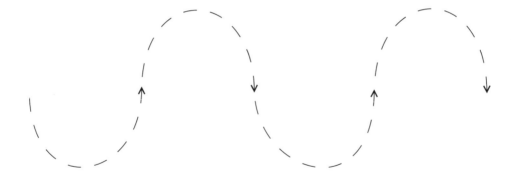

Serpentine

1. Visualize a figure eight as two circles joined together.
2. Ride your horse around the first circle, bending him around your inside leg . . .
3. . . . until you approach your starting point again. Then straighten him for a step or two . . .
4. . . . and bend him around your other leg to ride the second circle.

Fig. 77 Still on the track of the first circle—to the left—my eyes are looking exactly where I want to go. My hands are slightly in, and my inside leg is asking for left bending.

Fig. 78 As we complete that circle, we're very straight. My legs are even at the girth, my hands have even contact, and my eyes are looking straight ahead.

Fig. 79 Now I've begun to track right. My eyes are right, my hands are right, and my horse is bending throughout his body around my right leg.

5. Now put together what you've learned from half-circles and figure eights by riding a serpentine: a series of three or four loops connected by straight lines. (How many loops depends on how much space you have; although the greener the two of you are, the

Fig. 77

Fig. 78

Fig. 79

bigger your loops should be.) Make sure your loops are uniform—not a tiny loop followed by a large loop; eyeball a pattern and follow it.

6. Because turns come up more quickly during serpentines, doing them will refine your coordination. Your aim is to go from one "inside leg to outside rein" combination . . .

7. . . . to the other, without losing smoothness.

8. The more effective your aids become with practice, the tighter the loops you can make.

RIDING A COURSE ON THE FLAT

As a sort of summing up of your flat work, first visualize and then ride on the flat the kind of track you'd follow on a hunter course: an introductory circle at one end of your ring, a long side, a diagonal, the other long side, another diagonal, and a final circle. Choose a pace and stick with it all the way through. Focus on maintaining your rhythm, straightness, balance, and smoothness.

FINAL THOUGHTS ON BASIC FLAT WORK

You'll have accomplished a lot when you're correct and confident in all this work. You'll have learned how to influence your horse's pace going forward and how to influence him laterally. And because you've been working on awareness as well as action, you'll be able to answer for yourself, by "feeling," such questions as "Is my horse straight? Is he bent? Where are his shoulders? Where are his haunches? Where are his head and neck? What pace is he in?"

The better your flat work becomes, the more rewarding your riding will be—and the simpler your job will be in the next section, basic jumping. While you don't have to be perfect at everything we've gone over before advancing, you must at least be comfortable. And the bottom line is that, the better your flat work, the easier jumping will be for you and your horse.

When you begin jumping, don't abandon your flat work. Continue to make it part of your daily routine. (In the next section, I'll give you a suggested schedule.) Jumping is not something you should do every day; in fact, my horses do very little jumping between showing—but flat work and trail riding are an effective combination for every day.

My own riding routine includes doing all of these exercises almost every day. I don't do them in the same order (that would bore my horses as much as it would me!), but in different sequences and combinations that keep us fresh and enjoying our work. Use your own imagination to mix up the work you do to hone basic skills. If you identify a weak point, of course you'll have to spend more time on it, but don't drill and drill. Spend five or ten minutes on the problem, then switch to something your horse does well and enjoys, and then come back to the problem area after the two of you are refreshed and his self-confidence is restored. Remember, the sign of a great rider—and a good trainer—is a happy horse. Don't just ask yourself, "How can I get this across?" Ask instead, "How can we accomplish what we need to in a way that's entertaining for both of us?" The more "feeling" a rider you become, the more instinctive will be your ability to answer that question. One of my favorite sayings is: "Ask for a lot, be happy with a little, and reward often."

II.

BASIC JUMPING

Many riders think flat work is so simple that they don't really have to pay any attention to it, that the real meat of learning to ride comes only when they begin jumping. If you're a rider who picked up this book with that perspective but gave the exercises in the preceding section your honest effort, I hope that by now you've begun to appreciate, as I do, what flat work can do both for your horse and for you. The work I'll be giving you now—over poles, over simple jumps, and over simple courses (all of which you'll be able to put together without a ton of expensive equipment)—should confirm your appreciation for what you've learned through flat work.

If, however, you skipped that earlier section, go back—please! You aren't being fair to either your horse or yourself if you move on to jumping before you achieve a level of real comfort with basic flat work. As the great jumper riders and trainers will tell you, successfully negotiating even the most challenging grand prix course is, at base, a matter of flat work with jumps in the way. If you can't do flat work, you can't jump well.

GAUGING READINESS

When are you competent enough in basic flat work to move on to basic jumping? Physically, you're ready when you can apply all the basic aids you've worked on independently—such as using your legs without your hands, applying one leg while keeping the other still, and so on—and when you have your horse responding to these basic aids—such as moving forward and laterally from your leg, coming back to your hand—with a minimum of effort on your part. Responsiveness is a basic necessity for all riding sports, and if you've done all the flat work I've given you so far you should be achieving responses with a minimum of effort (no big spurs or long whips).

Mentally, you're ready to advance when you reach the point where you feel real trust in your horse, trust in your teacher, and confidence in your own ability to go on. (If your only teacher so far has been this book and you feel any uncertainty, you may want to spend a couple of sessions with a professional trainer, just to be sure you're starting off correctly. At the very least, remember that I've said you have to trust me and follow what I say. If you follow my instructions conscientiously, the program will work; if you pick and choose, you're on your own.)

If you're not yet feeling confident about the idea of jumping, continue working on the flat until you're ready to advance. If you like, you can expand your flat work to include the exercises in this section that use poles on the ground, and you can even substitute poles on the ground for the small fences in the other exercises. This way, you'll do a lot to develop your jumping skills without ever leaving the ground (there's no need to rush yourself!). Once you're relaxed, you'll be able to take what your horse can do and use it to your advantage; but as long as you're petrified, you'll ride badly; all your mental circuits will be so busy with your own worries, you'll never feel the messages he's trying to get through to you.

When you do feel confident enough about yourself to consider moving on, make sure you have a really safe school horse and a teacher you can trust. If you have any doubts about your own horse, get a professional opinion of his safety before you try any jumping work with him. Don't think that if your desire is great enough you can fix any problem. Some horses aren't meant to jump, just as some horses aren't meant to do dressage. A dead-green horse, no matter how innately talented he may be, isn't a good match for a green rider. And a horse that's really chicken or physically unsound or that has a bad technique just isn't safe to jump. The leg-hanger, for example, is likely to crash, and you don't want to chance being aboard when he does.

ATTITUDE

Attitude is even more critical to your success over fences than was true in basic flat work. The key to learning to jump is self-discipline, which means focusing on the principles I'm giving you and following my instructions completely. All the exercises in this section will be aimed at keeping things simple; what I want you to do is concentrate on maintaining your position, looking where you want to go, and *allowing* your horse to jump the obstacle. If you clear your mind and focus on just these things, the exercises will be easy. Let your mind wander, to what you need to pick up at the supermarket on the way home or even to the presence of a friend watching you from the rail, and everything will fall apart.

The good news is that you can learn concentration by repetition, the same way your horse learns to leg-yield or turn on the forehand. Position (eyes up, heels down, and so forth), rhythm, and pace are the absolutes you need to focus on; pick one or two components that you know give you trouble and repeat them, repeat them, repeat them to yourself ("Eyes, rhythm, eyes, rhythm," for example). Counting strides can also be a helpful technique, because it keeps you conscious of the rhythm and keeps your mind on the job at hand.

One more thing of which I'll remind you as we go along is that each of the exercises has a beginning, a middle, and an end. *All parts of the exercise are equally important.* Many of them, for example, end with a halt or a circle; the way you perform the halt or the circle is every bit as important as the way you negotiate the jump. I've seen riders at all levels who focus all their concentration and energy so completely on the jump that they have none left for what comes after—and what comes after is usually the approach to another jump. If you're not ready to prepare for that next jump, you'll immediately doom your chances of having a good fence; *you must keep riding.* Jumping well—remember—is flat work with jumps in the way.

PRELIMINARIES

One of the first things you need to do, once your horse has passed muster in the safety department, is to determine whether he *knows how to jump.*

Remember how you watched him without a rider at the walk, trot, and canter, and how you squeezed your hand in rhythm with his stride to develop a *feeling* for his gaits? Before you begin this section's work, spend a little time watching him jump.

Set a fairly low vertical fence, two feet six inches or three feet in height, in your work area, and then form a jumping chute with two poles, resting one end of each pole on the corresponding end of the top rail, just inside the standard, and the other end on the ground leading up to the fence. Longe your horse through the chute several times, and watch what he does. Left to himself, he sets himself up, finds his balance . . .

. . . and clears the fence nicely, thank you.

Watch him several times, noting how (and how well!) he does his job. That's the way you want him to jump with you on his back, just as naturally as if you weren't there. Your goal is to *accompany* him; to complement him, not interfere with him. The great hunter and jumper riders appear to be at one with their horses—almost centaur-like—because they've mastered the art of *noninterference*. You want to master it, too.

EQUIPMENT FOR JUMPING

Tack

Just as on the flat, less is better. I school even the most difficult horses in the simplest possible equipment. In most cases, lots of flat work gets rid of the bad habits (head tossing, for example) that might otherwise require extra equipment. If I'm really having problems with a horse, I may add a running martingale just for showing, but I do so rarely; even Starman, the stallion I rode at the Olympics in Seoul, shows without a martingale. Generally, I advise riders to try not to school in a martingale—to save the reinforcements for showing. Even if a horse is a little difficult to ride without help from additional equipment, you'll learn to ride better if you don't routinely depend on it.

If you'd really feel more confident with a running martingale, however, adjust it loosely, so that the rings can reach the withers. (I prefer a running to a standing martingale because it's less restrictive. But a standing martingale will give you a bit more control on a green horse. If you use one, be sure to adjust the length so that the leather will easily reach the throatlatch; you want to provide some boundaries, not "fix" your horse's head and neck position.)

For jumping, I always use open-front shin boots. I add bell boots only if my horse has a real problem with overreaching.

Aids and Half-Aids: Voice, Spur, and Stick

Used sparingly, the voice is a very effective aid. If you need to encourage a horse that isn't coming forward enough in response to your leg, or you want to keep a hot horse coming to a spooky jump but don't want to close your leg more and risk an overreaction, a cluck can produce just the degree of additional boldness or confidence he needs. With many horses, I use the cluck as a first aid on the way to a fence, following it with leg, then a stronger leg, and finally my stick. But I'm careful not to overuse the cluck so as not to deaden the effect.

A "Whoa," like a cluck, is a useful "half-aid." A quiet, slow, drawn-out "Whoooa" (not right in front of the judge, of course) can steady a horse that's growing tense, inviting him to relax and wait—with none of the negative effect that taking his mouth might produce.

I always wear a spur; it's another helpful backup if the horse doesn't respond to my leg aid. To use the spur, turn your toe out (not down), increasing and decreasing the pressure in rhythm with the stride, just as you'd use your leg, until your horse responds. Don't just jam the spur into his side and leave it there, without "feeling"; he'll both resent it and eventually become deadened to it.

A stick should be as much a part of your standard equipment as gloves and polished boots. I prefer a medium-length stick to either the little bats you see some equitation riders use (they look nice, but they can't do much) or a long dressage-type whip (which can be used with both hands on the reins, but at the cost of jerking the horse in the mouth).

To use your stick, put both reins in one hand (keeping your horse straight and maintaining a soft feel that will let him go forward), and use the other hand to apply the stick behind your leg. Practice at a standstill and then at the walk, the trot, and the canter, until you're equally comfortable using either hand for either job. A tap of the stick on your horse's shoulder can be an effective backup to your leg and rein in correcting a shoulder that's starting to bulge.

Your horse should always go forward in response to your stick. If he refuses a fence and you use your stick, I'd rather see him bolt away than just stand there. The correction must be forward. If you hold or jerk him in the mouth at the same time that you apply your stick, he has nowhere to go but up or sideways or back, none of which you want. If he ducks out to one side, turn him back the way he came—to the left, say, if he ducks to the right—and then circle in that same direction to approach the fence again, so that he knows he has to do what you tell him to do, not what he decides to do.

Which aid to use—voice, spur, or stick—and in what order or combination is very much a matter of knowing your own horse and using just as much as he needs but no more. Moderation is the key; overuse leads to ineffectiveness.

SCHEDULE

You probably don't enjoy doing the same old thing day after day, and neither does your horse. While ideally you'll work him six days a week, your partnership will be a lot more satisfying to both of you if you leaven your concentrated schooling with more relaxing work and an occasional trail ride or light hack. A schedule along the following lines should keep both of you fresh and interested in your work:

Monday: off
Tuesday: easy flat work
Wednesday: more demanding flat work or
     gymnastic jumping school
Thursday: easy flat work
Friday: jumping school or trail ride
Saturday: flat work
Sunday: light jumping school or flat work

While you're learning the exercises in this book you may want to jump two or three times a week, but most of the time you should mix up the flat work and jumping. However, if you feel it will help a youngster grasp a new exercise by jumping two days in a row, use low fences that won't pound his legs. If he responds well, maybe jump him just once or twice the following week.

CHAPTER SEVEN

JUMPING POSITION

Before you approach your first pole on the ground, I'm going to help you establish a balanced jumping position at the halt. Finding your balance is crucial now because you're going to depend on your ability to maintain that balance as you jump. Once you've developed a secure jumping position and committed to your muscle memory the way it should *feel*, you'll be that much freer to attend to the communication between you and your horse that goes on as you jump.

For the work in this section, you're going to want your stirrups a hole or two shorter than you've had them on the flat, which will put a little more angle in your ankles, knees, and hips. While doing flat work your stirrups were as long as you could comfortably have them and still keep your heels down. In jumping you'll find that the tighter angles a shorter length creates will help you maintain the more forward position needed to stay with your horse's more forward center of gravity.

Stirrups that are too long will glue you into the

saddle, behind the motion and out of balance—even making you fall back in the air. Some riders, particularly shorter ones, think they must ride long all the time. I disagree. Stirrups that are too long make you reach all the time, so you can't go with your horse's motion. That means you can't achieve your goal of interfering as little as possible while he gets on with his job.

As a rule of thumb, you'll generally want to raise your stirrups one hole to jump low fences (up to three feet six inches) and then another hole for every foot higher you jump. The bigger and wider the fences, the more you'll feel the need to get up with your horse by shortening your stirrups.

In grand prix competition, for example, I normally raise my stirrups three to four holes from the length I use in schooling on the flat. For the low fences you'll be meeting in this section, though, one or two holes should be plenty.

Just sitting in your chair, you can prove to yourself how critical your balance is to following the motion of jumping. First, put your legs straight out in front of you and try to get to your feet without using your hands, which is the equivalent of sinking your weight in your heels and lightening your seat to just short of two-point position as you approach a fence. You can't get to your feet unless somebody pulls you up—the equivalent of pulling yourself forward by yanking on your horse's mouth or getting "left behind." Moreover, his hind end would be strung way out behind because your leg wasn't there to help him stay "together" and balanced for the jumping effort.

Fig. 80

Fig. 80   Here I'm all out of balance: my lower leg is way out in front of me, and I can't get my seat out of the saddle.

Now try tucking your legs back behind the vertical, where they'd be if you were pivoting your upper body forward from pinched knees and swinging your legs back to compensate. If you keep your legs there and try to get up, you'll fall on your nose. But if you place your legs just comfortably underneath you, where they'd normally be if you were sitting up straight, you can stand up without help and without a struggle.

Fig. 81 Here my lower leg is too far back. The stirrup leather is angled rearward instead of being perpendicular to the ground, my knee is pinched, and my toe is slightly in. If anything untoward were to happen, I'd lose my balance and fall forward.

To keep your lower legs under you and achieve balance in the saddle, be sure that your heels stay down and your ankles stay flexible, so that your Achilles tendon can act as your shock absorber each time you

Fig. 81

land from a fence. This is something your shorter stirrup length will help produce. Your heels are your anchor; if they aren't down, your lower legs will almost certainly swing forward, back, or both when you go to jump, because you haven't set your anchor properly.

To give yourself an effective anchor, turn your toes out about twenty degrees and push your heel down so that you have useful contact with your leg from just below the knee to the ankle (as you did on the flat) and, remember, don't pinch with your knee.

Fig. 82 This is the position I want to be in over a fence. The weight in my heels keeps my legs quietly around my horse, and I'm pushing down in my knee, not pinching. My seat is out of the saddle, my hands rest firmly on his neck, and my eyes are up and looking ahead. You can see that my leg is very secure. The whole limb is down and around my horse, and my weight flows down through my knees and into my heels.

Fig. 82

If your horse rushes forward as soon as you release his mouth, he's telling you either that you are pinching and he thinks your leg squeeze means "Hurry up!" or that you're standing up too far in your stirrups, leaning forward, and sending his center of gravity forward. When your weight goes forward, you lose your balance, feel insecure, and so pinch to compensate.

When your horse jumps, his center of gravity moves farther forward than it moves when you canter on the flat. The position of your seat and the amount you'll need to bring your upper body forward to stay with him will depend on your level of accomplishment. If you are a beginner, stay relatively forward to keep yourself off his back and out of his way.

For now, while still at the halt, incline your upper body forward about 3o degrees, the same angle as in the posting trot. Push your knuckles down on the neck or grab the mane or a neckstrap so that you'll be able to stay forward. Take another look at the "ideal position" picture: my upper body is forward, ready for a fence; my eyes are up; my hands are firmly on the neck; and my legs are well anchored by my deep heels.

Send your weight down into your heels and let your seat come off the saddle, but don't stand way up in your stirrups; as in the "up" phase of the trot, think of moving your seat more "forward" than "up." This position isn't a very effective one for riding, but it will allow you to develop basic feel without interfering with your horse's jumping effort.

As you gain better control of your body and become comfortable with the jumping motion, you'll be able to move your center of gravity closer to your horse's. Drop your seat so close to the saddle that you just graze the leather with your breeches. You should be centered over the deepest part of the saddle, just behind the pommel, not pushed back in the old-fashioned fox hunter's pose, with lower leg ahead of the body and nowhere to go but backward.

Fig. 83   Here my seat is barely above the saddle, ready at any moment to drop into it and be effective either as a driving aid or as a retarding aid. My leg is under me, and my body is bent at the hips, ready to move forward. I'm neither ahead of nor behind the motion.

Fig. 83

You should feel ready to "go with your horse," neither jumping ahead of him nor sitting against him, behind the motion.

With your upper body in the more forward jumping position, you'll need shorter reins than you had on the flat to maintain a nice, elastic, *feeling* contact—your conversational link—with your horse's mouth. In the preceding picture you can see that, if I need to feel the mouth to slow or change direction, I can do so instantly.

While you're learning to find your balance, rest your hands on your horse's neck as a crutch so that you don't hit him in the mouth. *Rest* them there, don't lean—you should just be able to feel the neck with your knuckles. Once your balance is reliable, carry your hands just *above* the neck, with a feeling similar to the one you have in posting trot.

Now you have your *jumping position,* the position you'll use both between fences and in the air over them. Get used to it by practicing not just at the halt but also at the walk, the trot, and the canter, resting your hands on the neck or grabbing mane whenever you feel you're going to fall back or forward.

As you sense yourself becoming more secure, try this exercise: at a standstill, take your hands off the neck and quietly (not with a sudden rush that might spook your horse) raise your arms out from your sides like airplane wings. When you can do so without tipping forward or back, you'll know for certain that you really are balanced over your base and are not supporting yourself on your hands. You want your balance so firmly established on the flat that you *know* you can maintain it in the air and not hit your horse in the mouth with your hands or in the back with your seat.

Now, as you walk around in jumping position—hands on the neck, seat slightly out of the saddle, knees relaxed, ankles flexed—concentrate on *feeling* which muscles are holding you in place. I'm not going to tell you which ones; finding out the answer for yourself will make it more meaningful—and memorable. Ask yourself, "How am I doing this? What are the muscles and feelings that are keeping me in balance?" You don't need to know their names, but you do need to explore fully your sense of being in balance so that you *feel* all its components. Being aware of how you're balancing will build muscle memory; you'll be able to carry the feeling through this work and into the work to follow, bringing yourself back to the correct position by remembering how it *feels* when it's right. Lack of muscle memory is what makes you revert to ineffective ways of doing things.

THE ELEMENTS OF EFFECTIVE JUMPING

Most of the elements of effective jumping are things you've mastered on the flat: position and balance, eyes looking ahead, correct pace, and consistent rhythm. At first, as you put these elements together to work over fences, you'll focus consciously on one element at a time. Gradually, all these conscious efforts will become reflexes.

One major new element you're going to add to your work now is *smoothness.* And with the secure position that you've already developed, you'll find smoothness fairly easy to achieve. Think back to watching your horse jumping free on the longe. He can already manage smoothness on his own; your job is to make yourself enough of a partner so that you don't disrupt his smoothness. Do that, and you'll *both* be smooth.

What, besides noninterference, does your horse need from you in jumping? Guidance in just two areas: pace (including rhythm) and direction. It's your responsibility to tell him how fast you want him to go and what line you want him to be on. The jump itself is *his* responsibility, and that's how the great riders make it look. He sees a distance to the fence as well as you do; your job is not to disrupt his concentration by fussing with him. If you make yourself responsible for pace and line, and if you organize those elements in the turn before the jump, he can focus on the fence. Once you tell him what kind of line it is by creating and maintaining the right pace (forward, normal, or steady) and the line (straight, angled, or bending), the jumps themselves are easy for him. He'll balance himself and find a distance automatically. When you "do your homework" this way, by establishing your position, the pace, and the line before you even turn to the jump and maintaining them, the number of strides works out perfectly and automatically.

CHAPTER EIGHT

EXERCISE 1:
STRAIGHT LINE OVER RAILS
ON THE GROUND

Your horse's size and natural stride dictate the amount of pace you'll need, and this first exercise will tell you the natural length of his canter stride: a long 13 feet, a normal 12, a short 11 or less. Besides helping you identify his natural stride, the exercise will also give you a good feel for the pace needed to make it longer or shorter, and it will give you lots of time to establish your jumping position.

Exercise 1-A

Place a single rail, with a stripe painted in the middle, on the ground. From the beginning, you want to train yourself to jump across the middle of your fences, so it's to your advantage if all the rails you go over, on the ground or in jumps, are marked at the center.

In the jumping position that you've practiced, first walk . . .

. . . and then trot the rail.

On each approach, look *up* toward the fence line of your work area. (Looking up is the beginning of a habit you want to form; when you jump fences rather than poles you'll look to the next jump instead of the fence line.)

A few strides beyond the rail, make a smooth halt. Then assess how you did and what you could have done better.

Throughout, focus on maintaining position, line (in this case, straightness to the center), and pace (an even rhythm—don't get faster and then slower) *both in front of the rail and after it.* "After" is at least as important as "before," maybe more so, because it's where you begin to develop a tool you'll want to be able to depend on when you ride courses. Remember, right at the beginning of this section I told you that the end of every exercise would be as important as its beginning and middle.

WALKING THE RAIL

Fig. 84 I start with a nice walk rhythm and a straight line; to maintain my line, I focus on a point beyond the rail, not on the center stripe.

Fig. 85 As we pass over the rail, I maintain my position, not leaning forward or back. I follow my horse's head and neck with my arms and hands, all the while keeping my focus on the rhythm and the straightness of our line. *He's* responsible for getting his hooves over the rail.

Fig. 84

Fig. 85

Fig.86

Fig. 86 If he starts to rush, I make a half-halt to tell him to maintain his pace, then relax when he does—but I never lose the straight line or my position.

TROTTING THE RAIL

Fig. 87 Always, always, always *look* where you're going. My eyes are keeping us on the straight track. I'm in my normal posting-trot position, upper body 30 degrees in front of the vertical, maintaining a straight line from my elbow to the horse's mouth, and keeping a light contact in the reins with my legs under me.

Fig. 87

Fig. 88 My horse had to take a large step to clear the rail; the big step has made me post higher than necessary. However, I've kept my balance—no sign of falling forward or back—and I've maintained the straight line from elbow to mouth, and I'm still following his head and neck.

Fig. 88

Fig. 89 An instant later, we're together again. My seat is just about to touch the saddle as his right hind leg is coming down, my ankles are absorbing the shock down through my heels, and my eyes are still holding the line.

Fig. 89

Fig. 90 I'm keeping my eyes on my line and opening my hip angle slightly to prepare for our halt.

Fig. 90

Fig. 91

Fig. 91   To begin the halt, I anchor myself by sitting in the saddle and deepening my heels. At the same time I bend my elbows to raise the horse's balance. When we've halted, I relax and check my position.

After you've gone over the rail a few times at the walk and the trot, canter it, again letting the pole "get in the way." It's not a big jump, so stay relaxed and just allow your horse to take it in his stride.

CANTERING THE RAIL

Fig. 92   I'm just sitting the canter and letting my horse think about the rail. My seat is quiet in the saddle, my heels are down, and I have a light contact with his mouth.

Fig. 92

Fig. 93   I keep my position as he steps over the rail. My hips stay elastic, so I don't bounce out of the saddle, and my arms follow his neck and mouth.

Fig. 93

Fig. 94   Even though his hind legs made a little jump, my seat and hips elastically follow his back. My upper body remains slightly forward, "with the motion" but not thrown up and forward as if we had taken a jump.

Fig. 94

Exercise 1-B

When you and your horse are comfortable cantering the single rail, add a second rail sixty-six feet beyond the first. Eventually you're going to use this configuration to tell you whether your horse's canter stride is short, medium, or long; the distance you've set allows five normal canter strides after trotting the first rail for a horse with an average twelve-foot stride.

Before you work on determining canter stride, though, get used to the configuration by means of the following progression of exercises, which start in the trot. Pick a focal point at the end of your work area—one that lines up with the middle of the two rails—that you can use to help you stay straight. Then focus on maintaining *straightness* across both rails and into the halt beyond. Once again, the end is as important as the beginning and the middle.

Fig. 95

Focus on staying straight to the center of each rail, maintaining your rhythm and keeping your balanced jumping position as you trot in over the first rail . . .

. . . down to the second . . .

. . . over it . . .

. . . and out to a stop several strides beyond, still aiming at your focal point to stay straight.

Fig. 96

Fig. 95 I'm in my jumping position, my seat slightly out of the saddle. I'm thinking "Position!" really balancing myself over my leg and following my horse's mouth.

Fig. 96 As he steps over the rail, I maintain my balance, my line, and our pace—basically I'm staying out of his way.

Fig. 97 We're in excellent balance on the way to the second rail. I'm following his motion with a light contact that says, "No faster." My heels are down, and my legs are quietly "there," resting on his sides.

Fig. 97

Fig. 98 As he steps over the rail, I maintain my balance: my eyes are up, holding my line; my heels are deep, holding my leg quiet; hands are low with a following contact. I don't throw him off balance by leaning forward or back.

His expression in this sequence confirms that I'm accompanying, not disturbing him; he's free to concentrate on clearing the rails.

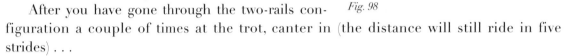

Fig. 98

After you have gone through the two-rails configuration a couple of times at the trot, canter in (the distance will still ride in five strides) . . .

. . . down to the second rail . . .

. . . out . . .

. . . and come to a smooth, straight halt several strides later.

Continue cantering the two rails until both you and your horse are negotiating the entire trip smoothly and calmly.

C ANTERING THE *R* AILS

Fig. 99 As we step over the first rail, my upper body is slightly forward, but my "following seat" is still lightly in the saddle. I'm focusing on regulating our pace, and my eyes are making the line work. I'm not looking down at

Fig. 99

Fig. 100

the rail or throwing my body or hands, but just maintaining what I have.

Fig. 100 After the rail, I remain quiet, my position the same except for slightly more supple arms. I'm thinking, "Eyes and rhythm"; my horse, once again, is totally concentrating on his job, which is to canter over the next rail.

Fig. 101   As he crosses the second rail, I stay with him, keeping my seat lightly "there." If I leaned forward or lifted my seat way up, he would speed up. I look as if I'm schooling on the flat with following arms and seat, perfect straightness and quiet legs, but there's a rail under us.

Fig. 102   "Police" yourself in the halt: keep your eyes up, bend your elbows slightly, and anchor your seat and legs down and around your horse—*every time.*

Fig. 101

Exercise 1-C

Now let's find out about your horse's stride length.

Canter over the first rail just as you did before, focusing on maintaining the rhythm and leaving your horse alone. Start counting strides aloud, but do not begin with the landing step (in which only his front feet land beyond the rail).

Begin with the first complete stride he takes inside the rail. That's "One."

Continue counting—"Two . . .

". . . Three . . .

". . . Four . . .

". . . Five"—and see where your horse is when you say "Five."

Fig. 102

If he fits the five strides in very comfortably, he has an average stride. If he's very close to the second rail, his stride is long. If he has to stand way back, or he adds a short one before the second rail, he's short-strided.

Don't stop, though. Continue out over the second rail, bring your horse to a halt on a straight line a few strides beyond, and think about how you did.

FINDING STRIDE LENGTH

As I begin determining my horse's stride length, I'm in a more forward position, similar to the balanced jumping position in the trot. You should be able to work over these rails smoothly in a half-seat like this as well as in the closer seat I used in the last exercise. If your horse is strong or fresh, definitely use more contact with your seat. When he relaxes, practice this balanced position.

Fig. 103   We're meeting the second of our two rails just right—the perfect takeoff spot—so I know he has a normal stride.

Counting strides has a very valuable side effect: it teaches you to feel rhythm and, subconsciously, to judge distances. The next time you go through this line you'll know when you say "Three" that you're just two

Fig. 103

strides away from the rail. You'll then begin to see what two normal remaining strides look like. With practice, by "osmosis," you'll develop an "eye," the skill that tells you whether a distance is going to work nicely or need a little adjustment.

(If you have trouble telling which is the landing stride and which the first full stride, start earlier: say "Land" as your horse touches down with his front legs on the far side of the first rail, then "One" when those legs land the next time, and so on.)

When you're able to keep your horse straight and stop smoothly, try varying the end of the exercise by halting on a straight line one time, then riding a smooth twenty-meter circle in one direction the next, and riding a similar circle in the other direction a time or two after that. In addition to keeping your horse from anticipating the halt, riding the circles will be useful preparation for riding courses.

As you begin the circle, *look where you are going.* Sit quietly in the saddle, following the canter stride with your hips and arms. If you have any trouble sitting in the saddle after being in two-point, drop your stirrups and ride the circle without them. You'll automatically sit correctly, and your horse will canter more smoothly, even with the stirrups banging on his sides.

Exercise 1-D

Next, try adjusting your horse's stride. It's something you did in basic flat work, but now you'll have the added factor of a rail to focus on.

Try *lengthening* first. To make the exercise work you must establish a longer stride *before* you cross the first rail, so build more pace on a big circle and then turn to the rails. As your horse "lands" over the first rail, keep your leg and lighter feel of his mouth to *allow* him to continue his more open stride . . .

. . . and cover the distance between rails in four strides. (Don't forget your straight halt afterward!)

Fig. 104

Fig. 105

Adjusting Stride — Lengthening

Fig. 104   I start in my basic canter position: seat in the saddle, heels down, upper body slightly ahead of the vertical, arms a continuation of the reins.

Fig. 105   A moment later I'm following more with my arms to encourage my horse to stretch his frame. To make four even strides between the rails, I must have his stride longer *before* we cross the first rail.

Fig. 106

Fig. 106   He lifts up to begin to stretch over the rail. I maintain my forward hip angle to stay with him, but I don't lean way forward or look down at the rail. My seat is lightly touching the saddle.

Fig. 107   As he stretches, I follow with supple arms, seat, and hips.

Fig. 108   He is maintaining a lovely rhythm. My arms and hands are very soft, following him as he lengthens.

Fig. 107

Fig. 109   Even now, in the "gathering" moment, he's longer in his frame and stride. I'm concentrating on our rhythm and line so the four strides works out nicely.

Fig. 110   With seat and leg, I say, "Keep stretching," and I feel his neck stretch, as well as his stride.

Fig. 111   As he steps over the rail, I follow, keeping a light seat and light contact with his mouth so that I'm not interfering with him.

Adjusting Stride—Shortening

Now shorten the stride. Again, prepare the length you want between the two rails *before* you turn to them by keeping just enough leg to maintain the canter and closing your fingers more firmly on the reins. When you feel the stride shorten, approach the first rail while *maintaining* the pace. Ideally, you'll fit in a sixth stride before the second rail. But if you see you haven't shortened enough to fit in that extra stride, just shorten some more—smoothly. Don't yank; sit deeper and close your hands more firmly on the reins, and see if you can make the "six" work. And in any case, finish the exercise with a smooth halt on a straight line.

Fig. 108

Fig. 109

Fig. 110

Fig. 111

Notice throughout the sequence how my leg stays down and around my horse and my eyes stay up.

Fig. 112 My basic position—eyes up, heels down, seat in the saddle—is the same as in lengthening, but now my reins are slightly shorter and I have stronger contact with the horse's mouth. He's "overflexed"—he has overreacted by dropping behind the vertical.

Fig. 113 Over the rail, I'm feeling his mouth to ask him to keep the shorter stride.

Fig. 114 He responds correctly, shortening his frame and balancing better, his poll now the highest part of his neck. Because he is carrying himself, my reins are lighter. Ideally, I should have my upper body back a few more degrees.

Fig. 115 Here I'm sitting better, more "into" my horse. My elbows are bent, helping to keep his balance up and short. My seat says "Stay in the canter," and my hands say "Shorten."

Continue working over the two rails, varying your striding requests and experimenting until you find the combination of pressure that produces what you're looking for. With repetition, you'll store this information in your muscle memory, too.

If you discover that your horse is going crooked instead of straight, look for the cause in your own riding first. Many riders have one hand that's heavier than the other or one leg that's stronger. Another possibility: does your horse have a physical problem? Any unevenness you noticed on the flat may be magnified in this exercise, and it will certainly be more noticeable when you progress to fences.

Fig. 112

Fig. 113

Fig. 114

Fig. 115

JUMPING ON A CURVING TRACK

EXERCISE 2:
CIRCLES OVER RAILS ON THE GROUND

When you're comfortable with crossing two rails on a straight line, move on to learning how to negotiate them on a bending line—a feature you'll meet in all equitation and jumper classes.

We'll start with one rail as the center of a figure eight, then move on to two rails on a circle, and finally meet those same two rails as part of a more sophisticated figure eight. Each of these exercises will develop your use of your eyes and further your ability to maintain position, rhythm, and pace on a bending line. And following a bending track will increase your horse's suppleness; he'll have to think about "jumping" and turning while he stays balanced and focused on the upcoming rail through a turn.

The key to making each circle round is using your eyes properly. When you drive a car, you go where your eyes are looking—your eyes automatically signal your body to make the adjustments that will take you where you're looking (that's why people swerve when they look at something off to one side of the road). The same thing happens in riding. When you look around a circle where you want to go, your body will follow the bending track that your eyes mark out. You won't need any consciously applied bending aids to push your horse out; the eyes will do it for you.

Exercise 2-A: Figure Eight Over One Rail

I think of this basic figure-eight exercise as having two perfect circles joining at the center of the rail. Each time I cross the rail, I angle my horse *slightly* in the direction of the new circle.

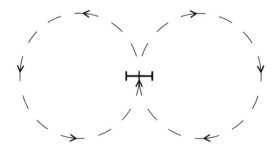

Figure eight over one rail

Fig. 116   Before my horse even steps over the rail, I anticipate the left turn, not by dropping a shoulder or collapsing a hip, but simply by turning my head and looking left. As I do so, my hands automatically shift leftward and tell him to begin turning.

Fig. 116

Fig. 117   My eyes hold us on my imaginary circle pattern. Both my hands are slightly left, so that my left rein is direct, my right supporting (against the neck). I continue to look where I want to go, so as soon as I reach the halfway point I'll glue my eyes back on the center of the rail where I want to cross it.

Fig. 117

Fig. 118   As we get close to the rail, I make him straight to the center of it. Again, I anticipate the new direction by looking right and beginning to turn him with both hands slightly right.

Fig. 118

Fig. 119   As I make my right-hand circle, I glue my eyes back onto the center of the rail. I don't lean in; I simply turn my head and so stay in line with my horse. My eyes are right, both hands are slightly right, my outside rein and leg are preventing the shoulder and haunches from falling out. And always—*always!*—I look where I want to go.

Fig. 119

Exercise 2-B: Two Rails on the Ground on a Circle

Now that you've practiced riding over one rail on a curving track, develop your feel further by negotiating two rails on a circle. Visualize a circle twenty meters across (about sixty feet), then place two rails across the circular track, one at the equivalent of nine o'clock and the other at three o'clock. (To help yourself keep the circle round as you ride it, you can also place markers just inside the track at six and at twelve o'clock and ride around them.)

First, walk the circle once. Remind yourself constantly to keep focusing ahead, around the circle, to keep the figure *round.*

Fig. 120   As I let my horse step over the rail, I concentrate on looking at the next rail, not down at this one. To turn him, I'm carrying both hands slightly left; my left rein, just off the neck, is directing, while my right, against the neck, is supporting. My inside leg prevents him from falling in; my outside stops him from falling out.

Fig. 120

Now pick up a posting trot and negotiate the circle again. Discipline yourself to go over the center of each rail . . . and to stay on the circle between rails. When you discipline yourself this way, your body language—what you do with your eyes, your reins, and your legs—communicates clearly with your horse to tell him where you want him to go.

Fig. 121   Without actually looking at the rail, I know we are about to go over it; that's my horse's responsibility. I know he's bent slightly left—I can feel it; I don't need to look at him. As we go over the rail, I'll remain focused *ahead.*

Fig. 121

When you're able to maintain your trot rhythm dependably and ride a truly circular track, go on to cantering the rails.

Again, stay straight to the center of each rail and keep looking around the circle. Maintaining the rhythm and shape of the circle is the important thing; don't worry about the number of strides between rails.

Concentrate on keeping the circle perfectly round so that your horse follows the same track *every* time, *smoothly.* Visualize *exactly* the same pattern and *exactly* the same feeling each time around.

Fig. 122

Fig. 122 In the canter, I ride and think just as in the trot, putting my eyes on the next rail and letting my horse concern himself with stepping over the obstacle. Because he's found a rather big distance, I've come farther out of the saddle than usual, but I am going with him, keeping my hands low. I keep my outside aids on him to be sure he turns as he goes over.

Fig. 123 As we continue around to the next rail, my seat stays in the saddle, following the motion of his back. My eyes are keeping us on the track. My horse is bent only as much as the circle we're on; my inside leg at the girth asks him to bend and keeps him from falling in.

Fig. 123

Fig. 124 He stepped over this rail, and my seat stayed close to the saddle. My hands, working together toward the inside, make the turn happen. Notice I'm holding the inside rein slightly off the neck.

Attention to detail and the ability that attention gives you to repeat a good performance again and again are assets you'll rely on as you advance. Whether you're going over rails on the ground or five-foot-six fences, the basics you're establishing now are the ones you'll come to depend on.

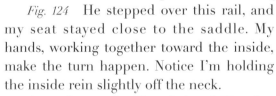

Fig. 124

Exercise 2-C: Figure Eight Over Two Rails

To develop your eyes' accuracy and your horse's suppleness still further, now ride the two rails on the ground as a figure eight, using three versions of the same exercise.

First, trot and then canter a simple figure eight. In the canter, cross the first rail . . .

. . . and land looking across the diagonal.

After landing, turn onto the diagonal . . .

. . . and change leads through the trot at the mid-point of the diagonal.

Keep using your eyes to define the track . . .

. . . and turn in time to let yourself cross the midpoint of the second rail straight. Then continue back across the diagonal again to complete your figure eight.

Fig. 125   I'm starting in the trot. This turn is much shorter than in the circle exercise, so you see more bending over the rail and around the turn that follows. My eyes look in as before, but now I'm looking into the imaginary line across the diagonal.

Fig. 126   As we get to the diagonal, we'll straighten. Notice that I'm not leaning in or out; I'm in the center of my horse.

Fig. 127   Now my eyes have shifted to the right to look at the second rail. My hands are slightly right, beginning to make the right bend; I'm changing my posting diagonal . . .

Fig. 128   . . . and riding my horse to the center of this new rail.

After a few simple figure eights, make the exercise a little more challenging:

At the trot, cross one rail . . .

Fig. 125

Fig. 126

Fig. 127

Fig. 128

. . . and ride a small circle to the inside that takes you back over the rail again. Then go on with the figure eight:

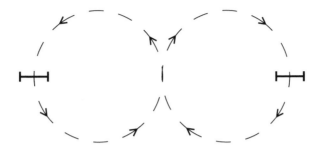

Figure eight over two rails

Travel the diagonal and turn for the second rail . . .

. . . and cross it a second time on a small circle before riding back to complete the figure eight.

After two or three figure-eights-plus-circles at the trot, challenge your horse's balance and your eye a little more by riding the same pattern at the canter.

You'll stay on one lead as you circle to the inside after the first rail . . .

. . . cross it again, doing your best to aim right for the center . . .

. . . and curve around for your diagonal path toward the second half of the figure eight.

Doing this exercise at the canter is especially effective for making your horse more supple and obedient to the directional signals you give with your eyes.

Fig. 129   Before we stepped over this rail I looked right; we land turning, into a tight arc.

Fig. 130   Now my eyes are back on the rail. My reins are asking him to turn and take short strides so that we'll make a small circle. My inside leg bends him while my outside leg helps to bring him around and keep this short canter.

Fig. 129

Fig. 130

Fig. 131   We're arriving at the center of the rail off our tight turn, and already I'm looking for the diagonal line I need to reach the second half of the exercise.

Fig. 132   One more thing to think about is a lead change at the midpoint of the diagonal. This is a simple change through the trot. My eyes keep the line while I feel for the trot. I take a half-halt with my arms, and as soon as I feel the trot rhythm I close my right leg and ask for the left lead, returning to the canter and all the while staying on my pattern. When you and your horse are more advanced, you can make a flying change through the diagonal.

Pick a spot to come to a smooth halt (never just a haphazard sloppy ending) and evaluate your ride. When you've been able to keep your horse consistently on track for two or three figure-eights-plus-circles without tugging at the reins or losing your position, you'll have accomplished enough for the day.

Fig. 131

Fig. 132

CHAPTER NINE

STRAIGHT LINES

EXERCISE 3:
TWO SMALL JUMPS ON A LINE

*T*his exercise, which provides your first experience of actual jumps, takes you back to focusing on straightness.

Exercise 3-A

Set a single low vertical—two feet high, or eighteen inches if that makes you feel more comfortable—with ground rails on both sides. Place the fence about a third of the way down the middle of your working space. (Set all your fences this way for the following exercises so that they can be ridden in either direction. That gives you added variety without added effort.)

As you've done before, pick a distant focal point that lines up with the middle of your fence. Then trot to the fence, all the way to the base without breaking to the canter before you jump. Focus on your focal point to keep you straight. You'll land in a canter stride, so close your hands firmly and bring your upper body back closer to the vertical to halt your horse smoothly on a straight line four or five strides after your fence.

Fig. 133   I'm in my jumping position, my upper body forward, and my eyes are on my line. My seat is close to the saddle and my weight is well anchored in my heels.

Fig. 134   My upper body has not moved at all. I'm still following his mouth; notice the straight line from elbow to bit. I try not to interfere; I want to keep our centers of gravity together.

Fig. 135   To prepare for the halt, I bring my upper body back to the vertical, bend my elbows to lift his head and neck, take a firmer contact on the mouth, and put more weight in my heels.

Fig. 133

Fig. 134

Fig. 135

Exercise 3-B

After trotting the single small vertical fence a few times, set a second one of equal size sixty feet away. You'll use the two jumps (as you did the two rails on the ground in the first exercise) for a progression of exercises.

Using your distant focal point again, trot the first fence and bring your horse back to a trot after he lands so that you meet the second fence in the trot as well. After landing from the second fence, bring him back through the trot to a halt on a straight line just as you did with the single vertical. Halting on a straight line keeps you straight, which helps develop the control you'll need later when you'll have to make a flying change between lines.

Fig. 136

Fig. 137

Fig. 136   In the landing, my hands follow his mouth, my arm is a continuation of the rein, and my leg stays down and around my horse. At this moment I'm already *thinking* of my trot transition.

Fig. 137   As he takes a canter stride away from the first fence, I deepen my heel, put my seat *firmly* in the saddle, and bring my upper body back. At the same time I take a strong feel of his mouth, lifting my chest and hands as a unit that says, "Trot now." As my horse finds the trot rhythm, I keep my seat in the saddle and relax my retarding aids, trusting him to maintain his pace and step over the second jump.

Exercise 3-C

Trot in again, but this time let your horse continue to canter after he lands and go on to meet the second fence in the canter. Again, halt him on a straight line.

Fig. 138

Fig. 138   As we land from the trot fence, I allow my horse to continue in the canter. I don't send him forward with my leg unless I feel he's dropping back to the trot.

Fig. 139   Now I've got my "following seat"—hips forward and arms supple, so I just follow my horse. My eyes are glued on fence two throughout.

Fig. 140   As he jumps, I rest my hands lightly on his neck so that I don't hit him in the mouth. I give

Fig. 139

him complete freedom with my arms as though they were part of the rein. Looking ahead, I think about my halting position.

Continue with this exercise until you get the feel of the canter rhythm. When you feel comfortable with the rhythm, start to count your strides to the second fence. For now, you're counting just to help yourself stay conscious of your rhythm. Because you've trotted to the first fence, you'll probably do five strides in the sixty feet, although at this point the number doesn't matter.

Fig. 140

Exercise 3-D

Reverse the order of jumps this time: meet the first fence at a slow canter . . . but come back to the trot after landing from it and trot out over the second fence.

Since your horse has been thinking "forward," getting the downward transition to the trot won't be easy; he's probably been "taking" you a little as he cantered out. You've already had experience in Exercise 3-B bringing him back to a trot for the second fence, so you should be able to manage. However, if you're having trouble with the added impulsion created by cantering in . . .

. . . try cantering in and halting . . . then trotting out.

With all the flat work you've done, you'll find you can halt easily, even if you couldn't get your horse back to the trot the time before. And once you've done *that,* you'll be able to use a half-halt and get a nice transition to the trot the next time.

Repeat these variations—trot in and trot out, trot in and canter out, canter in and trot out, always finishing with a halt on a straight line—until you're really comfortable jumping the two fences on a straight line.

Exercise 3-E

The next variation adds two new elements: cantering into the first fence as well as down the line and out, and meeting the line off a turn (as you normally would do in the show ring). Instead of coming to a halt after one of your trot in/canter out trips, you will continue around your work area and come back to canter the entire line.

The distance between fences, sixty feet, should translate into four normal twelve-foot canter strides between your first landing and second takeoff. So establish what you think is your horse's normal pace in the canter as you travel around the ring. For the sake of smoothness, you want your stride length in the approach to the first fence to match what you produce down the line to the second fence.

You want a twelve-foot stride and an established rhythm *before* you ever get to your first fence, so that all you need to do when you jump into the line is maintain stride and rhythm. If your stride is too short, you'll have to lengthen to get the four strides; if it's long, you'll have to shorten down the line. You don't want to do either, because the exercise won't be smooth. Moreover, your horse will be thinking about your hands or legs rather than about the jump in front of him. Do as little as you can in front of a fence. *Allow your horse to jump!*

Your accuracy going down the line will depend on how you ride the turn to the first element, so you want a very "straight" horse in the turn—his hindquarters following the track of his forelegs, neither leaning in nor bulging out. You'll get that smooth response if you keep things simple. As you approach the turn to the fence, use your distant focal point to define the straight course you want to ride (remember, you go where you look). Carry both your hands to the inside, just enough to put your horse on a straight track down the line. Maintain your own centered body position as you clear the first fence, ride four strides, jump the second, and halt on a straight line a few strides later.

Fig. 141

Fig. 141 In our first stride inside the line, I relax my arms and allow my horse to stretch, keeping a light contact with my seat and following the motion with my upper body.

Fig. 142 As he jumps, I hold my line with my eyes—I'm looking straight between his ears—and I keep my legs long and quiet.

At the halt, evaluate your performance. Not only how well you maintained your position and your straight track, but also the smoothness of your ride. Did you have to make a noticeable change of pace inside the line to get the four

Fig. 142

strides? If so, your ride lacked smoothness, so next time aim for maintaining that inside-the-line rhythm, speed, and stride length all the way around, so that you approach the first fence in the pace you want down the line. Repeat the exercise a few times, until you achieve the balance of aids that lets you feel a consistent rhythm all the way through.

When you do feel that consistency, you can develop your control and coordination further by varying the ending of the exercise. Alternate halting on a straight line with riding a circle following the second fence. As you land, look in the direction you want to go and anticipate a circle, so that your body language goes to work. In the first stride, sit in, lift your chest, and take a half-halt, just as you would on the straight. Shift both hands slightly to the inside, so that your inside rein is a little off the neck (a "direct" rein) and your outside is against the neck and supporting (your outside rein and leg hold your horse from falling out while you keep looking in).

Exercise 3-F

To build still more control and to help teach your horse collection, now canter the line in a slower, shorter stride, so that you fit five strides into the sixty feet between the jumps.

Approach the first jump in a very short canter stride. Your legs maintain the rhythm, so that he doesn't fall into the trot as your hands tell him, "Take shorter strides."

Keep that same short stride when you land so that you can fit in the extra stride. Count as you go down the line, and make the trip smooth.

After the second fence, halt on a straight line and assess your ride. Then do the exercise again, focusing on keeping your ride straight and smooth.

Fig. 143   We came into this fence in a short stride to find the short distance. I have a light, low contact with his mouth in the air, anticipating the shorter strides I want when we land.

Fig. 144   The instant we do land, I tell him, "Wait a minute, you must make shorter strides." I keep my hands low and increase the pressure on his mouth until I feel the shorter rhythm.

Fig. 143

Fig. 144

If you have trouble adding the stride, your horse probably hasn't learned to respect your shortening aids. Apply the same sort of remedy that you used back in Exercise 3-C to get him trotting out of the line after cantering in: land from the first fence and halt; then pick up your shortened canter stride and come around again. (As you did before, use a very definite goal, the halt, to enable yourself to achieve the related but more nebulous goal of shortening stride.)

EXERCISE 4:
DIAGONAL AND BENDING LINES

In this exercise, you'll ride the same line two ways, first as a straight line and then as a bending line. In both, the way you turn to the first fence is the most crucial part of the exercise—because it's in this turn that you establish your line, the guiding function of your eyes, and the rhythm and pace to take you through successfully. Study the diagram below and be sure you understand the line—the approach as well as the center section—for both variations. As long as you *do* understand, your correct position will enable you to use the other skills effectively; just by looking where you want to go, you'll automatically signal to your body how much hand and leg it must apply to take you there.

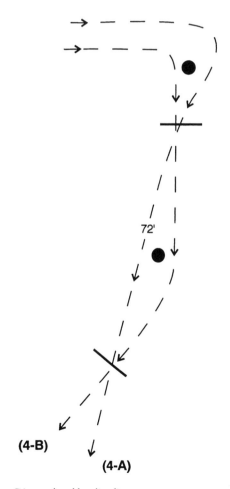

Diagonal and bending lines

Exercise 4-A

Set your second fence at a slight angle to the first 72 feet away (measure the distance by walking directly from the center of the first fence to the center of the second). To help you understand the lines I want you to ride, use two cones or markers. Set one cone just inside where you'd need to turn in to ride a *straight line* that meets the centers of both fences on the diagonal; put a second cone halfway between the two fences just slightly to the right of the straight line.

Coming around your ring at a normal canter pace, turn so that your track takes you just to the outside of the first cone. Looking ahead, you'll see a straight line across the middle of both fences (line A in the drawing) passing just to the inside of the second cone. If you find this line and maintain your normal canter pace, the distance between fences will ride as a smooth five strides.

Fig. 145

Remember to keep your line straight, which means that you're going to meet both fences in the center—but at a bit of an angle.

Fig. 145   Cantering around the cone in the turn makes me see a straight line over the two fences, even though I'm riding to the first fence at a slight angle. Once I find my line, all I need to do is stay on it, maintaining my pace and rhythm.

Fig. 146   Over this fence my eyes are glued on the center stripe on the rail. A horse with an average twelve-foot stride

Fig. 146

should easily get five strides in the seventy-two-foot distance.

Fig. 147   I have my straight line just inside the second cone, on my left. Riding around the outside of the first cone and inside the second has helped me keep my line. There's no need to steer because I made the line way back in the turn and I know the second fence will happen automatically.

Fig. 147

Finish the exercise with a halt on a straight line, evaluate your ride, and then repeat until jumping fences at an angle becomes fairly normal and you're consistent about meeting both fences in the center.

Exercise 4-B

Now ride the same two jumps as a bending line. At the same normal canter pace, make your turn to the first fence *inside* the first cone this time so that you meet the first fence at a 90-degree angle. From there, sight the center of the second fence and ride a bending line to it, passing to the outside of the second cone at about the halfway point. On this bending line, you should comfortably fit in six strides between fences if you maintain your rhythm and pace. Meet the second fence squarely and in the middle, and halt on a straight line a few strides afterward.

Fig. 148

Fig. 149

Fig. 148   Way back in the turn—and this time I'm turning to the *inside* of the first cone—I'm looking straight at the first fence. I also check out the second cone and second fence in relation to the first fence.

Fig. 149 As I land from the first fence, I can see my line around the cone to the second fence.

Fig. 150 Riding around the cone automatically makes the bending line, and it creates a straight line to the center of the second fence. Just as in riding a turn on the flat, if I look where I want to go, I'll get there. As always I'm counting strides and as I near the fence I see the six is there.

Fig. 151 The six worked perfectly, and now I hold my line to complete the exercise.

Once you're comfortable with the bending line and the six-stride distance between fences, ride it as a seven. Just as you did in Exercise 3, you'll have to

Fig. 150

Fig. 151

start with a shorter stride, which you'll have fully established by the time you make the turn to the first fence. Enlarge your bend just a little to be sure you have enough room for the seven. Again, concentrate on making the trip smooth, and remember to learn a little something from each less than satisfactory try until you're consistent all the way down the line every time you ride it.

CHAPTER TEN

EXERCISE 5:
JUMPING ON AN ANGLE

Now it is time to build on the fence-meeting skills you began to develop in Exercise 4. This exercise will help you increase the accuracy of your eye while maintaining your pace and track, and in more challenging circumstances than you've met so far.

Exercise 5-A

Again use two fences set 72 feet apart. This time, though, position the two jumps in opposite directions to each other and both at a fairly sharp angle, about 45 degrees, to the straight line (a sharper angle than the fences in the previous exercise), as you see in the diagram.

At a normal canter, ride the line so that you meet the first jump (labeled A in the diagram) on a left-to-right angle and the second (B) on a right-to-left. As before, meet each fence in its center, and work to ride the line in five strides.

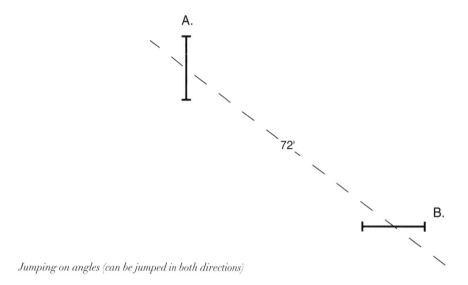

A.

72'

B.

Jumping on angles (can be jumped in both directions)

From your horse's point of view, what's different about this exercise is the fact that he's meeting each of these fences at a sharp angle, so pay close attention to keeping him straight and going forward. If he approaches a fence to one side of the line, or if your hands move at all left or right instead of staying perfectly still and centered, he could run out. And if he jumps the first fence off center, the deviation will affect your ability to make the second fence in a smooth five strides.

Fig. 152   I am on a left-to-right angle, holding my line with my eyes and steady contact on his mouth. Think "Straight"; no turning, no pulling left or right.

Fig. 153   I have held my line and simply allowed the second fence to be in my path. He is between my hands and legs.

Fig. 152

Fig. 153

Finish the exercise by halting on a straight line and reviewing your ride. Then repeat it a few more times, aiming for a smooth five strides between the fences and a steady pace throughout.

EXERCISE 6:
A SHORT COURSE

Now, to give yourself experience in putting together all the components of basic jumping that you've been working on, practice making your own short course. Like everything we've done before, this exercise requires no special equipment; the diagram below shows two courses that use just four fences and combine the now familiar lines of Exercises 3, 4, and 5. The fences can be any height you find comfortable—2 feet, 3 feet 6, or just rails on the ground if you'd rather start with getting the basic idea down before adding height.

For example, you might start with the straightforward four-stride line from Exercise 3 (fences 1 and 2), continue around a right-hand turn to the bending six from Exercise 4 (fences 3 and 4), and then make a left turn to the direct five strides on the angle (fences 5 and 6). Use the straightforward four-stride line to get your "speedometer" going; then focus on maintaining the same rhythm but a *different* track (wide on a curve) around the bending six strides of the second line and keep those qualities all the way around to the third line.

Another course could start with fence 1 on an angle and then the direct five strides to fence 2, followed by a left-hand turn to the straight four-stride line (fences

1.

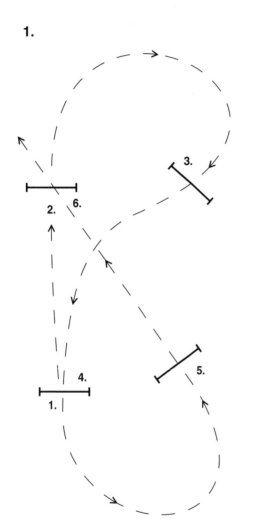

2.

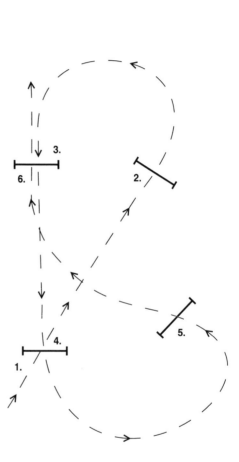

Short courses

60' between **1** + **2**
(make 4 strides)
72' between **3** + **4**
(make a slow–bending 6 strides)
72' between **5** + **6**
(make a direct 5 strides)

3 and 4), and finish with a deeper left turn to ride fences 5 and 6 in a bending six strides.

Variety keeps you and your horse alert and fresh, and you can mix up the recipes to give yourself lots of variety in pattern and in striding. After you've ridden this course in a normal twelve-foot-stride canter, for example, you can practice shortening and coming back by adding a stride in the second or third line, working on adding it so smoothly that your pace change would be invisible to anyone watching.

Don't worry if your horse picks up the wrong lead after a fence or cross-canters down a line; simply make the change (through the trot if he isn't up to flying changes yet) in the turn between that line and the next, so you're set up properly by the time you turn to the next fence. Your focus, remember, is simple—position, pace, and line—and your goal is just to "keep going" smoothly.

Each time you finish riding a course, stop on a straight line and analyze your performance. Ask yourself whether your lines were really smooth. A rough performance indicates that you didn't do your homework somewhere. Maybe you had the wrong pace in the turn or the wrong line coming out of the turn. Resolve to use your turns to make future lines ride smoothly. Watch a top rider very closely and you'll see that's what she does: she makes all the needed adjustments in the turn—correcting position and straightness, changing pace, finding her line, applying the aids with *feel*. Down the line, she doesn't seem to do anything—because she doesn't *have* to do anything. Then turn your attention to her horse, and you'll see that he's concentrating on the jumps. He's able to do so because his rider hasn't jumped into the line with too much pace and then had to tear his head off, or jumped in too slowly and had to run. By being prepared *before* the fences, a top rider can allow her horse to get on with his job.

That's how you want to be, and you can. Establish your pace and line in your turns and you'll find the jumps are simple.

EXERCISE 7:
A GYMNASTIC

The preceding six exercises focused on developing your jumping skills. With all the work you've done by now in this area, you're ready for an exercise that's good for both you and your horse: a gymnastic that will help him set himself up and jump round, while simultaneously giving you the freedom to concentrate almost exclusively on your own position. Gymnastics will also develop your feel for flowing from one fence to the next in quick succession, as you'd do in the case of in-and-outs and combinations.

The exercise consists of several obstacles in close succession, set so that, once you've steered your horse to the center of the first one, the momentum of the jumps themselves will carry him the rest of the way. And as he goes through, you'll have repeated opportunities to develop reliability in each part of your jumping position. Over and over, as you go through, you'll tell yourself "Eyes up," or "Heels down," or "Give with your hand," working on your weak points one at a time.

To set the gymnastic, place two "trot" rails on the ground, four and a half feet apart; place standards for a crossrail nine feet beyond the second rail, another set of standards— no rails—for a low vertical eighteen feet after the crossrail, and finally a double set of standards for what will be a low, square oxer twenty feet after the vertical. Since you'll start by just trotting the rails on the ground, and then add the fences one by one, alongside each set of standards place enough rails to build your jumps later on. You'll need two rails for the vertical, three for the oxer, plus one ground-line rail for each fence. (The distances are "normal," so your horse should find them very comfortable.) This arrangement, crossrail to

Fig. 154

Fig. 155

Fig. 156

Fig. 157

Fig. 158

vertical to oxer, has the effect of gradually stretching out his frame while still helping him to set himself up for each new effort.

Fig. 154   Here I am letting my horse figure out the trot rails to the crossrail. I can concentrate on my jumping position—heels, hands, eyes—and my line.

Fig. 155   In the one-stride to the vertical, I go with him—with low "following" arms and upper body tipped forward.

Fig. 156   As he sets himself up to jump, I don't interfere. Our centers of gravity are in line.

Fig. 157   As he lands, my weight sinks into my heels and my upper body follows his motion. My arms and hands give his head and neck the freedom he needs to balance himself.

Fig. 158   During the canter stride to the oxer, I keep light contact with my seat and hands just to be with him. As he jumps, I'm still with the motion—upper body forward; hands very light, low and toward the mouth so he can concentrate on his jump as I concentrate on myself.

When your horse's performance over this original configuration is reasonably reliable, challenge him a little by raising the fences six to twelve inches. You can also vary the order of the fences and the distances between to keep his attention and develop his jumping skills. For example, switch the positions of the vertical and the oxer; now the gymnastic will make him first lengthen and then compress his frame; after the oxer, he'll have to work harder to get his hindquarters under him and round up over the upright vertical. Increasing the degree of difficulty another notch—by shortening the distances by one to two feet—will make your horse pay even more attention to himself in front of a fence, in the air, and on landing.

EXERCISE 8:
AN IN-AND-OUT

An in-and-out can be challenging, but you're going to free up your concentration so that you can focus on it. Do this by starting the exercise with a trot fence set three canter strides in front of the "in." When you land from the trot fence, you'll count "One, two, three," and the distance to the "in" will be right there.

Set a low vertical for the trot fence. Then measure forty-two feet, set another low vertical for the "in," measure twenty-four feet, and set a third for the "out." You've practiced counting strides, and the gymnastic has developed your feel for jumping fences one stride apart, so you shouldn't have any trouble with this exercise.

Focusing ahead to keep yourself straight (as always), trot in . . . take three canter strides (counting to keep the rhythm) . . . jump in . . . take one canter stride . . . jump out . . . and bring your horse to a smooth halt a few strides beyond.

Ride this exercise just as you did the gymnastic, with your seat close to the saddle between elements—no standing in your stirrups!—so that even in the one-stride your seat touches the saddle. (You don't want it either down and driving your horse forward or way above him.)

If you feel your horse getting quick between fences, say "Whoa" and take his mouth more strongly. If he hangs back jumping the "in" and it looks as if you're about to do a stride and a half, use your legs in the air as well as when you land. In either case, the setup of the three strides to the one should make sure you get there at the right distance.

When you're riding this exercise consistently smoothly, remove the trot fence and ride the in-and-out on its own. Establish your pace—a regular canter—and line way back in the turn, and you'll find the exercise will ride just as smoothly as it did when you had the aid of the lead-in trot fence.

JUMPING WITHOUT STIRRUPS

Jumping without stirrups is an exercise I recommend for two reasons. One, of course, is that it's an insurance policy. Everybody loses a stirrup at least once or twice in a riding career; if it happens, you want to be able to continue riding without losing your position, your composure, or your chance at a ribbon if you're in the show ring (where, in observance of Murphy's Law, you just might be). But the other—and the really important reason—is what it does for your balance. Like riding your horse on the flat without stirrups, jumping without stirrups is a great way to solidify your balance, so that you never find yourself getting ahead of your horse and jumping up his neck.

Don't try jumping without stirrups before you're ready, though. If the idea terrifies you, just continue with your regular work for a while longer. Eventually you'll build the confidence to give it a try.

A good way to begin is to go down a line using your stirrups, then drop them after the last fence, so that you ride your turn or circle without irons. The moment you take your feet out of the irons, you'll feel yourself riding more "with" your horse, the best antidote in the world for riders who habitually want to make a move up the neck. Your hips and seat will relax and begin following his back better. Your legs will feel longer, and your lower leg will stay quieter at his side.

Ride just the turn or circle without irons until you've established your balance enough that you feel secure. Then remove the stirrups from your saddle, so that they don't bang your horse's sides, and try a single fence without them. As you feel more confident, you can increase the number of fences.

Start with the simple, straight line of Exercise 3. Ride the line once with your stirrups and drop them as you land from the second fence. Immediately you'll sink into the saddle and have a following seat. This really helps your balance. Circling after the fence will help you bring your horse together. Feel how much more effective you are when you're sitting down on him this way. My horses usually go better when I ride without stirrups, because I naturally sit more correctly.

Fig. 159   Here I am jumping a single fence with the stirrups removed. My balance and my firm leg keep my position

Fig. 159

secure; I don't need to lean on his mouth to pull me over the fence. My position looks the same with or without stirrups.

Gradually work up from this single fence to a simple line and then to the more complicated ones. Finish by jumping a small course without stirrups, as riders in equitation classes are sometimes asked to do. The more you can feel that your balance and your ability to stay with your horse are all yours, not dependent on supports like stirrups and reins, the more secure and effective a rider you'll be—and the more prepared for the advanced work of the next two sections.

FLYING CHANGES

Before moving on, introduce your horse to flying changes with the following simple exercise. It's helpful if you're working with a green youngster that isn't quite ready for

Fig. 159A

advanced flat work but that does need to know how to do a flying change for hunter courses; it can also help with the older horse that has a "thing" about changes and gets himself all in a knot when you apply your leg to ask for a change of lead. It works best in an indoor ring; if you're working outdoors, you'll find setting it up close to the fence line gives the best results.

Place a rail on the ground just before each corner of your ring, about four strides from the end; put a single low jump on one long side and a line of two fences down the other.

Fig. 159A   Jump the single fence and continue toward the corner. Your horse will see the end of the ring coming up and know he's going to make a turn. Maintain your body position to and over the rail—seat close to the saddle, upper body just slightly ahead of the vertical. Don't throw yourself at the rail, which would throw him on his forehand and prevent him from changing. You're not jumping, just cantering.

Fig. 159B   Just before you meet the rail, move both hands a little to the inside to encourage the turn; the inside rein indicates the direction of the turn, and the outside rein brings his shoulders around. Keep a hint of outside leg; use any more and a baby might

Fig. 159B

well not understand, and a scared horse may get upset. But gradually the exercise will give any horse the idea; that outside rein against the neck and hint of outside leg will support his outside shoulder and haunches enough to help him change. In most cases, as he steps over the rail into the turn, he will change.

If the exercise doesn't produce a change after a couple of tries, you may be throwing your body around more than you realize or pulling his head around too much. Try giving him a tap with your stick behind your outside leg as you go over the rail. Another good correction is to take off your stirrups, which will force you to sit in the saddle and in balance with your horse, and try again. This time it should work if you let the rail make the change.

Continue around your work area, crossing jumps and rails, until your horse is making his changes calmly and smoothly. Then you can gradually increase your outside leg—still over the rail for the first few times—and finally ask for your changes with the normal hand and leg aids.

III.

ADVANCED
FLAT WORK

Chapter Eleven

A New Level
of Feeling

You've progressed from Part I's slow, steady, basic flat work—transitions, bending, lengthening, and shortening—to Part II's basic jumping, going from poles on the ground to a simple course that let you call on all the riding skills you've been developing. You're comfortable with a number of variations on that course now, ready to take on the next challenge—but when you turn the page to Part III, you find the words "flat work" staring up at you again. "Didn't we do that already?" you may be muttering. "Why are we going back to flat work?"

The answer is that you're *not* going back. You're going *forward*—to a level of flat work that you wouldn't have been able to do, or to appreciate, when you started my program, and that will fine-tune your ability to *feel* and interact with your horse as never before. If you think of learning to be a feeling rider as learning to converse with your horse, what you'll be doing in advanced flat work is adding both more words and more color to the language of your conversation: more precision in both what you want and the way you convey your requests to him. Whatever your sport—eventing, dressage, equitation, show jumping—your basic goal is to get your horse to move forward, come back, turn left or right, and so on, with a *minimum amount of effort*—no big spurs or long whip. The flat work I'll be giving you is the way to reach that goal.

Some of the exercises you'll be doing in this section are a refinement or extension of work you did in Part I. Others will be new in themselves but will build on the understanding and skill you developed in your earlier work. And all of them will put extra sensors in your antennae and extra buttons on your control panel, enabling you to recognize problems earlier, deal with them more effectively and efficiently, and produce a smoother performance in whichever discipline you ride—dressage, hunter-jumper, or cross-country.

You aren't the only beneficiary, though. The work you'll cover in this section is work I wouldn't do without on any horse, from green to Olympic veteran; it's good for him as well as for me. In particular, the lateral work that you'll start off with will have the effect of getting the horse to go naturally on the bit, connecting him from back to front by putting his haunches to work, and making him a livelier and easier-to-ride partner.

Think back to when you watched your horse traveling loose on the flat and jumping on the longe: the more animated he was, the rounder his body; even on the flat, his hindquarters were engaged, his back came up, and he carried himself. (Unless he's extremely young and inexperienced, you will never see him going faster and faster to maintain his balance because he is falling onto his forehand.) Advanced flat work will strengthen the muscles in his hindquarters and topline, not just teaching him but also *enabling* him to travel round and carry himself (and you) in balance.

KEEPING IT SIMPLE—AND REWARDING

You'll find there's a lot to learn in this section—but if you stick with the step-by-step approach I give you, you *won't* find the work overwhelming. For one thing, I'll be encouraging you to think of your horse as divided into four major sections—left shoulder, right shoulder, left haunch, right haunch—and work on just one section at a time. This close focus will magnify all the information available and enable you to become aware (perhaps for the first time, and certainly with greater clarity than ever before) of the exact position of the part of your horse's body you're focusing on—whether it's straight or crooked, in balance or leaning. You'll find out just how much leg and/or hand you need to apply, and in what manner, to direct or correct a shoulder or haunch, and whether one side is less responsive (and in need of more attention) than its partner.

While I'm taking you through each exercise and showing you the way to new levels of understanding and feeling, I'll also be showing you simple solutions to common riding problems. For example, I'll show you how to use your hips to sit the trot in a way that will make you feel secure, and how to use the rhythm from your own body to generate the rhythm you want in your horse's (and so banish forever the dread of downward transitions tugging you out of the saddle and out of balance). Instead of awkward "Well, which is it?" steps as you go from one gait to the next, you'll be increasingly able to maintain the harmony you want through both upward and downward transitions.

Better yet, as you progress through these exercises, expanding your body-language "vocabulary" and learning more and more about how your horse works and how you can best communicate with him, you'll find that you're persuading him to adopt your attitude about riding. Taking his cue from your consistent aids, he'll begin to think "forward" instinctively, and to respond at the first indication that you want him to do something new; you'll begin getting results from "whispers," not "yells." You'll even find that, as a by-product of the work you're doing, he's developing those sought-after qualities of "on the bit," roundness, and ability to collect.

One more bonus: your increased effectiveness as a rider is transferrable. If you put in the time to fine-tune your grasp of the language in which you and your horse communicate, within a few months you should be able to ride *any* horse—equitation, hunter, jumper, green or old, hot or dull—communicate with him in the same terms, and have him as relaxed, round, and happy as the partner with whom you've been doing all these months of slow, steady work. With any horse, you'll know when you need to be aggressive and when you should be quiet—because you'll hear what he's saying to you and be able to respond in a language he understands.

READINESS CHECK

Before you begin this section's work, though, I want you to do some honest self-evaluation—because this new work will deliver the tools I've promised you only if you're ready to learn how to use them. What that means, of course, is that your basic flat work must be truly solid; if you find it isn't, go back to the work of Part I until you're confident and comfortable with all of it.

Most important: your position in the saddle must be secure (in flat work, remember, you want to ride a couple of holes longer than in jumping, so take your stirrups down to anklebone length again). If it isn't, spend time on it now. You'll be doing a lot of the new lateral work that this section covers in an active sitting trot, so that secure seat will be even more essential than it was in Part I.

A lot of riders react to the idea of sitting the trot with dread. They're just not comfortable doing it—which means they're stiff in the hips. Riding without stirrups is the best way I know to develop relaxation in the hips and to turn an unbalanced seat into a deep, secure one. Without the crutch of stirrups, you naturally *have* to position your center of gravity over your horse's or you'll fall off—and you'll know when you've found the right spot because you'll *feel* in balance.

I ride without stirrups regularly, and every horse I ride goes better when I do: I use my seat, legs, and entire body more correctly, so I need my reins less, and that lets the horse relax and concentrate on his job. I suggested riding without stirrups earlier in this book; by now, if you've worked through all the exercises I've given you up to this point—no skimping—you should be a confident and practiced enough partner with your horse that dropping your stirrups shouldn't faze you. Make riding without stirrups at the walk, the sitting and the posting trot, the canter, and even over low fences a routine part of your riding—and don't start this month's work until riding without stirrups *feels* routine.

(The one thing that might interfere with your ability to ride without stirrups is lack of fitness—and as I've said before, if you're serious about riding, you have to be serious about *being an athlete,* which means doing whatever you need to do to be at your physical best. Fitness is a matter of regular physical exercise, so set yourself a realistic program of swimming, or running, or vigorous walking, or bicycling, or working out at the gym, and stick with it. It doesn't have to cost money, but the payoff—in the way you'll feel about yourself as the weight comes off and the muscles firm—will be worth every bit of the effort it does cost. And your horse, who'll be increasing his own strength, fitness, and suppleness through the work *he's* doing, will appreciate having a fitter, better-balanced rider who doesn't hang on his mouth.)

At all gaits, you need to be able to let the muscles of your seat relax and your hips swing in rhythm with your horse, following his motion and absorbing shock, inviting his back to relax. At the walk, your whole hip region should stay relaxed and move forward and back in harmony with his motion—so that when you tighten your seat muscles and sit a little more strongly to increase his impulsion, he'll notice the difference. In the trot, the motion should be a little quicker, but the whole hip region should move. Watch any top rider closely and you'll see him or her following with seat and lower back, the side seam of the breeches going behind the vertical and in front, behind and in front. The legs may close and the seat muscles may tighten to push for a moment in each stride, but then it's relax and follow again. That kind of suppleness in the hips is what will give you a good seat—so it's worth whatever effort you expend to achieve it.

Along with a secure seat, by now you should have learned to use your aids independently—to apply your legs without using your hands, and one leg without the other. To accomplish the turn on the forehand, for example, you employ an active leg but only a little bit of hand. (If you used too much hand the first couple of times you tried the movement, your horse backed up.) The degree of independence you can manage may not be complete yet, but you should at least be able to *feel* when you clash aids (that is, you ask your horse for two contradictory things at once) or get the wrong balance between one aid and another—and be able to reorganize and try again.

For the work we'll be doing in this section, your seat and legs will be your principal means of communication with your horse. Your hands' primary function will be to receive and guide the energy that your seat and legs create. After all, you can't come down to a big fence with a thousand pounds in your hands and expect to jump well. Your horse's balance needs to be focused over his "rear-mounted" engine. The more you learn, through these exercises, to use seat and legs to engage that engine, the lighter in your hands (and more ridable) he'll become.

We'll be focusing more than we have before on the use of the seat as a mediator between your legs and hands. It can reinforce your legs as a driving aid—swinging with and emphasizing the rhythm of the gait you're in (or even, as we'll cover later, the gait you want to go to) or reinforce your hands as a retarding aid.

One more thing: be honest about weak points and strong points, yours and your horse's. People and horses are both naturally one-sided; your horse, like you, probably feels a lot more comfortable working to one side than to the other. You may have noticed *which* side in your basic flat work, or maybe it became more obvious in basic jumping—if, for example, he consistently wanted to jump to the left. Or it may not really become apparent until you're working on this section's more challenging movements. Wherever you find one-sidedness, try to deal with it then and there by working more to the side the horse is less comfortable about. Overcoming one-sidedness is a slow process, but it pays off in better maneuverability and straighter jumping.

Besides, with your increasing awareness of *feel*, recognizing a problem will create a "do something about it" reflex. If you've acknowledged that your horse has a tendency to travel bent slightly left, for example, you'll be increasingly on the alert for signs that he's exhibiting the problem and you need to do something about it. This will be a conscious awareness at first, but with time you'll feel the telltale imbalance unconsciously and automatically apply aids to bend him slightly right, incorporating your corrections into whatever you're actually concentrating on. The great riders are constantly and unconsciously straightening their horses, making them livelier or more athletic, or otherwise countering minor imperfections; they *feel* and automatically respond. (That doesn't mean that they fiddle constantly with their horses' mouths, of course—or that you should with yours. But with practice, as you develop your reflexes and become better able to envision how your horse feels when he's straight, your educated body will automatically make most or all of the subtle adjustments needed to match reality with the ideal.) With practice, you'll develop your reflexes and be able to do the same.

YOUR
ALL-IMPORTANT
ATTITUDE

Approach each day's work by reaffirming to yourself that the kind of feeling riding you're aiming to achieve is a partnership between friends. You're not a dictator, and your horse isn't your subject; neither are you trying to stuff into him information that you alone possess. The two of you are on a mission together, learning things that are new to both of you.

As I told you right from the beginning, your attitude is all-important. You want to succeed, but tell yourself, "If I—or we—don't get something right the first time, I won't worry. We'll try again tomorrow, and the next day, and success will come if I'm patient." Resolve that if you do run into a problem that you can't solve today you'll wind up the day's work with something that you know the two of you can accomplish, ending the session in harmony and restored confidence.

And even if you're making terrific progress, resist the temptation to do too much. Work on an advanced exercise for a little while and then give your horse a break with some simple forward work on straight lines—say five or ten minutes on shoulder-in and then a few minutes of going straight and forward in a posting trot. Stay positive and patient, trust your horse, and treat him like a partner. If you keep in mind the saying "Less is more," your aids will be simple and clear, and the program will work.

Start each session by walking on a loose rein for five or ten minutes, just letting your horse ease into his work—like any athlete, he needs to stretch out and warm up his muscles. (This time is good for you, too: it lets you start out loose and relaxed, clearing your mind of outside concerns so that you can focus on yourself and him.) Don't underestimate the amount of training you can do and information you can gather at the walk. When I warm up a horse in the walk, I'm unconsciously doing little exercises that identify and counteract that particular individual's tendencies, whether to be crooked, lazy, or too quick. We're carrying on what amounts to a nice little conversation about the boundaries and attitude I want for the day—not a big seminar, just a little honest discussion between friends. I'm saying, "Hi, it's me, and we're about to get to work. How are you feeling today? Oh, you're a bit stiff here? Well, let's see if we can help you loosen up a little, shall we?" And so on. Still on long reins, spend another five to ten minutes in posting trot; try a little lengthening and shortening to make sure he's going forward and coming back in response to your basic aids.

LEG-YIELD REVIEW

Now, still as part of your warmup, move on to a little review work that also acts as a test of readiness to go on: leg-yielding at the walk. This is *the* exercise I use whenever I get on a new horse. It's an excellent way to say, "Good morning; how are you?" and check the horse's responsiveness, understanding, and honesty to my leg aids. Used as part of your warmup for advanced flat work, it lets you check yourself as well. (If the response you get now isn't as good as when you worked on the movement in Part I, take a good look at your position and the way you're applying the aids.) The leg-yield also focuses on one of the major concepts we'll be working on in this section: putting your horse from your inside leg onto—and having him accept—your outside rein.

Let's say you're on a track to the right, with the fence line to your left. First use your right leg to leg-yield your horse left, so that he travels laterally toward the fence as well as forward, for six to ten steps.

Sit straight in the saddle; don't collapse your right hip in an effort to push your horse left. As you press your right (inside) leg against him, you should feel that the energy your leg is creating travels to the left (outside) hand, respects the feel of the bit, and stays there, neither pushing through so that you feel your outside hand being tugged, nor dropping behind so that you have nothing in your hand. This sensation is what I mean by "putting your horse on"—or "making him fill out"—your outside rein (the left rein in this case).

Fig. 160 You can see my horse is slightly bent around my right leg as he moves away from it to the left. (As you give the aid, though, think "Straight" so that you don't overdo the bend—a common mistake.) To move his haunches over, I've slid my right leg behind the girth; my left leg stays at the girth, keeping us moving forward. You can see how he is filling out the outside rein with his neck.

In a dressage test, the horse's shoulder is supposed to lead the haunches *slightly*. But in training I try to keep the horse's hips and shoulders very even—to counter what is most horses' tendency to lead with their shoulders and lag with their haunches.

Do six or ten steps of leg-yield to the left, using your right leg to send your horse toward the fence as well as forward, then a few steps of forward only to double-check that he is staying straight and parallel to the rail, and then six or ten more steps to the right, away from the fence, pressing with your left leg and sending his energy to your receiving right hand.

Don't rush. Do ten steps or twenty, depending on how comfortable he feels, and work toward a balanced degree of forward and sideways. It shouldn't be a big production; if it *is*, you're probably not ready to go on to advanced flat work just yet. Spend more time solidifying your basics.

If your horse is really honest to

Fig. 160

your leg, and if you're using your aids correctly and sitting in the middle of him, he will be light in your hand. *Leg*, not hand, is what makes a horse light; that's something I didn't understand for years. Your legs make the haunches active; that's what we mean when we say the legs "engage" the haunches. When you use your right leg, right away your horse contracts the joints in his right hind leg and uses it actively to step to the left, stepping more under himself with that leg—which means he carries himself. He can be light in your hand because he's supporting himself, balancing himself, and not leaning on you. Like a dancer, he can move lightly wherever he wants to go; you don't have to push him there.

If your horse feels heavy and you do have to push him, then he isn't carrying himself or being honest to your leg. Use your spur or a whip behind your leg if the spur alone doesn't do it—to make him lighter, so that you can get back to guiding him with invisible aids. Once he's responsive and light to your leg, he'll be responsive and light in his mouth.

HALT AND REINBACK

The first new work in this section expands on the simple halts we did in Part 1, refining the aids and continuing on into the reinback. You may be wondering why we didn't get around to backing until now—a lot of teachers introduce it in the first couple of lessons with their beginners. The answer is that it's a "backward" movement, and I wanted your "forward" skills to be solid before you tackled backing. By now, you should have achieved that point.

We'll start by halting from the walk and then go on to trot-halt and canter-halt. We want these all to be clean transitions, with no "in-between" steps of some other gait before you get the halt. And the secret of clean transitions is to maintain impulsion even as you're halting—which means going from the front-to-back halt that you did in Part 1, where you simply closed your fingers, to a back-to-front halt that activates the hindquarters and then contains the forward flow of energy.

In a good working walk, close your legs—or even tickle with your spurs a little—to energize your horse's hindquarters and bring them under him. Then ask him to stop his forward motion by resisting with your hands (helped by maintaining a bend in your elbows) and stilling your seat. Remember to sit in and up, and to keep some elasticity in your arms so that he can stay round and soft as he steps into the halt, not inverted and resistant.

The heavier your horse is in your hands and the more he pulls against you, the more you need to stretch up, lift your hands a couple of inches, deepen your heel, and leg, leg, leg him . . . until he lightens into the halt.

In this sequence watch the horse's topline as I "coil his spring" by activating his hindquarters and then resist him firmly.

Fig. 161 In a relaxed walk, with elastic, firm contact, I begin to apply my legs and resist with my back and arms.

Fig. 162 The horse responds by lightening his forehand, raising his poll. Notice I haven't changed the position of my arms; my leg and back have made him lift in front.

Fig. 163 He halts with all four legs under him, in balance, and soft in my hands—not with his head way up or down.

To halt from the trot, begin by using your legs and seat to make the trot a little more active . . . and then shorten it a little: squeeze, squeeze with your calves to call your horse to attention and make him a bit quicker while you feel his mouth just enough to compress the energy into an active trot.

Finally, resist the impulsion (keeping your seat deep and your leg long, so that he doesn't pull you out of the saddle) by blocking him with your back and arms. Be sure to keep your joints firm but elastic; follow each brief but firm "take" with an equally brief lightening (you don't want to pull) . . . so that he halts *up* into your hands.

Halting from the canter works the same way: tickle, tickle, tickle to call your horse to attention and push his haunches under, then resist, resist, resist . . . until he canters right down into the halt, keeping his forehand elevated and "sitting down" to stop—in balance and not falling on his nose.

The Reinback

As in the halt, to rein back I use my *legs*

Fig. 161

Fig. 162

Fig. 163

more than my hands; legging your horse into the bit is what makes him go backward. The joints in your arms should remain elastic; your arms resist and relax, resist and relax as your legs create energy that he tries to send forward. As he bores against you, you resist and leg him to lighten him; when he starts to lighten, you lighten immediately, and repeat.

At the halt, use your leg aid for an instant before you close your fingers on the reins, so that your horse thinks "forward" for an instant before your hands block him.

Although you may need a *little* backward feeling on the mouth while you're teaching the reinback, pulling on the mouth is not the way to send your message; again, your horse's movement comes from back to front, so your signal shouldn't go the other way.

Your hand and leg are sending two different messages, of course—your leg saying "Forward" and your hand saying "Keep the energy, but don't send it forward; use it to go backward." (And as always, the right "volume"—degree of pressure—for each of those messages can vary from step to step, depending on what *he* tells *you*.)

You want your horse to walk up into the contact . . . and then walk back away from it, still thinking "Forward" enough that at any moment you could increase your leg, relax your feel of the mouth, and send him right into a forward gait.

Going forward or coming backward, he should be stepping up under himself all the time, his impulsion "spring" coiled and ready to use.

If your horse gets heavy as he steps back, close your leg (and use spur if necessary) to make him lively again. The moment you touch him with the spur, he'll pick up his hind leg more energetically.

In the opposite problem, a horse that runs backward is trying to evade your aids. Use a stronger leg and lighter hand to reestablish "Forward" and put him back on the aids. Do two steps back . . . and go forward . . . two steps back . . . and go forward . . . and then change to some very forward work—a posting trot, perhaps—for a while, coming back to the reinback later.

Fig. 163A I've closed my legs while resisting with my arms and hands and *thinking* "Step backward," and Top Seed steps back smoothly. Notice in this and the next photo you see no pulling or leaning way back on my part.

He has a lovely shape: no resistance, simply obeying my aids; not overflexed, above the bit, or rooting. His poll is the highest point on his neck, and his haunches are slightly lowered, engaged—ready for any command. This is the balance your horse should work from; again, engaged haunches mean a lighter forehand.

Fig. 163B To continue back, I simply repeat my closing legs and resisting hands, sitting in the center of the saddle and using both legs and both reins to keep him straight. With a well-schooled horse like this, when I say I "close" my legs, the closing is only a thought. He understands immediately and is pleased to work with me, responding to invisible aids. Green horses may need a strong leg—even a spur—and much firmer resistance. But through correct repetition, even the dullest horse will respond to lighter aids as he comes to understand what you want.

It's up to you to be smarter than your horse—and with some horses, that may mean keeping reinback work to a minimum. You can achieve the objective of lightening a horse in lots of ways, and in most cases I tend to prefer forward transitions, such as going from a working trot back to a very active, short sitting trot, to the reinback for lightening, and forward again—or simply riding the transitions without the reinback. (And I certainly wouldn't do this with a three- or four-year-old just off the race track—it's way past his level of thinking. He won't be able to grasp anything this sophisticated until he gets a lot more training under his girth.)

Fig. 163A

The reinback can be useful in the ring. If you have a horse that's a little numb in the mouth, you might want to canter into the ring, stop,

Fig. 163B

and back a step or two to get him light before going into a jump-off. And the judge of an equitation class may call for you to halt and rein back during the work-off. If your horse is on your aids, simply close your legs and he'll respond to invisible aids, backing smoothly and staying round. One last thought on the halt and reinback: to many riders, these transitions may sound irrelevant or even silly. But to me this is a very exciting and fun part of riding and training horses. How well and clearly can I communicate? How effortless can I make our work together? Riding at this level is also beautiful to watch and appreciate because it is not *easy* in the sense that just anyone, any time, can perform it classically, as a work of art.

Horses are reflections of their riders, not only in the way they are turned out, but also in the way they carry themselves, respond, and in their expression while they work. When a horse is light, willing, and happy, we know he has a quality rider for a partner.

Shoulder-in

The shoulder-in is a difficult movement for your horse, so he's not going to want to do it. But the reason it's difficult for him is also why it's so good for him: like all horses, he naturally wants to travel with his shoulders *out* and his haunches *in*. The shoulder-in makes him do just the opposite, so he'll find it difficult—but it will also be great for making him straight. If you could do only one straightness exercise with him, this should be it. And once he *is* straight, so that he's in balance and not popping one shoulder one way and his haunches the other, all his work is going to be easier.

Early in this chapter I talked about one-sidedness and the need to overcome it. The shoulder-in is one place where one-sidedness will announce itself loud and clear: if you have particular difficulty getting your horse to bend around your right leg in a right shoulder-in, he's telling you he likes to travel with the left shoulder *out* and his haunches to the right. (When we move on to haunches-in, the next exercise, you should find getting his haunches in to the right an easy movement.) Think back over how he jumps and you'll probably also realize that he jumps to the left, cuts in on most left-hand turns, and bulges his haunches to the right. The way to overcome the problem is to do a lot more shoulder-in to the right than to the left (and not much haunches-in to the right). Progress may be slow, but gradually you'll discover that his turns are better controlled and his jumping is straighter.

Because the shoulder-in is a difficult exercise, I suggest you read it through twice, visualizing yourself doing what the text and pictures describe, before you actually try it with your horse. You may also find it helpful to think of the shoulder-in as the first step of a turn on the haunches—a movement you did in basic flat work—with your legs preventing the haunches from moving in or out as your hands swing the shoulders around. (Two words of caution, though: before you can have any success with the shoulder-in, your horse will *have* to be honest to your leg, doing turns on the forehand, turns on the haunches, and leg-yields well; and you will have to be able both to apply your aids independently and to coordinate them.)

Fig. 164 In the shoulder-in, you want your horse to be at a 3o-degree angle to the rail, bent slightly to the inside and away from the direction he's traveling in, so that you can see just the corner of his inside eye. He should be bent evenly from poll to tail and moving on three tracks: the inside foreleg and outside hind on tracks of their own, and the outside fore and inside hind sharing a single track. In this configuration, with his spine bent, he flexes and bends the inside hind leg more than he would if travel-ing straight. He carries more weight on the inside haunch and begins to "sit" a little more on his hind end, espe-cially the inside hind.

The easiest way to estab-lish the bend of the shoul-der-in is to start on the turn from the short to the long side of your ring. Going into

Fig. 164

the turn, take both hands slightly to the inside. The inside, direct rein leads him into the turn—and on into the shoulder-in—and the outside rein, against the neck, brings the shoulders in off the track, the same way it does in the turn on the haunches.

Fig. 165 As you bring the shoulders off the track, your legs must keep the haunches on it and tell your horse to continue in his normal walk rhythm, neither rushing nor stopping as he bends onto the three tracks. My inside leg at the girth keeps the horse's haunches from following his shoulders and sees that they stay straight on the track; my outside leg makes sure that the haunches don't fall out and keeps our forward impulsion.

As you firm up the pressure in your hands, your inside leg is at the girth telling him, "I want you to bend in your rib cage, so that your shoulders are to the inside, your haunches stay where they are, and your energy constantly flows to the outside rein."

While the inside leg is at

Fig. 165

the girth, the outside rein is against the neck; it's that rein that really makes the half-halt work and controls the degree of bending. Once again, you're controlling your horse between your inside leg and outside rein.

Fig. 166 If your horse is listening to you, your inside rein should be very light; in fact, you should even be able to move your inside hand slightly toward the mouth—as I'm doing here—and have him continue in shoulder-in. This horse is beautifully connected from back to front, light as a feather.

Fig. 166

Fig. 167 The outside rein should have a little more weight, keeping him from bending his neck too much as he brings his shoulders to the inside and regulating the pace so that he doesn't speed up. My outside "neck rein" is playing its dual role nicely, supporting and bringing the shoulders over. My feel on this rein is not backward; it's slightly lateral, toward the inside, so that the rein is always in contact with the neck. And because I'm using just enough pressure—not overdoing my feel on either rein—he is neither overflexed nor laterally overbent. Just as in the leg-yield, I'm creating and sending energy from my inside leg to my outside hand.

If you're having trouble getting the shoulders off the track, stop a moment and think about what's happening. Your moving both hands to the inside allows the inside rein to "lead" your horse off the track and the outside rein to press his shoulders to the inside. While the inside rein indicates what you want, the outside rein against the neck is actually what brings the shoulders over—so you have to make sure that the bend is even and that the outside rein is working for you. (Many people haven't a clue how important the outside rein is here; they just pull the horse's head in with the inside rein.)

If the outside rein isn't working, stop your horse and break the movement down into components you already know:

Do an actual step of turn

Fig. 167

on the haunches, in the same direction as you want your shoulder-in to be; one step will bring the shoulders about thirty degrees off the track.

Then stop him again, and this time ask for a step of turn on the forehand—to put the haunches back on the track, where you want them to be.

Breaking the movement down this way—so that you know exactly what each shoulder and each hip is doing, which way it's bent, and how you got it to go that way—will help you be very clear about both what you're doing and how your horse is responding. That will let you isolate the aid that either he isn't responding to or you aren't giving clearly enough to let him respond the way you want.

Once you can manage the shoulder-in in both directions at the walk, move on to doing it at the sitting trot. In the trot, your leg should be active when your horse's inside hind leg is in support (the moment you would be sitting if you were posting) and about to lift into the new stride—the moment you can influence what he does with the leg. If he's responding nicely, you can relax the aid every other step; squeezing on alternate steps will be enough to maintain the movement. Concentrate on keeping the rhythm constant, though—squeeze, relax, squeeze, relax.

The quality of the steps you get in the shoulder-in, not the quantity, is the important factor. Continue down the long side if you have the correct bend and nice rhythm; you may only get two steps at first. When you lose that quality, go straight forward until you've restored balance and lightness—or even give your horse a real break by making a complete tour of your ring in posting trot—and then try again, starting off on a turn or circle to reestablish the inside-leg/outside-hand link. Don't drive him crazy by trying to get thirty minutes of shoulder-in, though; try it just a few times and then go on to something less demanding.

Later in my program we'll work on doing shoulder-in at the canter, but for now don't worry about going beyond the walk and trot. The movement is difficult enough at those gaits and even harder in the canter—but it's one of the most effective means I know for really getting a horse on the aids and in self-carriage. Use it to deal with one-sidedness by giving him about twice as much shoulder-in time going in his weak direction at both the walk and the trot.

Chapter Twelve

Haunches-in

The logical next step in my program is haunches-in—a movement you'll probably find somewhat easier than the shoulder-in because most horses have a natural tendency toward traveling with their haunches in. Like the shoulder-in, haunches-in relates to a movement you worked on in Part I: it's an advanced version of the turn on the forehand, asking the horse to bend his body as well as move his haunches. And also like shoulder-in, it will contribute to your horse's straightness by refining your ability to control a particular part of his body.

In haunches-in, you position the haunches to the inside of your track at about a 30-degree angle (the same angle you wanted the shoulders to have in shoulder-in). The horse's forelegs travel straight along the track in the normal manner, and his head and neck should also be straight or even bent ever so slightly to the inside, so that you can just see the corner of his inside eye. If you're doing the exercise correctly, you'll get that hint of bend without trying for it, though, so just think about keeping the head and neck straight.

Like shoulder-in, haunches-in is a diagonal-aids exercise. Your legs should create the bend: inside leg at the girth, encouraging your horse to bend around it, and outside leg back a little to help the haunches move in and stay there. Your hands should simply receive his energy, indicate direction, and control speed. That's not the way a lot of riders do it, though; they try to achieve haunches-in by pulling the head around to the *outside.* Doing so does make the haunches swing in, since shoulders-out/haunches-in is a natural way of going, but the horse's body lacks all bend—and the movement does nothing to promote control and straightness.

As you did with the shoulder-in, you can use a turn onto the long side of your work area to get your horse into the position you want. Before you begin, picture the point (just as you're about to complete your turn) at which his inside foreleg and outside hind are on the same track; that point, where his hindquarters are at about a 30-degree angle to the straightaway, is where you're going to want to apply your aids. Think about how your horse and your surroundings look at that point, so that you'll recognize it when you're actually riding the movement.

Fig. 168 Here I've applied my inside leg at the girth and my outside leg a little back to ask him to bend in his ribs, keep his shoulders on the track and haunches inside the track. My legs are also keeping

Fig. 168

him marching down the rail. (I also think of these aids as my outside leg asking him to curl around my inside leg.)

Fig. 169 You should feel even contact in your outside and inside hands, which are just holding the head and neck straight. (On a green horse, you will need an indirect inside rein against the neck to hold the shoulders out, but the ideal is to have the inside leg alone be adequate to keep him straight.)

Don't let yourself use an indirect inside rein to drag the shoulders out so that the haunches come in. An indirect rein only bends the horse from nose to withers, and you want to bend the whole horse.

Keep your shoulders straight— your shoulders and his should be parallel—and your weight even on both seat bones. Don't let your having your outside leg farther back weight your outside seat bone more than your inside.

To help you maintain your haunches-in as you go down the long side, I want to introduce a concept that you may never have come across in your riding work before: the need for a *range of pressure* in your aids.

The kind of focus and awareness that you'll need to recognize and respond to this need is at the heart of everything I mean by being a "feeling" rider. From one stride to the next, the amount of pressure you need in your outside leg to keep your horse in the bend and on the track you want can vary—maybe three pounds, then one, then two—depending

Fig. 169

on how responsive he is (which translates into how much pressure you're feeling from him). The more aware you are of the feeling he's giving you, the better you'll be able to apply just as much pressure as he needs, no more and no less.

Just being aware that you need to focus on the message he's sending you will start to develop your sensitivity here; the more conscious you stay of it—and of how he responds to the messages you send back through your leg aid—the better you'll become at recognizing exactly what he's saying and how to answer him.

Keep that need for awareness in mind as you continue. At every step, apply your outside leg . . . closing and relaxing, closing and relaxing, to keep your horse where you want him to be. (You may glance back at the hindquarters once or twice to be sure you have the haunches in to the degree you want, but eventually you should be able to feel where they are and not have to look.)

Use your inside leg in the same rhythmic way to keep your horse going forward. You will feel him shorten stride *slightly* to accommodate the position of his quarters . . . but don't let him drop behind your leg. Keep him coming forward in an even rhythm.

Resist the temptation to overcorrect—*perfect* practice is what makes perfect. Some riders figure that they need to start out with the haunches at a 45-degree angle to end up with a 30-degree one, but I don't recommend your doing so unless your horse is extremely stiff. Even if he is stiff, don't overcorrect more than a couple of times; what you want him to get used to is traveling on three tracks with his haunches at a 30-degree angle. In fact, an overdone angle is the biggest problem I see with riders doing haunches-in; if your horse swings his quarters in too far, go back to shoulder-in to counteract the tendency.

After you're comfortable doing haunches-in at the walk, go on to doing it at the sitting trot and then a little at the canter—but not much, because most horses want to canter with the haunches in naturally. (Horses are more than ready to use anything you teach them against you if it helps them evade work—and too much haunches-in at the canter makes it too easy to avoid cantering straight.) If your horse wants to canter with his haunches *out,* of course, do as much haunches-in work in the canter as you need; if you're having trouble with flying changes, holding the shoulders straight and doing haunches-in to both the left and the right should make him much more proficient at doing a correct flying change.

At walk, trot, and canter, use your seat and legs to keep your horse's rhythm steady and his impulsion coming, so that he can't evade your aids. You want his energy working steadily from behind, so that he bends all the joints in his hindquarters, carries his weight rearward, and is *able* to lighten his forehand.

A PAUSE TO
ASSESS

Your flat work has begun to move beyond the basics. As a result of the two inside-leg-to-outside-rein exercises you've been doing, shoulder-in and haunches-in, and maybe even since you went back over the leg-yield, you should have begun to notice that your horse is going in a better shape—without any conscious effort in this direction from you. The improvement is a natural result of the lateral exercises you've been doing. As your legs get the haunches actively engaged, all of a sudden he starts to give all over—hind legs, back, neck, jaw. He's a little rounder than he used to be with you on his back: not resisting the bit but accepting it, not pulling on the reins. The next step (and one you'll get very soon, if you haven't already) is that he'll start to come on the bit.

"On the Bit"

That's a phrase you've heard a few times, isn't it? What it means is a condition in which the horse is *connected* back to front. Your seat and legs make the hind end active, generating energy that comes forward into your hands, and your horse accepts your contact, completing a circular flow of communication from him up to you and back again. You're riding the back of him up under the forehand and making him straight at the same time; he breaks at the poll not because you're dragging his head down and in but because he's carrying himself over his hindquarters. Achieving and becoming aware of that state is what *feeling* is all about. A lucky few riders can recognize the feeling automatically; it's a gift they're born with. But those who aren't born with it can learn it.

What tells you that your horse is on the bit? You feel as if he's a little shorter from back to front, because you're moving his hind end up under him. His steps feel and sound a little livelier, and they're regular. And his back comes up underneath you a bit more (something I didn't recognize until just a few years ago).

Creating "on the bit" can be something of a balancing act. I like to think of it as a little like plumping feathers in a pillow: your legs are almost tickling your horse, making him straight and forward and more animated; your seat is pushing a little, accentuating the natural motion of his back in the stride, telling him he's got to be more active from behind; "but," your hand is saying, "I don't want you to go faster, even though I'm asking for impulsion. I want you to let my hands package that impulsion, contain it, while you stay light and lively."

That's the ideal. But, to me, "on the bit" is a result of correct riding and a means to an end—that of being able to execute more sophisticated movements fluently. It's not an end in itself. And while you're asking your horse to stay a little rounder, you may have to do a lot of resisting with your hands as he tries to run away from accepting the bit pressure. Half-halts are the way I get my message across. As I feel the inside hind leg come under and support him, I use my leg to say "Come on" at the same time that my hand takes a squeeze of contact; then I soften the hand and relax the leg; on the next stride I half-halt again. I'm containing his energy, establishing parameters, telling him not to go faster or longer but to use his impulsion to carry himself. And I'm doing these things continually and to various degrees depending upon his responses and the movement I'm doing— whether shoulder-in, transitions, or jumping, for example.

Asking your horse to be round and on the bit is another time to be aware of the need for varying pressure in your aids. As your awareness grows, you'll find there's almost never a time when both legs should apply exactly the same amount, or when either legs or hands should apply the same amount from one stride to the next. You might need nine pounds in one leg and nine and a half in the other, or seven and nine; two pounds in the "squeeze" phase of your hands' first squeeze-release and one or two and a quarter in the second. The message you send to each of the four sections of your horse depends on the message each of those sections is sending you.

If you pull on your horse, he's going to pull back. Therefore, what you're always working toward is the lightest possible aids: being able to create energy with a light leg, send it into a light hand (more of a "tap, tap, feel, feel" than a "squeeezzze, puuulll") and yet have the energy stay contained within the frame.

At times, you may need to give a fairly strong first half-halt, but apply it quickly and remove it quickly; repeat the aid, if necessary, but then return to using lighter pressure. Use the same range of pressure with your leg aids: in some cases a horse needs a very strong leg, or even a sharp prick with the spur (and if he's a deadhead, he may need that sharp prick more than once), but you'll never see me stick my spur in any horse's ribs and leave it there for six or eight strides at a time.

Your horse will pick up on the quality of your aids; if they're light and elastic, he'll be light and elastic. If his steps get a little dead, you can use a quick spur to get him lively again, but then go back to your light aids. And never puuulll back with your hands: I resist with my hands, arms, and back as a unit, and always with different degrees of pressure in rhythm with my horse's steps. I move my two hands as one, keeping a constant distance between them as I shift them to one side or the other, so one is always more indirect (against the neck or near it) and the other more direct. That way, my pressure is always more sideways than straight back; remember, I'm always riding the horse slightly from inside leg to outside hand to make him straight and round.

L O N G   A N D   L O W —
A   S T R E T C H I N G   E X E R C I S E

Want to find out how successful you've been in teaching your horse to use his haunches and his back in the lateral work you've done so far? End a work session by letting him relax.

Bring him to the walk and let the reins slide through your fingers to the buckle. If you've been connecting him from back to front correctly—and if he's really accepting your seat and leg and is coming through from behind, seeking the bit—he should stretch his head and neck, following the bit to the ground.

If he isn't really connected, or isn't loose in his back, he'll sort of half-stretch . . . and then *raise* his head (and you'll know you need to spend more time on the earlier exercises).

Stretching isn't just a test, of course. Letting your horse stretch out and down this way is something you should do whenever you take a break in a work session. (Few things irritate me quite as much as seeing a rider giving herself a break but holding her reins in a fixed little cross in one hand, so that her horse has to stay flexed.)

Stretching also isn't just something to do at a walk; it's something you can do at the halt and at all three gaits—walk, trot, and canter.

Try it at the walk first. Close your leg and use your seat to emphasize the rhythm of the walk and send your horse's energy forward. (Your legs and seat pushing him up into the bit are like fingers squeezing toothpaste from a tube.)

When you feel him coming up onto the bit, lighten your contact to encourage him to poke his nose out; see if he'll follow the impulsion forward, stretching out and down. To be successful, you must truly *feel* what he's doing and be very supple in your arms.

Fig. 170 I've encouraged Starman to take the bit by sending him forward from my seat and leg while keeping a passive contact with my hand. As he starts downward, I follow with my arms and hands. He's stretching as far as he can go, and I'm continuing to encourage him with my light, elastic contact with his mouth.

If he gets above the bit, take a steady, equal pressure of both sides of the mouth (with supple, elastic arms that follow as he nods his head) and close your legs to get him to take hold of the bit again.

Fig. 170

When he does, reward him by giving and letting him stretch. As soon as he starts to come up again, reapply the aids, taking a steady, elastic feel of his mouth and using your legs to ask him to stretch. Keep squeezing and giving, encouraging him to drop his head farther and farther. Focus totally on what you're doing, so that you respond instantly. You want to reward him the moment he stretches, and catch him the moment he comes up, in both cases staying very supple and soft so that you don't scare him from taking the bit.

If he roots *up*, he's trying to escape the pressure; he hasn't figured out that he'll be rewarded with a lighter rein if he stretches downward. Be patient and keep asking; be alert for the second when he happens on the response you want and reward him by giving immediately.

You can play with him all the way down to the ground. Each time he comes up or drops behind the contact, take an equal feel and add leg again. That pressure, applied equally and steadily on both sides of his mouth, will encourage him to root and push against it, just as an old school horse will root against a child who hangs on his mouth.

Fig. 171 In the posting trot (posting, rather than sitting, so that his back muscles can stretch freely), I have a light, equal pressure and very elastic arms. My horse has begun to stretch down, but I feel him hesitating and thinking about coming back up, so I'm keeping a little contact.

Fig. 172 As he stretches fully, I give completely, extending my arm so that there's a straight line from my elbow to his mouth. He's truly relaxed and using himself beautifully because he understands that if he stretches he gets a reward of less pressure on the reins. (Remember, a horse will only put his head down if he is relaxed; if he's frightened, or even nervous, his head comes up immediately.) When he stretches all the way to the ground like this, he

Fig. 171

Fig. 172

uses the same neck and back muscles I want him to use on top of a jump.

Fig. 173 In the canter, I'm using seat and leg to send Starman forward and have lowered and widened my hands to encourage him to stretch down. I follow as much as I can without

Fig. 173

dropping the contact completely. My fingers are open to let the reins slide through and not hit him in the mouth; notice the straight line from elbow to bit.

Once your horse gets the idea, you won't have to play with him. If he's really on your seat and leg, he'll happily stretch all the way to the ground as soon as you give him the chance.

Veterinarians will tell you that working in this long-and-low shape does a great deal of good for the back and hind end, stretching and strengthening all the muscles. It's an excellent corrective. For horses that go with their polls way up and overflex, so that they're short in the neck and in some cases a little behind the bit, lots and lots of stretching at all three gaits helps counter the tendency. For hunters and jumpers that want to jump hollow, hours and hours of stretching will develop a whole new set of muscles to promote rounding. And stretching is a great relaxer for hot horses that go upside down because of tension. One horse that had a big under-muscle on the neck when I started working with him now can walk, trot, and canter with his nose on the ground thanks to this work.

When to do it? If you can get this kind of stretching at the beginning of your work session, it's a great way to help your horse loosen up—but you may not be able to. Stretching is easiest at the end of a session, when his muscles are well limbered. And it comes as a welcome reward after all the work you've been asking those muscles to do—it *feels* good, and it *is* good.

CHAPTER THIRTEEN

FLEXION AND
COLLECTION

The next step in your horse's advanced flat work will be using transitions to improve his balance and self-carriage. Before we begin that, though, I want to take a few minutes to talk about two terms that come up frequently in talking about balance, and that many people don't really understand.

I can't say often enough that the back-to-front connection of your horse—creating energy in the hind end and sending it forward—is the basis of all good riding. You're learning that by experience, through the improvements you're beginning to see in his way of going. Yet many people don't understand that true roundness has to come from behind (they think it can be achieved simply by cranking the head in), or don't want to spend the time and effort to build the back-to-front connection. Instead, they focus on the front end, and on making the horse break at the poll and bring his nose in on the vertical by pulling on the reins, hoping that some of what they produce in the front will somehow travel backward to round the back and activate the hindquarters.

But energy doesn't travel backward in a horse; it has to start from the hindquarters because that's where the engine is. You can create flexion with reins alone, but it won't do a thing to the rest of the horse's body; he can travel along quite easily with his nose tucked in but his back hollow and his hind legs out behind him. For that reason, I don't even think about trying to create flexion as such.

Instead, what I aim for—and what my program will deliver, if you work steadily and honestly at the exercises—is a horse that's *naturally* round from nose to tail, as he would be if you watched him free in the field. This horse is round because his whole body is working together, the hindquarters (his rear-mounted engine) coming under him actively, lightening his forehand and creating a natural roundness—a compressed frame that's like a coiled spring, controllable and ready for use. That's *collection*—and if you have that, anything you ask your horse to do will be easier for him. (You'll also have flexion, which comes naturally when you ride the whole horse from back to front. You can produce flexion without collection, but you can't achieve collection without flexion.)

These qualities of roundness and energy are what you'll be aiming to create even more of in our next exercise when you go from working gaits to collected gaits. Taking your horse through a program of this type of flat work (or basic dressage) is like taking him to the gym each day: lengthening him, shortening him, bending, and stretching him, to make him a better athlete.

TRANSITIONS

Transitions—particularly downward transitions, both within a gait and from one gait to another—are a great way to encourage your horse to keep coming from back to front and to carry himself. You use leg to create whatever energy you need, hand to receive the energy and tell your horse what you want him to do with it, and seat to reinforce either the driving message of your leg or the containing message of your hand.

Whether the transition is upward or downward, you can also use your seat to make the change smooth rather than jarring—by communicating to your horse the rhythm of the new gait that you want. Each gait has its own rhythm, of course: the four-beat walk, the two-beat trot, the three-beat canter, with variations depending on whether the gait is working, extended, or collected. I find that if you *think* the rhythm of the new gait that you want (like humming a song in your head, without making any audible noise), your seat and legs will automatically start telling your horse about it as you ask for the transition—or even as you're just preparing to ask. The higher the level of communication between you, the more quickly he'll pick up on your message and the smoother the transition will be.

If you want to go from the walk to the trot, thinking the trot rhythm will make your legs close a little more

Fig. 174

quickly, in the one-two of the trot, and help him pick up the rhythm in his body.

Fig. 174 Here I am in the walk thinking "trot." I automatically use my aids in the trot rhythm. My seat and legs are collecting him, bringing him to attention, and preparing him for the trot transition.

Fig. 175 As I feel the one-two rhythm begin, my upper body automatically tips slightly forward to stay with his center of gravity. He steps smoothly into trot, not losing his shape or balance.

In a downward transition, say from the canter to the trot, standing in your stirrups and stiffening on the reins will give you a very poor transition, but putting the rhythm of the trot

Fig. 175

stride into the half-halts that you give while still cantering will let you make a smooth, balanced transition.

Downward transitions tend to be the bumpiest, because your horse has to shift his balance backward from where it's been in the faster gait. (For the same reason, downward transitions are also where he's most likely to become crooked—so you, as the brains of the operation, have to be on the lookout for straightness problems and be ready to apply appropriate corrections.) As you start taking his mouth to tell him to slow, he's probably going to grab the bit—and pull you out of the saddle if you're not ready for him. Here's a place where thinking the rhythm really helps:

Fig. 175B   Quiet the swing of your hips and sit against your horse more, using your almost passive seat—a very short push against rather than with the motion—to tell him you want shorter strides. I'm keeping my hips relaxed, eyes up, elbows just in front of my hip bones—so my reins are a comfortable length—and I'm thinking about my half-halt. I deepen my heels (think of yourself "growing" in the saddle), close my legs against him so that he gets off his forehand and comes up under himself (remember, any time he pulls against you, leg is what gets him light), and then take his mouth briefly, bending my elbows to ask him to stay light in front. Keeping your elbows bent prevents him from pulling you down and forward and keeps his poll up so that he stays off his nose.

Fig. 175B

Fig. 175C   When he answers the half-halt, I reward him by relaxing my elbows and easing my feel on his mouth, so that he knows this is what I wanted. I relax my legs as well, to tell him to trot, and "think" the trot rhythm with my seat. As he gets the trot rhythm, I make sure we maintain the nice, light balance, closing my legs to keep him moving actively into the bit from behind.

If your horse is very heavy, your first couple of "takes" may look rather jerky, because he's going to expect to have something to lean on—so *he'll* take more when he feels you give, which will make your next take have to be more forceful. Think of the motion as "lifting" him into the slower gait—so that he "sits" more behind and doesn't fall down in front.

Fig. 175C

As your horse finds out that you aren't willing to let him balance himself by pulling against you, he'll lighten and not fall forward so much. And if you strengthen your leg or even add a prick of your spur the instant you feel him pull, you'll accelerate the "Carry yourself!" learning process.

Keep sitting and lifting him slightly with your half-halts, bending your elbows. As you feel him trying to fall on his nose, sit in and sit up to bring his center of gravity back. With repetition, he'll come to recognize that, when you open your hip angle and sit a little more deeply, you're going to be asking him to come back—so he'll start to do so on his own, and you'll have less of a tug of war.

(That lifting feeling in your arms during the downward transition, by the way, is not a static pull but a little circle, resisting very slightly toward you, up, and forward again. The canter, particularly, is a circular gait in the way the horse comes off the ground into a moment of suspension, through the air, and then down again; your hips and your arms should have that same motion of lifting and giving, lifting and giving. You're resisting in rhythm until he lightens, taking and giving in direct response to how strong he is against you.)

Collecting and Extending Gaits

Back in Part I we worked on lengthening and shortening your horse's stride at all three gaits, a tool you should have found useful in jumping our little courses at the end of Part II. Now we're going to take that idea a step further and introduce collected and extended gaits—required in dressage tests, and useful for all types of riding because they let you rebalance your horse and repackage his energy as you may need.

Fig. 176

Let's say, for example, that you're in a working trot and you want to bring your horse back to a very collected and animated sitting trot.

The rhythm of a collected trot is actually a little quicker than that of a working trot, so think a slightly quicker "one-two" as you close your legs in rhythm with his steps and push with your seat to shorten and enliven them. As your horse responds to your leg and seat and begins to go forward, resist with your hands to keep the liveliness inside a shortened frame.

Fig. 176 I'm just beginning my half-halt to ask for a collected trot: closing my legs in the trot rhythm, then resisting with my arms and back.

Fig. 177 As my horse responds, his hind legs come under him, he raises his poll, and his steps—and frame—become shorter and more animated.

Repeat your half-halts, accentuating both forward pressure and resistance until you feel

Fig. 177

the horse becoming shorter and more animated. When he becomes light, with more jump in his stride, and you know he's carrying himself (maybe in three steps, maybe in eight), reward him by giving, relaxing your aids and going on to a forward posting trot or canter for a couple of minutes before asking for another transition.

While he's learning, don't hold a collected gait for more than a few strides. It's hard work—you're asking him to bend the three joints of his hind legs further than he's used to, and to call on some muscles he may not even know he has. At first he may leap, or plunge, or stop, or run sideways—anything to get out of working so hard—so make your requests short and repeat, repeat, repeat. When you do get him to collect, think about keeping him straight; use your skills to correct any crookedness—for example, do a step or two of shoulder-in to correct a bulge. Over time, you'll come to assess for straightness and apply any appropriate correction without even consciously having to sort out what it is.

Just as you should feel your horse's frame shorten in a collected gait, in a true extended gait you'll feel it lengthen—as his stride grows longer, his back seems to lengthen and his neck stretches forward, so that he's stretching into his bit.

Fig. 178 Here in the trot, for example, I think the longer rhythm I want, building more impulsion in Top Seed's stride with my seat (each time I sit) and my legs. I have a light, elastic contact with his mouth, encouraging him to stretch into the bit.

Fig. 178

In the canter, again think the longer rhythm of an extended canter and follow that rhythm with your seat (hearing the music in your head), at each stride giving a longer push for a second . . . just before you close your leg against the horse's side to get a longer canter stride. Maintain the lightest of contacts with his mouth. Pushing isn't pumping; it's just in your hips and seat, like the motion you'd use to activate a swing, emphasizing the stride motion.

If you're tempted to pump to get more lengthening, don't; instead, add a touch of your stick. (The reason you're tempted is probably that nothing is happening; you have to get your horse's attention a little more forcefully and make him understand that when you give these aids you're telling him to stretch and go.)

If your horse is sulky and throws his head, use a touch of spur and stick—just enough to tell him, "Come on, let's get going"—and then lighten your aids to calf and seat pressure alone. You want him to learn to respond to calf and seat, knowing the stick will follow if he isn't honest.

Fig. 179 Here I've asked Starman to lengthen. He happily responds, stretching his stride to the maximum, as I follow with my arms and hips. Because he's extending fully *and* staying light, my aids are light too.

Fig. 179

Is He Carrying Himself?

Like the stretching work you did a little while back, this next technique will sharpen your awareness of your horse's balance—the *quality* of his back-to-front connection and the pressure in your hand. Every so often, when you think he's carrying himself, find out for sure: for two or three strides, move one hand forward, so that there's a loop in the rein, and see whether he stays the same or falls forward looking for the contact. If he stays the same, his balance is good; if he falls forward, he's leaning on you.

When you feel his balance slipping, apply a half-halt with seat and leg to rebalance him . . . and then test his balance again.

Keep your elbow joints oily and elastic throughout the take and give—you don't want to snatch or grab at your horse. Even if the movement looks obvious, it should never be rough. And stay mindful of just how much leg and hand he needs to come back into balance and stay there: it will change *by the step,* so the pressure you apply should change accordingly—maybe ten pounds in your hands the first time, four or five the second, then nine, then six, two, six, two, but never five, five, five, five. You'll know how good your estimate was by how your horse responds.

The more accustomed your horse becomes to your give, the easier he'll find it to maintain his self-carriage without your contact containing him up front. Most of my horses end up balancing themselves practically on loose reins, with very few rebalancing reminders.

GETTING USED TO A SHOW-RING PACE

A lot of riders who are very comfortable with collected work practically freeze up at the idea of getting into the galloping pace they'll need (400 meters per minute for FEI jumper classes, 350 for hunter classes) to jump a course in a regular twelve-foot stride. I can understand that, since when I first came East from California I wasn't comfortable galloping the grand prix courses in the big fields, with tight time allowances.

I knew I couldn't just hope that with enough shows I'd eventually get used to the pace; not only would I put myself at a competitive disadvantage, but my own nervousness would communicate itself to whatever horse I was riding. So what I did to conquer the problem was to allocate time in my practice sessions and *make* myself go out and gallop around and around until I became really comfortable with going fast. That approach worked for me, and it can work for you (*and* your horse, who'll benefit a great deal by learning that he doesn't have to get excited to gallop; you want him to stay relaxed).

Fig. 180 To encourage Cannonball to gallop forward, I have my seat out of the saddle and I'm giving him freedom with my arms and hands.

Fig. 181 As we go even faster, my arms remain relaxed, allowing him freedom to balance himself with his head and neck. To strengthen my position—and stay with his center of gravity—I've sunk slightly into the saddle, pushing my deep heel slightly forward as a brace.

To develop your confidence as well as your horse's ability to gallop calmly while staying adjustable, the following exercise mixes fast and collected work. After you've been doing some

Fig. 180

Fig. 181

collected work (or, better yet, at the end of a work session, when any edge either you or your horse may have had at starting time has worn off) pick up your regular twelve-foot canter stride, sitting down in your saddle but closing your hip angle just enough to stay with his center of gravity. Do a few transitions down and back up again, keeping your elbows and hips very elastic to follow his mouth (with the same light contact) and back. Then return to your working canter and ride a small, neat circle around a jump in your work area.

Pick up the pace to a hand gallop, keeping your seat close to the saddle but your hips forward. As you near the jump, sink your seat down, open your hip angle a little, and apply several half-halts to bring your horse back to a working canter and circle the obstacle.

Fig. 182 As I gallop Starman toward the fence, my eyes are on the imaginary line I will make around it. My upper body is forward, my seat is light, and my contact with his mouth is light.

Fig. 183 Now I prepare for my turn: I sit in, deepen my heels, bend my elbows, make a half-halt—and look where I want to go.

Fig. 182

Fig. 183

Fig. 184 Maintaining my seat and a light contact, I keep looking in and ahead to where I want to go. Notice how effectively my outside rein and leg against the horse regulate the size of the circle and keep him from drifting out or changing leads.

Fig. 185 As we complete the circle, I find my straight line to the next fence, close my legs, and prepare my upper-body position to gallop forward again.

This time you might pick up the pace by closing your legs and giving with your hands, lifting yourself a little more into two-point. If your horse gets very strong, close your legs and give a little half-halt to assure yourself that you're still in control . . . but then try to relax and maintain the pace around another jump, or down one side of your ring or field.

Fig. 184

Fig. 185

Next, sit down and take several half-halts and shorten stride until you're definitely at a slower pace—eight or nine miles per hour instead of the fourteen of the extended gallop or even the twelve of the hand gallop.

At this slower pace, make another circle on a very light rein . . . and then gallop off again, before gradually opening your hip angle . . . and making a series of downward transitions . . . to a halt.

The kind of course I've described will prepare you for doing transitions at higher rates of speed than you're used to, going fast in a jump-off, making short turns, or galloping cross-country and then coming back before a fence. (If you're uncomfortable circling the jumps, you can work without them until you get used to the basic idea of speed, then gradually introduce them.) Once you're feeling comfortable with the pattern, and your horse is under control, change direction every few jumps, throwing in a lead change, to add another dimension to the exercise.

Some horses get very excited the first few times around such a course, others have to be pushed into galloping, but most of them find it a welcome change from their regular work. If you stay calm about it, your horse will accept it as no big deal fairly quickly, no matter what attitude he starts out with—and as soon as he feels you begin sitting in and stretching up, he'll understand your body language and slow down.

This exercise is a good place (and a good time in your horse's training) to introduce vocal aids—"whoa" for downward transitions, and a cluck as you gallop forward to the next fence. Use them with your hand and leg aids first, so that he learns to associate each one with the proper response, and then on their own. They're milder and more relaxing when used on their own, and a way to strengthen the physical aids when used together with them. Once your horse learns to respond to them, he'll be easier to ride at both higher and lower rates of speed.

Chapter Fourteen

Advanced Turn on the Haunches

After the exhilaration and stretching of galloping work, it's time to get back to some increasingly sophisticated lateral work. This exercise, the advanced turn on the haunches, refines still further your control of both the shoulders and the haunches by taking a movement you learned to do at a standstill and putting it in motion. Instead of keeping your horse's head and neck straight as you take his forehand around one step at a time, you'll curve his whole body evenly to the inside as you take his shoulders around in a full circle (or, while you're learning, a half-circle) and his haunches travel their own tiny circle inside the larger one.

In performing this movement, you'll have to maintain impulsion at the same time that you use the bending skills you've been honing in both the shoulder-in and haunches-in. Doing so will require you to coordinate your aids to a greater degree than you've done before. Though challenging, this coordination will pay off by increasing your horse's suppleness and responsiveness. (Don't challenge yourself *too* much, however; read through the exercise and see yourself performing it before you actually give it a try. The more kinks you can work out before you actually meet them, the more good practice you and your horse will both have.)

Begin by establishing *shoulder*-in position at an active walk; this gives you part of the bend you'll want and some impulsion. Keep using your inside leg at the girth, in rhythm with his step, to keep him active and ask him to bend his body around, and your outside leg (the most active of your aids) to keep his haunches stepping under him or a little to the inside (and *not* to the outside).

With your position established, begin the turn . . .

Fig. 186

Fig. 187

Fig. 186 After walking forward in shoulder-in, I take a half-halt, using my legs to keep his forward impulsion and with both hands moving left—just enough so that the inside rein comes *slightly* off the neck and directs him into the turn, and the outside comes against the neck and helps to swing his shoulders around.

Fig. 187 As he contin-
ues to swing around from
my outside (right) aids, his
hind legs step slightly forward, as well as to the left,
generating impulsion and
helping his body to main-
tain a "U" around my
inside leg.

Fig. 188 As he takes
his final step to the left to
finish a 180-degree turn,
he's still bent evenly left
from nose to tail. In the
next step we'll be walking
forward again on a
straight line.

Fig. 188

Think about keeping the rhythm and your horse's steps even, taking one step at a time
but *not* stopping. If you start to lose rhythm or impulsion, give a cluck and a little spur, but
let your degree of contact with the mouth tell him, "Don't run forward."

If you feel him stepping *into* your outside leg, press harder with that leg, to make him
step *away* from it and move his haunches in more.

If he wants to stop or back, be sure your hands aren't too heavy. This exercise requires
that you use your hands and legs quite independently. To give yourself more time to refine
your coordination, make a larger half-circle, thinking haunches-in, and gradually tighten it
up, concentrating on keeping impulsion.

SHOULDER-IN
AT THE CANTER

Fig. 189 In this right shoulder-in in the canter, you can see I'm really "sitting in" and following with my hips. My left leg is firmly on his side, but not way back. My right leg is slightly
forward. My left rein is firmly against his neck, holding the shoulders to the right. Starman is
responding well to all these aids, traveling smoothly on three tracks.

You'll remember that, when we worked on the shoulder-in early in this section, I told
you not to try it at the canter just yet; that you needed to have the movement really down

pat at the walk and trot, with both you and your horse understanding and being comfortable with the feeling of moving 3o degrees to the rail, before going on to shoulder-in at the canter.

The reason: since horses tend to travel with their haunches in at the canter—and their shoulders out—your horse might mistake your telling him to keep his haunches *out* (on the track) as a request for a flying change unless he's very familiar with the movement in the other gaits.

But the shoulder-in at the canter is a lesson worth teaching: it makes a horse use his haunches *under* his body and so he becomes better balanced, more supple and stronger behind—just the tools he needs to travel straight.

Fig. 189

Because having your horse keep his hindquarters straight is crucial to good shoulder-in work, do this work down your fence lines. By now you should be able to feel when he's straight (head and neck, shoulders and haunches), when he's out of alignment, and which way what part of him is popping, but having the fence as a guide will give you a little extra help in this department. (As I mentioned earlier, many riders don't do a correct shoulder-in at all. They think kinking the neck around and pulling the head in do the job—but that position has no resemblance to what I mean by shoulder-in.)

For shoulder-in at the canter, another crucial element is your keeping your seat in the saddle and your weight centered. In any gait, the minute you lighten your seat you lose a lot of your ability to influence your horse's hind legs; that's why I so strongly stress riding without stirrups to deepen your seat and learning to follow the motion with your seat and hips. In shoulder-in at the canter, your horse needs you to maintain a secure, following seat that's even a little bit heavy and that stays right in the saddle to tell him, "Stay on this lead; stay on this lead." If your seat lightens, you'll get flying changes—because he'll feel your active inside leg but he *won't* feel your seat and hips telling him to stay on the lead he's on, so he'll think you want a change.

In three-point position, your seat firmly in the saddle and your hips moving in time with your horse, pick up a working canter—but as you do be aware that your horse is going to want to shift his haunches in, and use your inside leg at the girth—or, if you must, *no more than an inch or two behind the girth*—to keep them out, on the track. Any farther back and you're sure to get a flying change.

At the same time, shift both hands to the inside to the same degree as you did on the advanced turn on the haunches, so that the outside rein lies firmly against his shoulder, and both reins lead his shoulders to the inside. You should be able to see the corner of his inside eye—but, remember, *don't* pull the neck in; the feel you have on both reins, coupled with your inside-leg pressure, will give you the bend you want.

(You have him on the diagonal aids again—inside leg to outside rein—and the outside rein is what tells him that your inside leg doesn't mean what he may think it does and he's to maintain the bend and not change leads. The inside rein, remaining light and off the neck, frees his inside shoulder and reaffirms that he should stay on his inside lead.)

Keep your seat deep and your outside leg resting at the girth, reinforcing your outside rein's message that you want him to stay on this lead. But be aware that he may stay on the correct lead in front and change behind the first few times. It's not unreasonable for him to be a bit confused—he's been taught "left leg, right lead; right leg, left lead" up to now.

Instead of bending his hocks and rounding his back in response to your active leg asking him to maintain impulsion, he may cheat and swap leads because it's easier for him to understand. If that happens more than once, bring him back to a walk and reaffirm the basic shoulder-in aids, then try the movement in the canter again. At first, ask for just a couple of shoulder-in strides at a time, returning to the walk for more reinforcement in between. When he's consistently comfortable with two or three strides at a time, gradually increase the number as you did in the slower gaits.

Stay aware of the degree of pressure you're exerting with each hand and each leg at every step, and what effect it's having. Your horse's needs can change from one stride to the next, and they'll almost certainly change several times in one trip around your ring or course as he bulges one way or the other, or goes from heavy to light and back again. Keep reading him constantly, using what you see in comparison to the fence line and what you feel in each hand and each leg, and be ready to make corrections the instant he needs them.

CHAPTER FIFTEEN

COUNTER-CANTER

The counter-canter is a terrific exercise for improving your horse's balance and his ability to do lead changes. Although the term "counter-canter" may have struck dread in your heart when you began my program, you'll find it's an easy movement to do now—because you have your horse dependably on your aids. (The key is to think *normal aids* for the lead you want and not let yourself get all tugged out of shape by the idea of direction.)

Pick up the outside lead—let's say it's the right lead—on a straight track that gives you plenty of room before you need to make a turn. Choose a distant point at which you can make a wide left-hand turn (the more familiar you become with counter-cantering, the smaller your turns can be; for now, though, keep things simple).

Approaching the point where you'll begin your turn, make sure you're sitting deep in the *center* of your saddle, not leaning in or out or forward. If you aren't, just as in the shoulder-in at the canter, your horse will give you a flying change; you want to sit even deeper to convince him that you really do want him to stay on the right lead.

As you head around the turn, keep your right leg at the girth and your left leg (the one to the inside of the turn, although it's the *outside* leg in the sense of the lead you're traveling on) back, to maintain the lead. Thinking "Haunches-out" may help you stay wrapped around the lead you're on despite the direction you're going.

Apply your aids carefully, feeling for the right balance of hand and leg; too much of one or the other will give your horse mixed signals. (I'm often able to produce a nice counter-canter where a student has had great difficulty, solely because my position is balanced and my aids come across with feeling.)

To guide him through the turn, keep *sitting* in (tell yourself, "Sit! Sit! Sit!") as you look where you want to go, your left rein against his neck, your right a little out from the neck (as always, move them to the side as a unit, keeping your touching-thumbs distance between them), bending him just enough that you can see the corner of his right eye, and your left leg—very firmly—behind the girth, telling him to maintain the right lead. The aids tell him, "Keep your shoulder there and stay on the right lead"—and by keeping the haunches right, you free the right hind to maintain the lead.

The combination of aids is what gets your horse around to the left successfully: your right leg at the girth, your seat in the saddle, your eyes looking up and around the turn, your hands forming something of a chute to channel the impulsion forward and around the turn—with just a slight bit more feel in the left hand to indicate direction. (Your eyes are

Fig. 190

so important to your balance: when you look where you want to go, your horse responds to your body language, *automatically*.)

Fig. 190 Starman is on the right lead, making a circle to the left. Since my seat is *the* most important aid to hold the counter-canter—it guards the hind legs, preventing them from escaping and switching leads—it is glued to the saddle. And to be sure I don't throw his balance off, I'm in the *center*, not leaning in or out. My contact is light because that is all that is needed to hold the lead. Notice how he's bent, slightly and evenly toward the lead he is on.

Fig. 191 This angle shows the aids clearly: he is bent slightly right, my right leg is at the girth, my left slightly back. My left rein, on the neck, supports the left shoulder and frees the right shoulder, helping to hold the right lead.

Occasionally one of my students can't get a horse to pick up the lead she wants on a straight track. If this

Fig. 191

happens to you, stop, move the haunches to the outside (to the right in our example), as if doing a step or two of a turn on the forehand in that direction, so that he's really listening to your left leg. Then ask again. This time you'll probably get the lead you want. If you don't, quickly follow through with a firm tap of your stick behind your left leg, reinforcing the aid so that your horse cannot mistake what you want. And don't go on too long: do five or six strides, come back to walk, repeat the exercise, and go on to something less demanding. Then, later in the session, come back to it again.

Practice the counter-canter on both leads; as usual, one will probably be harder than the other, so give your horse more time in that direction—and relax him with forward work in between. Because he's learned to be so much on your aids, you should be able to keep him both traveling straight and bent in the direction of your lead. In the end, the counter-canter should be just another movement; when he's honest to your aids, it's not a big deal.

FLYING CHANGES

We've talked a lot about avoiding flying changes when you *don't* want them. Once you've mastered all the preceding flat work, it will be time to focus on producing them when you do—for example, when you ride a course of jumps at show speed. (If your horse already does flying changes on his own, however, let him do them; don't make a big production of them.)

Don't start this work too soon, though; you'll probably need at least a couple of months of advanced flat work, and maybe more, before you and your horse are ready to tackle it. He needs to be clear about all the steppingstones that lead up to flying changes: the haunches-in, the shoulder-in, the turns on the forehand and the haunches.

You need to understand the logic of the progression of things I ask you to do; you also need to make and keep a firm resolution not to lose your temper. *This work is difficult,* so recognize that you're going to need to be patient. Think about how long it takes *you* to figure out how to do it. It'll take your horse that long and more.

Besides, there's an advantage in taking lots of time: the added practice time will make you a better rider—and you'll find that, the better you become at your part of the partnership with your horse, the better he'll work for you. I know this from experience. My horses go much better today than they did ten years ago. They were pretty good then, and I received compliments on my flat work then—but my flat work is *much better* today in terms of *feeling* what each individual horse needs, how far to go with him, and how to get the job done with less pushing and better-quality work. That's what's exciting to me about riding: you can always learn more; there's always room to improve.

Simple Changes: Canter-Walk-Canter

Start with simple changes. Pick up a right-lead canter on a straight line, moving your left leg back and keeping your right at the girth.

About a third of the way down your work area, apply a half-halt: sit in with your seat, put your legs on, and resist his mouth to bring him back to a walk for two or three steps.

Then ask for a left-lead canter—right leg back and left at the girth—staying on the same straight line.

Fig. 192 In the right-lead canter I begin to call him to attention with a half-halt, sitting in, looking up, closing my legs, resisting with my arms and hands and bending my elbows to lift him.

Fig. 193 This is a great canter-walk transition: he's working off his hind legs, bending his joints rather than falling on his nose.

Fig. 194 He steps into the walk rhythm and I prepare him for the left lead, bending him left, and closing my right leg behind the girth (my left is at the girth).

Fig. 195 I kept my position and my elbows bent so that he couldn't fall into the canter (or into a long trot). As I feel the stride begin, I send him forward, giving a little with my arms.

Fig. 192

Fig. 193

Fig. 194

Fig. 195

Keep practicing this simple sequence until you can do it very cleanly, with no in-between trotting steps, and no falling in or out either way around. When your horse is managing this nicely, substitute a complete halt for the half-halt and walk steps.

Simple Changes:
Canter-Halt-Canter

Here Top Seed and I demonstrate a right-lead to left-lead canter transition through the halt.

Fig. 196 I have my right-lead canter and am beginning my halt transition: I sit in and *up*, deepening my heels, closing my legs, and firming up my back so that I *don't* let him pull me forward.

Fig. 197 He halts with great balance, prepared to canter at any moment. I reward him briefly, relaxing my aids a little.

Fig. 198 Then I close my right leg and ask for a prompt canter on the left lead. In response to that pressure, he raises his poll and steps under with his left hind leg. I stay in the center of him, with eyes up, keeping my aids—mostly seat and leg—subtle throughout.

Fig. 196

Fig. 197

Fig. 198

The Flying Change

From this point, the flying change—left lead to right lead with no halt in the middle—is the next logical step. If your horse is really listening to your aids and you're really applying them correctly, a flying change should be easy to get—but with most horses and most riders, it doesn't happen quite that simply (so don't feel discouraged if it doesn't for you).

Before you start asking for flying changes, be very sure that your horse understands the haunches-in aids. Your moving the haunches over is what helps him change behind—and, once again, because he's a rear-engine animal, what happens behind is the crucial component. If you don't move the haunches over, he may give you a change in front but not change behind—and a horse that changes just in front is very hard to persuade to change behind. If you get the change behind first, though, the change in front follows automatically.

When you are smooth in both simple-change sequences and confident of your horse's haunches-in work, it's time to ask for the flying change. Begin by cantering down the center (or across the diagonal) of your work space—let's say on the left lead, so that you'll be changing to the right lead.

Give a half-halt, lifting and straightening the shoulders (if you let him fall forward, you'll never get the change), and alter your leg position to ask for the right lead: bring your right leg forward to the girth and move your left back a little, asking him to move his haunches slightly to the right.

Continue alternating half-halts (keep thinking "Straight shoulders"—and make sure your hip angle is open, so you aren't getting ahead of him with your body and weighing him down in front) and left-leg pressure to keep sending the haunches right, making sure your aids are consistent, repeating at every step until your horse gives you the right-lead change behind. (Don't just try once and give up, as so many people do; keep him cantering up and round so that he can change when he figures out that he should change.)

Once the hind end changes, the front will follow.

Here is the change from the side view:

Fig. 199 We're starting on the right lead. As his right hind leg comes under him I close my right leg to ask for the change (just as I did in the simple change); a moment later his hind legs will be airborne, so this is my opportunity to influence what he does with them.

Fig. 199

Fig. 200 And to be sure he does come forward with his left hind to begin the new lead, I keep my right leg closed as both hind legs are off the ground. He's carrying himself nicely, so I can keep my arms very relaxed. I stay centered—not leaning forward, or left or right. And I don't pull his head way around.

Fig. 201 A clean change: front and hind legs have come forward *together*. I *feel* the change; I don't need to look down; I can relax and continue on in a nice canter rhythm. Ultimately, all flying changes should be done in a normal canter rhythm—not slowing way down or speeding way up. You'll reach this point only when your horse is honestly on the aids.

Fig. 200

If your horse runs off with you because he's afraid of your leg, slow everything down and isolate your aids. Canter into the halt. Then do a couple of steps of turn on the forehand to position the haunches, setting him up so that the response you want is easy . . . and then ask for the new lead. Once he understands that he can get the change when the

Fig. 201

new inside leg comes up underneath him more, he'll be able to respond in the canter as well as at the walk or halt.

Keep the head and neck straight as you prepare and ask; if you pull him one way or the other, you'll unbalance him and he won't be able to change.

Flying changes easily upset a horse that's had bad experiences, so mix in plenty of simple changes and straightforward flat work. That way your horse won't be able to anticipate a flying change and get nervous.

HALF-PASS

The next step in our logical progression of advanced flat work, the half-pass, is the most difficult, which is why I've placed it last. In this movement, your horse travels forward and sideways on two tracks and is bent in the direction he is going. It develops the skills he'll use when he goes through a turn: it enhances his degree of collection, teaches him to engage his inside hind leg better for turns (particularly important in fast turns), and refines your use of and his responsiveness to the outside aids, so that you can control him better and let him look where he's going through turns. (A jumper coming through a fast turn with his head to the *outside* won't see the fence until the last moment and, because he's incorrectly balanced, will probably have it down.)

The half-pass I'm talking about *is* a dressage movement, but the degree of perfection necessary for dressage competition—the shoulders leading the haunches by just the right amount, for example—isn't as important to me as the horse's true acceptance of my aids. I want to be sure that he's reliably *on the aids,* all the time. And with a little polish, my half-pass—like all my flat work—could go to the dressage arena. As I mentioned early, the horse is bent in the direction he's going: if he's moving ahead and to the left, for example, he's bent around the rider's left leg. You've already moved your horse forward and sideways in the leg-yield, where the bend was opposite the direction of travel—leg-yielding to the left, for example, he was bent slightly around your right leg. You've also bent both ends of his body: first separately in shoulder-in and haunches-in, then together in the advanced turn on the haunches. Now you're going to put the fruits of all this bending work together.

Work on the half-pass at all three gaits, starting with the walk. Let's say you're going to do a half-pass to the left, away from the track of your work area. Traveling to the left, establish the bend by riding through a turn: use your inside leg at the girth, confirming the bend of the turn, and your outside leg just slightly behind the girth, to hold the haunches on the track.

Prepare to move the shoulders over by bringing your hands left, to the inside, just enough so that the inside rein is slightly *off* the neck and you can see the corner of your horse's left eye, no more. You're not depending on the left rein for the bend; you're creating it with your diagonal aids—inside leg to outside rein—so you should *feel* him reliably on that outside rein. This is important because it's the pressure of that rein against his neck and shoulder that you'll use to move his shoulders over; if he isn't honestly on your outside rein, you won't be able to use it effectively.

As he feels your rein pressure and begins to come off the track, think "Shoulder-in" and use your outside (right) leg to push the haunches over so that they're just behind the shoulders.

In a finished half-pass, the shoulders should lead a little, counteracting the horse's natural tendency to travel with haunches in and shoulders out. In training, though, I prefer to have shoulders and haunches as equal as possible—or maybe even the haunches a little bit ahead. (If a horse normally wants to travel with his haunches way to the outside, I may overcorrect and push the haunches farther to the inside than the shoulders.)

The hard part of the half-pass, for both your horse and you, is that at the same time that you're trying to send him left with the pressure of your right leg (which is probably your stronger leg aid) you have to use the left leg to keep the bend and forward impulsion. That idea probably sounds as contradictory as using leg to energize your horse when he's pulling you out of the saddle. Only if you and your horse already have all the pieces of this exercise down pat (as you should, since you've worked on all of them) will you be able to follow through with it.

Your goal is to establish the bend and then maintain it as you move your horse forward and sideways. In the beginning, you're going to fumble, either falling on the inside shoulder and letting the haunches lag or traveling with the haunches first and the nose to the outside. Your job, as a *feeling* rider, is to coordinate your aids, experimenting with how much of each you need to maintain both the bend and the forward movement.

It's a wonderful feeling when you find it: discovering that you can actually push with your legs, quite hard, at two different spots and feel your horse really bend *and* move into that bend, filling up the outside rein with your left-leg pressure and at the same time moving him left with your right. You want to be able to feel and talk to each part of your horse to influence his movement.

Apply both legs at the moment the gait naturally draws you deeper into the saddle— when his inside hind leg is on the ground, supporting him. The pressures are different, of course; normally the outside leg is stronger. However, if you feel your horse falling onto his inside shoulder, think "Shoulder-in" and use your inside leg more strongly to restore the bend and put him back on the outside rein. Or, if his haunches aren't coming over enough, think "Haunches-in."

Make sure you sit in the middle of your horse and don't fall forward. I've seen a lot of riders start looking down at the bending and fall forward as they do—which, of course, puts the horse on the forehand.

Fig. 202

Fig. 203

Think of the aids as *lifting* the horse (inside leg) and taking him over (outside leg), lifting and taking him over, with *his* inside hind leg doing most of the work.

Fig. 202   In the trot, I'm preparing for a half-pass to the left coming through the turn: both hands to the inside, inside leg at the girth, outside behind it. Notice the *even* bend, from nose to tail.

Fig. 203   As we begin the half-pass, he accepts my leg pressure. Both hands are to the inside and I'm sitting in the middle, my center of gravity in sync with his.

Fig. 204   He's making a "U" around my left leg. Notice my left leg at the girth, my right one back. I remain in the middle of my horse—not leaning.

Fig. 205   He's honestly filling out the outside rein well with his neck, and at the same time I'm pushing him over with that rein. This photograph shows what a good suppling movement this is: to cross his legs fluently while keeping his shoulders and haunches pretty much in line, he has to carry himself.

Fig. 206   To the right, he shows excellent engagement and balance, crossing his hind legs deeply as he travels forward and sideways.

Fig. 204

Fig. 205

Practice the half-pass in both directions, and be patient about the amount of progress you achieve in a session. This is a difficult movement for your horse and for you; I needed years of work to learn to do the movement correctly. Remember, your inside leg is creating the bend and sending him forward, while your outside leg and rein are bringing him over—so the better your half-pass, the lighter your inside rein should be.

Fig. 206

FINAL
FLAT-WORK THOUGHTS

This section has put a lot more words into the vocabulary of communication that you and your horse are building up. Use them all. Like a dancer, turn your practice sessions into interesting times by alternating collected and extended work, advanced maneuvers and simpler ones, and physically demanding work with relaxing and stretching.

No matter how involved or difficult, all the movements you've been learning to do are a matter of creating and regulating impulsion: generating it behind, sending it forward, and letting it out or containing it. That's why you have to ride both ends and both sides of your horse. He's a living, breathing entity that you are constantly molding and changing with energy: longer, shorter, faster, slower, left, right—whatever. For that molding and changing to take place harmoniously, though, you and he have to be speaking the same language—and the richer that language grows, the greater the range of what the two of you can do together and the better prepared you are for whatever riding discipline interests you.

IV.
ADVANCED JUMPING

CHAPTER SIXTEEN

You've progressed through the first three stages of my program, strengthening your partnership with your horse by improving both your riding and your communicating skills. In this next stage, advanced jumping, you'll once again be working on straight lines, bending lines, and curving lines, but the lines and the fences will be more challenging and your approach will be more sophisticated. You'll learn to analyze the technical questions that different types of fences pose, and the effect that the distances before and after a fence should have on the way you meet the fence. While you'll spend most of your time on stadium-type fences, I'll also be introducing you to natural obstacles. Throughout, of course, you'll continue to refine your ability to communicate with your horse through seat and hands as well as legs.

Are you ready for this new work? Well, the better you and your horse are in the advanced flat work of Part III, the better you'll do with the new work in this section, but you don't need to be perfect yet, because you aren't going to abandon flat work when you go back to jumping. By now you understand that flat work is something you'll do throughout your horse's career to keep him fit and supple, so you'll continue to do Part III's exercises as part of your daily routine—and keep improving your flat work as you proceed with jumping.

At this point you do need to be completely solid in the basic jumping work of Part II. The skills you honed there should be second nature to you before you try to advance. You shouldn't need, for example, to think about counting strides in a line, or have to stop and analyze what you need to do to ride a bending six. Those responses should be automatic; if they're not, stay with the basic jumping exercises (along with your flat work, of course) until they are.

Riding
Readiness Check

To be certain that you are secure enough in the basic skills you need, set up one of the simple courses that you rode at the end of Part II. When you ride it now, keep the following questions in mind:

1. Are you riding forward in rhythm? If you set the pace and then gallop forward in rhythm, the distance will always be there: your horse will jump out of stride. But if you start fussing at him, taking and nipping and stopping the impulsion, or take your leg off and let him slow, or stiffen up to look for a distance, you'll end up getting to the fence on a half-stride. Then you'll either have to stand way off and leap or take his mouth and fit in a short stride. Either way, you'll destroy the smoothness of your ride.

Think back to what you saw when you watched your horse jumping loose in the jumping chute or on the longe line: left to his own devices, he doesn't stop and then speed up, he looks and goes forward. Even if he has to pat the ground, he does that going forward. He knows how to get over the jump smoothly and successfully. If you can just set the pace and then stay out of his way, trusting the rhythm, he'll do fine.

Watch four top hunter riders at the next show you go to. Look for where and how their horses take off. The actual distance will vary, but the impression of smoothness won't— because such riders concentrate on maintaining pace and rhythm and don't even think about distance. They just focus on their jobs and let the distance happen. If they do any adjusting, it's by making the turn a little longer or shorter (something we'll discuss soon), not by making a major pace change. That leaves their horses free to study their fences and jump from any distance—comfortably, boldly, and cleanly.

2. Do you relax into the jump? Just as you shouldn't be fussing with your horse on the way to the fence, you shouldn't be fussing with him right in front of it. When you've established your rhythm and pace, and you can sense that he's one or two strides from the take-off, relax your arms and hands and give forward with them. Keep your driving aids—the seat and leg that tell him, "Yes, we're going to jump"—but soften your hands and arms.

In most cases, letting your horse figure out the distance himself is great for his education; in fact, letting him hit a jump is one of the best ways to make him a more careful jumper. If he hits, he stings himself; next time he'll pay more attention and pick up his feet more. On the other hand, if you manufacture every distance for him, he'll rely on you and stop trusting his own instincts. When you find yourself in a jump-off, where you have to go fast against the clock, or in a class where the jumps are bigger or more difficult than any you've faced before, you won't be able to ask him to help out. His sense of self-preservation will have withered away from disuse.

Of course, if you're on a horse that is a stopper or that has a bad front end, giving with the hands isn't an option. If you have to hold him off the jump and lift him a little with your hands to get him over, do—but recognize that you're baby-sitting a problem, and that you'd rather not have to help him this way. Always, as much as you possibly can, you want to trust your horse. If you don't, you can end up making even the most talented horse lazy and/or dependent on you. You want to ride each horse in the most positive way you can. If a bad jumper needs a defensive ride, fine; but don't let that style spill over into all your riding.

3. Is counting strides second nature to you? For this part of the checkup, set up three lines in your work area: one at seventy-two feet (a normal five strides) down one side, another at sixty-four feet (four feet longer than a normal four strides) down the other side, and a third at forty-six feet (two feet short of a perfect three) across the diagonal. Ride the three lines as a course, and count strides aloud in each line.

Counting is important for several reasons. First, it functions like a speedometer. If you go down the first line, which is supposed to be a normal five, and find that you end up doing it in a very long five, or in six, you know your pace is too slow; you aren't creating the impulsion you need. If you do it in a tight five, or even in four, you know you're too fast. You can use that information in the turn to the next line, picking up your pace or slowing it down to suit your needs. The smoothness you want to feel (and you want the judge to see in the show ring) all the way around comes from preparation—establishing rhythm, pace, and track in the turn before the fence, so that you can maintain it all the way down the line, giving the impression that every line is riding twelve feet to a stride.

Another useful thing about counting is how conscious it makes you of your horse's rhythm. Timing your "one—two—three" and so on to the first footfall of the stride, you hear whether the rhythm is staying regular, speeding up, or slowing down. The great riders have a natural sense of timing and rhythm, working off a clock in their heads: not just down the line, but through the turn, they keep that motor purring steadily, no matter what's coming up next—even through the final circle and halt at the end of a course. It's starting and stopping the rhythm that makes for a rough ride—taking a rough half-halt in the turn, releasing all leg pressure, and then spurring to reestablish forward pace again. You want to reach the point where there's a metronome ticking away in your head. The second your horse loses impulsion, on goes your leg—automatically, reflexively—because you feel his balance change and his rhythm alter. When you reach that level of sensitivity, you'll also be able to judge accurately where you can gallop a fence and be brilliant and where you should choose the conservative, steadier option that's more in keeping with your horse's skills.

A third benefit is that counting makes you conscious of how a three-stride line looks (and a four-stride, and a five-stride). The stride counting you did in your Part II work has helped establish the look of standard distances in your mind and given you a sense of how far out from the fence your takeoff area is for each. Now, in these more advanced exercises, my saying "If you see you're going to be a little long" will be meaningful; you will know that you're going to be long (or short, or whatever) and do something about it (steadying, turning shorter or wider, and so on)—earlier and more subtly as your sense for such differences improves.

In these advanced exercises, the takeoff distances will in some cases be a little more challenging, but the exercises use the same aids that you've honed on the flat. Some of them call for adding strides, leaving out strides, and choosing bending over straight lines, but you've already had some experience with these techniques, too. The specifics will be a little more complex now, but the theory is the same.

MENTAL
READINESS

Success in advanced jumping requires you to recognize and deal with your own and your horse's weak spots. In my case, for example, I discovered I had a tendency to be an aggressive rider and get stiff; when things got tough, I'd tend to lock up in my arms and add strides. I dealt with the problem by telling myself over and over, on the way to the ring,

"Let go. Let go. Let go." Now I don't even have to think about it; letting go has become second nature—but only because I worked on it. Riders I've worked with have been successful using the same approach and telling themselves "Get tough," or "Count," or "Soften"—whatever was appropriate for their particular weaknesses.

Just as recognizing your own weak points helps you deal with them, identifying your horse's lets you keep them from interfering with his performance. One of my horses, for example, is heavy on the left rein and tends to drift to the right. If I school him on the flat with left shoulder-in and half-passes from the right leg (sort of an equivalent to my pre-class "Let go" injunctions to myself), he's much better. The tendency is always there but, by being aware of it and working to counter it, I keep it in check. You'll come to recognize more of your horse's weak spots, and devise ways to compensate for them, as you work through the upcoming exercises.

The mental side of riding is very real. If worries are keeping you from performing your best, I strongly suggest that you consult a sports psychologist. In 1983 and 1984 the United States Equestrian Team encouraged its riders to work with sport psychologist Robert Rotella before their gold-medal 1984 Olympics win. As a Team member, I learned a lot about making the mind work for me instead of against me. As Dr. Rotella pointed out, you can't expect to solve all your problems by saying "Think positively," because nonpositive things do happen. You know your horse, and his history, so you should mentally rehearse a perfect ride around the course—and then, without dwelling on what might go wrong, have Plan B ready as well.

Let's say, for example, that there's a liverpool on course and your horse has spooked at liverpools in the past. You know that if he spooks at this one you'll need to make a prompt shift of gears and ride him more aggressively. Fine. The remedy is now in your bag of tricks. Rehearse it several times, but keep the rehearsal positive—"He dumped me at the liverpool in that last show, so here I'm going to have to be very, very strong," rather than "If he spooks, I'll go to the whip." Then rehearse the jump as if it's going to go right—because if you rehearse it going wrong you can make it go wrong, a self-fulfilling prophecy.

That's an example of the kind of handle on your riding problems sports psychology can help you get. Some of the great natural riders have developed instinctive remedies for potential mental hang-ups. For the rest of us, though, expert advice can provide a helpful shortcut to a sound solution.

All right: you've decided that your jumping basics are solid, and you've looked back over your work so far to figure out what weak spots you need to compensate for in your performance and your horse's. You're ready for the new work of this chapter, so let's move on.

IMPROVING
COMMUNICATION

EXERCISE 9:
ADVANCED COMMUNICATION
WITH YOUR HANDS

This is actually a group of exercises to help you increase your ability to feel with and use your hands more skillfully in riding.

Riders can use their hands in any of four basic ways over a fence:

Fig. 207 Grabbing mane (or grabbing a neck strap) is for the beginner: a way to keep the rider from hitting the horse in the mouth and maintain balance.

Fig. 208 The long crest release, in which the hands rest on either side of the crest close to halfway up the neck, is the next step up from grabbing mane. It protects the horse's mouth and provides security for the rider over the fence, but the big loop that hand position puts in the reins eliminates all contact.

Fig. 209 In the short crest release, the hands are just a couple of inches up the neck but still resting on the crest. It pro-

Fig. 207

Fig. 208

vides some contact with the mouth but little influence.

Fig. 210 The automatic release, also called a following or out-of-hand release, creates a straight line from the rider's elbow to the horse's mouth. Look at pictures of such great riders of the past and present as Bill Steinkraus, Mary Mairs Chapot, Kathy Kusner, George Morris, Michael Matz, or Joe Fargis, or most of the top European riders, and you'll see that same straight elbow-to-mouth line.

The automatic release, which is the one I've always used, is my favorite because it's the most classic, it "goes with the motion" and allows the horse the most freedom, and it's perfectly acceptable in equitation, show jumping, and eventing. Because it doesn't glue your hands to the crest, it enables you to influence your horse in the air: you can encourage him to stretch his neck and reach across a wide oxer, or you can take his mouth a little to steady him and encourage him to land a little shallower.

Fig. 209

Fig. 210

Like any sophisticated tool, however, the automatic release does require more finesse for correct use: a secure base and the ability to apply aids independently of one another, elastic arms, and sensitivity to the mouth.

You can develop the feeling hands you need for the automatic release with a couple of over-fences exercises I prescribe for my students:

The Teacup

Hold your reins between thumb and forefinger, as if you were holding a cup of tea. Maintain a light feel of the mouth and a straight line from your elbow to the mouth. Spread your hands out, away from the neck, so that you can't lean on the neck or the crest as a crutch. Think of the feeling you'd have in your arms and elbows if you were pushing a wheelbarrow; that's the feel you want as you're following the mouth.

Keep your hands this way as you approach a fence of comfortable height (two feet six or three feet), in the air, and into the landing, so that you really are following the mouth, not touching the neck. Keeping your hands spread is the key to learning to follow the mouth.

Fig. 211

Fig. 211 I have a straight line from my elbow to his mouth, and I'm not using his mane or neck for my balance.

If you find yourself falling on your hands as you land, your balance may need work, or you may be pinching with your knee, so that your lower leg slips back and your upper body pivots forward.

Most riders want to jam their hands back on the horse's neck in the landing; even in top Medal and Maclay competition, you see people falling on their hands all the time. But hands really aren't necessary. The more you can improve your balance and your security (and your confidence in your balance), the more you'll be able to eliminate this tendency in yourself. Riding without stirrups will help; so will the work in the next two exercises.

Driving-Style Reins

A variation on the teacup exercise, this is another tool to help teach you lightness.

Turn your closed hands so that they're vertical, thumb on top, as they would be if you were driving your horse. Try this hand position on the flat first, at the walk, trot, and canter. You'll find your arms are much more elastic; the position isn't nearly as strong as the normal one, so your elbows can't lock up as much.

Fig. 212

Now, with your hands still in driving position, head for your fence. You'll find the position encourages you to follow your horse to the jump, not pull back on his mouth, and relax into the jump even more effectively than you've ever done before, going with your horse and not interfering with him.

Fig. 212 My "driving-style" fingers are closed on the reins. My hand slides along the side of his neck, following his head and neck elastically.

Lifting in the Turns

As you may have discovered already, whenever things get complicated—you're putting lines together in a course or you're thinking about rebalancing in the middle of a line to meet the second fence better—your horse tends to fall on his forehand. Many riders react to this by stopping and backing the horse. Backing is a good correction, but it does interrupt the "forward" that you want your riding to have, and it's not something you can do in the show ring, so a better choice is the half-halt—closing your leg and taking your horse's mouth. With many horses, though, you don't even have to do that much; you can accomplish the same objective by lifting the horse—a sort of upward half-halt, which will change his balance from front to back without you even having to slow down.

At the moment when your horse's inside hind is on the ground, so that he's carrying his weight on his hind end and his front is at its lightest, lift him by bending your elbows and raising your hands, quickly but not roughly, and then giving immediately. Depending on how much your horse is on his forehand, you may want to add a little leg to bring his hind end up underneath him.

Repeat the movement once or twice, if necessary, until you feel him lighten in response and start carrying himself again. The technique works in the turns as well as between fences. I like to maintain a relatively even contact on the mouth; I don't pull the head around through the turn.

The horse's neck should be straight, not way to the outside or inside, but part of a uniform curve from nose to tail, conforming to the track of the turn. (If you pulled the head either way, he'd end up popping the opposite shoulder.)

If you feel him leaning, lift and let go once or twice, adding leg for a full half-halt if you need to. He should return to carrying himself on a very light contact.

All the time that you're rebalancing your horse, of course, you must also be looking where you're going, toward your next fence. You mustn't stop riding forward, or allow yourself to look down, any more than you'd look down to watch yourself depressing the gas pedal or shifting gears if you were driving. You may be able to allow yourself the merest fleeting glance down, but that's all. To keep riding forward, you have to keep focusing forward.

EXERCISE 10:
IMPROVING COMMUNICATION
THROUGH YOUR SEAT

Back in your flat work, you encountered—and made use of—the fact that your seat is the mediator between your hand and leg aids, telling your horse whether, for example, you're half-halting him to slow him or to rebalance him for better forward movement. And you'll remember that one big advantage I stressed about riding without stirrups was the way it helps you deepen your seat and move with your horse. The more you've developed a correct following seat, the less likely you are to produce any of three common mistakes that create a stiff, uncommunicative seat: riding with a hollow back, perching on the crotch, or slouching along with your hips way forward of the rest of you.

For jumping, you want a seat that allows you to follow your horse's back and either simply go with him, calm him, or "sit in" to drive him. You want to be able to feel through your seat what your horse needs on the way to a particular fence: to have the same kind of "oneness" in your jumping that you had without stirrups on the flat. It's an elasticity—the same kind of elasticity in your hips as you're striving to maintain in your arms with your "teacup" and driving-rein exercises.

Fig. 213

Fig. 213 Here I'm galloping with my following seat. I'm in the center of my horse, not way ahead or way behind the motion.

In my clinics, I frequently come across riders who think that the right way to ride to fences is standing in the stirrups, out of the saddle. "If I don't get out of the saddle," they say, "my horse goes nuts." If your horse is going nuts, it's not because of the fact that you're in the saddle; it's the *way* that you're in the saddle. Choosing to keep your seat in the saddle or to lift it out shouldn't be a conscious decision; rather, it should be your response to what's happening under you. If you're relaxed—if all your joints are relaxed—you'll go with him naturally.

Experiment to prove this fact to yourself. On a long gallop across a field or around your work area, notice that you automatically lean forward from the hips to stay over your horse's center of balance as it moves forward. That automatically brings your seat out of the saddle a bit, although you're certainly not standing in your stirrups.

Now turn your horse toward a jump, maybe in the center of the work area, or ride him toward a turn and you'll find yourself straightening a little (less if you're still asking for speed—in a jump-off, for instance) and bringing your seat closer to the saddle with each stride, "sitting in" to help create the balance and impulsion he'll need for the fence.

How much you use your seat on the way to a fence depends what you're riding, of course. A heavy horse, or a green horse, or one that's on the chicken side will probably need plenty of both seat and leg from you to keep his engine engaged and him in front of you. On a hot horse whose engine is already in gear, you can ride with a lighter seat and be more out of the saddle—he doesn't need you to motivate him. Still, even he needs your seat to be there, reminding him to keep thinking "forward" even when you're adding a stride or making a short turn.

The more you focus on feel, the more you'll be able to follow your horse and help him. Look at my position in these photos, and watch the top riders carefully every chance you get (I always watch the riders that I respect for their position and the feel they seem to have in their rides). As you watch, ask yourself what it is about that particular rider that makes his or her position look so great. What's there for you to try to incorporate in your own riding? What's the seat doing? The hips? The eyes? The hands? The leg? The upper body? Why does that rider look so harmonious? Or, putting it another way, why do his horses love him? When you see a poor ride, be equally analytical about why this rider looks so unattractive or ineffective or stiff. The more you see what works and doesn't work, and imagine doing the "what works" yourself, the better your body will respond.

IMPROVING
COMMUNICATION —
WITH YOUR EYES

EXERCISE 11:
JUMPING WITHOUT LOOKING

Think back again to when you watched your horse jumping free in a chute or on a longe line. Did you ever see him get to a wrong spot? Probably not. Instinctively, he knows more about jumping than you do—so doesn't it make sense to use what he knows, rather than to try to tell him how to jump?

When I was growing up and riding with Jimmy Williams, he'd have his students go around and around the jumping chute wearing sleeping masks over our eyes. He'd turn the horse loose, crack the whip, and we'd just hang on. With no visual information coming in, we had to depend on feel. The experience helped to teach us perfect balance, perfect position—and it let each of us feel the horse finding the jump without any help from the rider. It also taught us to trust the horse to do the job, and to go with him. (If you've tried jumping on a longe, without reins, you've had a similar "trusting" experience.)

The fact that you can trust your horse to jump the jump doesn't mean that you have no input in his jump, of course. You are responsible for telling him where you want him to go, and how, by establishing the rhythm, the pace, and the line. If you're clear to him about defining your intentions before the jump—no changing your mind and fussing with him as the fence comes up—he'll work successfully within them.

You can accomplish the same end that Jimmy achieved by having students jump blind if you set up your rhythm, pace, and line several strides out, and then focus on something

Fig. 214

in line with, but other than, the jump—say a tree beyond the rail around your work area, or a helper while you let your horse find the distance. Don't leg him; don't pull on the reins; don't interfere with him in any way but go with him to and over the fence. You'll find that your peripheral vision is adequate to let you know he's staying on the line.

Fig. 214 I've galloped to this oxer and looked away from it for five or six strides. At the takeoff, I'm still looking away, and in the air I'll continue to do so.

Continue with this exercise until you really are jumping without looking—no last-minute sneaking a peek, but keep "looking away" in front, over, and after the fence. (Remember, the end of every exercise I give you is just as important as the beginning and middle.) You're developing your ability to gallop to a jump and not take back, letting your horse find the distance—and proving to yourself that you don't need to interfere as you feel him doing it for you. That way, you won't be tempted to tear your horse's head off in front of a fence—or suddenly leg him and run him through the fence. Like the great riders, you'll develop the smoothness of approach that comes from feeling your horse take the rhythm and pace tools you've given him and use them to set himself up successfully.

CHAPTER SEVENTEEN

REFINING YOUR SENSE
OF DISTANCE

EXERCISE 12:
ADVANCED COUNTING

While you're going to leave the final responsibility for finding a takeoff spot to your horse, to do your job of establishing rhythm and pace well you must be able to see what will give him the smoothest and most uncomplicated trip to the fence. Thus you do need to be aware of distance to the fence. This exercise will give you that awareness.

I've waited until now to introduce this exercise because one of its two crucial components is rhythm. You wouldn't have been able to ride it successfully until you learned to trust your horse's ability to take care of you, and until you developed a clock in your head to keep your rhythm steady and your pace accurate. If you've reached that point, so that you'll be able to resist the temptation to take back or gun him in front of a fence, this exercise will work for you.

Place a rail or a small jump in the middle of your work area, where you'll have plenty of room to jump it as the center point of a figure eight. You'll begin by riding a large figure eight, giving yourself long approaches to the rail. Each time you approach, you'll count strides aloud. The first time you ride to the rail or small jump, say "One" when your horse's hooves hit the ground just before the takeoff. Next time, start a stride sooner—"One, two" as his hooves touch the ground. And the third time start when you think you're three strides away. Then try four, then five, then six; you can go all the way up to eight or ten. Continue the figure eight and with each new number start counting further back.

Whether you're right or wrong about the number of strides is not the most important point. The major thrust of this exercise is to take your mind off the fear of being unable to see distances; the counting does that by giving you a job to do. Besides, your counting will further develop your sense of rhythm and improve your consistency—and out of those

Fig. 215

things plus the experience of comparing your judgment with the actual number of strides you get will come the ability to see how many strides away you actually are.

Fig. 215 I am just saying "One" as his hooves hit the ground just before takeoff.

In the meanwhile, though, if you're wrong, don't cheat by fussing with your horse's rhythm and stride. Instead, move your line very slightly by shortening or opening up your turn. Let's say, for example, that you think you see five strides. You start counting, but then you realize you're going to be tight—so quietly help him wait with your hands and let him drift out just slightly, without ruining the rhythm, to the point where you can see the five.

Be careful, though, not to overdo the drift. Not only would you be teaching him to bulge through his turns, but you'd be likely to end up with five and a half or six strides before the fence.

Don't worry about what lead you land on, either. If it's the wrong one do a simple change: come back to the trot for a step and then pick up the canter again on the correct lead.

The most common problem I find riders having with this exercise is forgetting to look in through their turns and focus on the jump early enough. But if you do look in and start thinking early, you'll automatically get a lovely rhythm, you'll start seeing the number of strides accurately, and your horse is likely to relax more because he feels you being more relaxed and confident on top of him. More often than not, this exercise turns even hot horses into calmer, softer movers that consistently find good distances. Ideally, you should be able to count up to eight or ten strides while staying relaxed and maintaining the rhythm of your stride.

EXERCISE 13:
COUNTING OFF
TURNS TO LINES

Now you're going to apply the counting technique to the simple "mini-courses" you set up at the end of Part II, "Basic Jumping"—and discover how your new skill helps you find distances. You'll establish the rhythm you need for each line going into the turn before it; then you'll look in through the turn at your fence and, when you're comfortable with your rhythm, start counting out loud. Start with "One," and it doesn't matter if you say "One, two, three, jump," or "One, two, three, four, five, six, jump"; the very *act* of counting gives you your rhythm—and because you focus on the fence and start counting early, coming through the turn, you'll suddenly find you're hitting good distances, just as you did in the figure-eight exercise.

Let's say the course you decide to set includes a first line at normal distances, a steady second line, and a forward third.

On your opening circle, establish a normal twelve-foot canter stride. Then look in on the turn and start counting aloud: "One, two, three, four, five, jump . . . one, two, three, four, jump." Land and sink into your saddle a little (without opening your angle), and take a little contact with the mouth—an invisible "Are you listening?" half-halt.

Then start to shorten the stride—smoothly, gradually—each stride becoming a little shorter until you have whatever pace you'll need down the next line. You have the whole turn to shorten. That way, you don't have any major adjustment to make coming out of the line. Start counting at "One" again when you look through the turn to the next line. Once you've got the correct stride and rhythm, start counting again as you look through the turn to the first fence of the second line.

For that forward third line, take another little half-halt, just to be sure you have your horse's attention, after you land from the second line. Then gradually start to increase, making each stride just a little longer than the last, so that again you come out of the turn with just the stride you need, or maybe even a little more. You're much better off having a little more pace than you need, so that you can slow down some, than not enough, which would cause you to run your horse off his feet and end up with a long, flat jump or a chip.

Always be looking in to the next jump—never look down!—by halfway around the turn. Because your mind has plenty to occupy it, and you know your horse is taking care of "finding a distance," all of a sudden you'll discover that your jumps turn out great!

EXERCISE 14:
CIRCLES FOR
SUPPLENESS AND "EYES"

This next exercise improves both your skills and your horse's. For you, the benefit is improvement of your coordination and your reflexes; for him, it's an increase in his suppleness. What you need before beginning it is a secure seat. If your leg swings instead of anchoring you, or if you can't use your hands independently because you're leaning on them for support, you won't be able to manage the exercise—so make sure the basics are there before you begin.

The exercise consists of riding a circular track over jumps, making the whole trip as smooth and even as you can. How big the circle should be, and how high the jumps, depend on your horse. If he's green, give him plenty of room: make the circle big enough to allow at least four or five strides between fences. If he's a more seasoned performer, three strides may be enough. (You're not trying to trip him up, but you do want him bending consistently.) The fences don't have to be spaced evenly—in fact, for the sake of experience, it's probably better if they aren't—and their height can be anything from rails on the ground to three feet or more, depending on what you and your horse are comfortable doing. Whether you set three fences or four depends on how much space you have to work in and how many strides you want between fences.

By now you know whether your horse has an easier time going to the left or to the right. To make things simpler the first time through, circle him to his easier direction. Establish a smooth canter and bring both hands to the inside to put your horse on the circular track. Your inside rein functions as a direct or even an opening rein, and (even more important) your outside rein against the neck brings the shoulder around, so that his body follows the curve of the circle.

Fig. 216

Fig. 216 Before I jump the first fence, I'm already looking at the second fence. I ride this fence from feel rather than eyes. And I am preparing with my leading rein to turn right in the air. The earlier I focus on the

Fig. 217

next fence, the better I'll do at keeping my horse consistently on the circular track. (Watch the top riders and you'll see that they're always looking ahead to the fence beyond by the time they're within a couple of strides of the nearer one.)

Even if you're still having trouble making yourself look ahead this early, do it as soon as you can—and certainly no later than when you're in the air. If you wait until you've landed to look ahead, you'll be too late to influence your horse's turn; worse yet, if you look straight ahead, that's where you'll go—off the track. You'll have to struggle to get him turned to the next fence.

If you see that your horse is going to land a little to the outside, turn him to the inside with your outside rein against his neck, your outside leg holding his haunches, and a little more inside direct rein leading him in. (Think of your aids for the shoulder-in and the leg-yield.) On the other hand, if you feel him cutting in, use more inside leg to ride him more to the outside rein and the outside of the circle.

Fig. 218

Fig. 217   Over fence 1 I'm looking at fence 2. My right opening rein is turning him right in the air.

Fig. 218   As I ride to fence 2, I'm totally focused on it; my horse simply follows my eyes.

Fig. 219   Even before I jump 2, my eyes are on fence 3.

Fig. 220   As I jump 3, I'm

Fig. 219

looking at fence 1 again and using my right opening, or leading, rein to continue our circle.

Fig. 220

As you're improving your use of your eyes and your direct and indirect rein, your horse is enlarging his experience of meeting fences at different distances—and he, too, is learning to look ahead to the next fence by the time he's in the air. He's also learning to use both ends of his body athletically, jumping and turning at the same time—with hitting the jump behind the negative reinforcer if he forgets.

This is hard work, so your horse may try to stop. If he does, first use the cluck, then be more aggressive with your legs and add a tap on the shoulder with your stick. If he goes the other way and gets faster, apply steady half-halts to bring him back in a nice, even rhythm, using your voice in a soothing "Whoa."

Ride the exercise in both directions, with more repetitions to your horse's stiffer side. He'll need more work in this direction to be able to follow your opening rein and overcome his tendency to drift out.

CHAPTER EIGHTEEN

ABOUT FENCES

Before we go on to some more exercises, which will further develop your sense of distance, let's take a few minutes to talk about different kinds of fences and their effects on your riding plan.

When you walk a hunter, equitation, or jumper course, you make a couple of assumptions: that your horse will take off six feet out from the base of each fence, and that he'll land six feet beyond the fence. Thus to walk a line you start by taking two strides (which you've drilled yourself to make as close to three feet each as you can) from the back rail of the first fence to the "landing" and pausing, then walking the distance to the next fence, counting off four of your three-foot strides for every one of your horse's twelve-foot canter strides (and leaving two three-foot strides in front of the second fence for takeoff).

In hunter and equitation classes, making your actual takeoff and landing distances consistent (or at least making them look that way) is vital for the smooth trip the judge wants to see. In a jumper class, where the fences are more imposing, meeting them deep—close to the base—gives you an advantage over meeting them long. However, meeting them forward is even more important: you want to make the deep distance by getting "into" the base of the fence with energy, not nipping at your horse's head and adding strides. (It's always better to be going forward, even when you make a mistake, because impulsion covers a multitude of sins. As long as a horse has impulsion, he's got a tool he can use to get himself out of trouble.)

You want to be able to ride your horse to any fence at any distance, of course, so you need to give him practice at home in meeting everything from normal to long to short, at all sorts of angles and off all sorts of turns. You won't find the same distance every time in the show ring, so you need to be ready to deal with (and trust him to deal with) whatever you find. Rhythm, pace, and trust remain critical—and a variety of experience helps build consistency in all three.

In a jump-off, you'll have to be able to ride your horse *at* the fences to save time—continuing at a fast gallop rather than adding to make certain each distance is perfect—and be confident that he'll respect the jumps. You want to feel that you can meet a fence at any distance, out of any pace, and have him jump it, not stop or knock it down. The way you ride him can make him both bold and careful; by adjusting your ride to accommodate the particular demands of each kind of fence, you'll increase his ability to meet it successfully.

Oxers

Coming close to the base is particularly important when you're jumping oxers. If you asked your horse to take off six feet away from a six-foot-wide oxer, you'd be asking him to jump twelve feet (the normal takeoff-plus-landing allowance), not including the arc over the fence, before he even started to come down; what you'd end up with would be a flat, hollow-backed jump and a short landing or a crash. If you bring him close to the front rail, you'll enable him to make a rounder jump and land at a distance more like that of his takeoff. As long-time great jumper rider Rodney Jenkins says, the front rail "should be your best friend"; by galloping right up close to it, so that you arrive with plenty of impulsion—not taking back and stuffing in a short stride—you'll be sure of having enough power to make it across the back rail. Get to an oxer riding backward, however, and you take a chance of landing right in the middle of it.

Verticals

The big difference between jumping verticals and jumping oxers is the kind of balance you need. In general you want to go over each of them in a symmetrical arc, but the shape of the fence dictates the shape of the arc: lower and broader for the oxer, higher and narrower for the vertical.

Triple Bars

A triple bar is a relatively easy jump, because the angle of the jump itself gives you the arc—unlike an oxer, where your horse has to jump up and around the first rail. You can really gallop him at the first rail, ride "right to the bottom" because the front rail is low, and have him jump up and across the back. Horses land farther out from a triple bar, sometimes with more impulsion.

No matter what kind of fence you encounter, and whether you're competing in hunters or jumpers, you'll do your job better if you meet every fence smoothly, neither snatching your horse in the mouth nor running his feet off. Looks aren't the only reason; if you interrupt the flow with roughness, especially in front of a fence, you take your horse's eyes and mind off his job, so he can't do what you should be trusting him to do. The secret to smoothness? Preparation. Think about how you're going to ride the line and meet the fences while you're still just making the turn.

How to Ride All Types
of Combinations

EXERCISE 15:
TWO OXERS, SIXTY-SIX FEET APART

At sixty-six feet (measured from the back rail of the first oxer to the front rail of the second), this line is either six feet long for a four-stride or six feet short for a five-stride. What will make it work, whichever striding you choose, is not so much the distance you get to the first jump but the pace you establish in the turn. If you have plenty of pace and a big stride in the turn, you'll jump into the line with more rpm's behind you, and you'll land going forward more. But if you come through with a very short, backward ten-foot or eleven-foot stride, instead of a forward twelve-foot or thirteen-foot stride, you'll land with fewer rpm's and have to add a stride to make the second oxer work.

Because a horse typically lands in a little farther over an oxer, you'll probably find it easier to aim for the long four strides than the short five, but this decision certainly depends on your horse's natural stride—long or short. Once you've landed, you can gallop aggressively at the second oxer. (If you were dealing with two verticals, you'd be landing closer to the first one; you'd still aim for the four, but you'd need to leg your horse more strongly to make him lengthen a little more.)

Now let's look at a few variations on this basic setup:

• If you're on a short-strided horse, you might ordinarily be more inclined toward the five. Let's say, though, that you're in a jump-off, so you want to do the four for the sake of time. Start thinking about getting the four *before* your first fence and establish an open stride. Then start riding the four *in the air over the first oxer,* so that you start legging him even before you land. (In today's show jumping, even the time allowed in the first round is much tighter than it was ten years ago, so time faults are more likely. Even in first rounds you've really got to be able to gallop and jump, adjusting your speed to meet every jump as efficiently as possible.)

• If for some reason you want to ride the sixty-six feet as a steady five instead of a forward four, get your galloping pace to the first oxer but use no leg in the air—or even say "Whoa"—so that your horse lands a little slow and immediately you can fit in an extra stride.

• If the second oxer is followed by a short turn, gallop to both oxers but use no leg in the air over the second, so that your horse lands a little "dead." You'll have an easier time making the turn.

MAKING FOUR STRIDES WORK . . .

Fig. 221 I'm in a very open, galloping stride. My upper body is slightly inclined forward, but my seat remains close to the saddle.

Fig. 221

Fig. 222 As he lands I follow him with my low arms, allowing him to stretch his neck while my leg says "Longer strides."

Fig. 223 Now I simply follow him to the fence.

Fig. 224 We meet the second fence still moving forward. Because of our pace the distance is fine. I just go with him.

Fig. 222

Fig. 223

. . . AND MAKING FIVE

Fig. 225 In the same line, adding a stride, my gallop is somewhat shorter, with more contact.

Fig. 226 We meet the second fence at a closer distance, on a shorter stride.

Fig. 224

Fig. 225

Fig. 226

EXERCISE 16:
OXER TO OXER TO VERTICAL —
A TIGHT ONE- OR TWO-STRIDE IN-AND-OUT

You can set this exercise a couple of different ways. Start with your two oxers sixty-six feet apart; then set a vertical either twenty-three feet beyond for a tight one-stride in-and-out or thirty-five feet beyond for a two-stride.

Think about this configuration for a minute. You're going to want enough pace to get over both oxers, but not so much that your horse ends up taking you through the vertical. What's the best way to get this result?

• In this case, doing the sixty-six feet as a forward four will be a difficult test for you and your horse. Because you'll land over the "in" with more pace than you want, making the distance to the "out" even tighter, your horse will have to shorten and be very responsive to get out cleanly over the vertical. (It will certainly be easier if you're on a big scopey horse with a long stride: gallop the first oxer, close your leg in the air, and on landing get into the four strides early, then say "Whoa" as he lands from the "in" to make the in-and-out work.)

• You also don't want to land from the first oxer, wait a stride, and then ride backward so that you can fit in the five—because, if you're late and off pace, you may not have enough power to make it over the second oxer.

• On most horses, then, the best choice is to "ride" (the word trainers use for really galloping at a fence) the first oxer, give a little "Whoa" and feel the mouth a bit in the air so that you land steady, steady for a stride or two, and then think "Continue" for the next two or three. If you shorten early in the line, you can ride the last couple of strides forward, and even add a little leg to get yourself over the back rail of the second oxer but not land too far in toward the vertical.

• Now, suppose you were riding the line the other way: vertical to oxer to oxer. You'd want to come to the vertical very slow and then "ride" the first oxer a little; the distance is already short, so you wouldn't want to jump in very big and make it even shorter. If you jump in a little slow, then you can close your legs and ride across the oxers. (In a jump-off, you'd keep your leg in the air over the first oxer, land going to the second oxer, and do the distance in four.)

Fig. 227 Riding the sixty-six-foot line in the forward four strides (something you want to be able to do to save time in a jump-off), I've galloped to the first oxer and met it perfectly.

Fig. 227

Fig. 228 Then we gallop quite forward to the second oxer.

Fig. 229 We meet this oxer a little long, but we have plenty of pace to make the fence work. I trust him as he studies the fence.

Fig. 230 As we come into the vertical, he slows himself down, helped a little by my hands and seat and voice . . .

Fig. 228

Fig. 229

Fig. 231 . . . and jumps out easily.

How you ride a line, then, has to do with what's in the line, what comes after it, what type of class you're in (in other words, what the judges are looking for), and what kind of horse you have. If you're on a nice little inexpensive horse with an eleven-foot stride, don't try to ride the line the same way as the fancy Medal contender with the huge stride and great adjustability. By the same token, if you're on that fancy horse, go ahead and show off by doing the brilliant ride—but only if you're sure you can bring it off. Whatever you're riding, ask yourself how your horse can look and do his best, and make your decisions accordingly. And don't be discour-

Fig. 230

Fig. 231

aged if you have to choose the steady, unspectacular way. If the rider on the brilliant horse blows the brilliant ride, your conservative, classical ride may just be the one that wins.

EXERCISE 17:
TRIPLE BAR TO TWO
VERTICALS

This exercise teaches you the principle of galloping to the *deep* distance. Set your triple bar; sixty-four feet beyond that, set one vertical, and put the second thirty-four feet beyond that. The sixty-four feet is four feet longer than a perfect four strides. The thirty-four feet is two feet shorter than a perfect two strides.

As I mentioned earlier, you can gallop right to the bottom of a triple bar—and you *want* to do that here, so that your horse has a round jump. If you stood back six or eight feet, he'd jump long and flat; then he'd have trouble making the sixty-four, the long four strides. When he lands, *let him continue* for the first couple of strides; relax and don't interfere. If you set the right pace before the triple, he should be able to maintain the rhythm down the line (although, if he's a limited mover, you may want to encourage him more by actively giving, even closing your legs to make sure he's coming forward and "getting into" the four strides. You want to be very deep to the vertical because a deep distance will encourage your horse to make a rounder jump and land short inside, which will help you with the tight distance inside; if you stand back at the first vertical, you'll jump flatter and land that much farther inside, making the tight distance even tighter.

Your plan of attack, then, should be this: on top of the triple bar, close your leg a little, so that your horse lands going; then close your leg for at least the first two strides after you land. That way, you can take a normal third stride and a short fourth one (what trainers call "patting the ground") that puts your horse together with his hocks under him, so that he can hop over the vertical and make the in-and-out work.

Fig. 232 I've gal-

Fig. 232

loped on quite a big stride to this triple bar with a wooden liverpool under it, and my horse jumps it well. Even now, in the air, I'm thinking of the forward four strides —knowing we must land and *continue*.

Fig. 233 We are continuing on quite an open stride into the first vertical, and my horse is beginning to balance himself for the jump ahead.

Fig. 233

Fig. 234

Fig. 235

Fig. 234   Because of my preparation, we meet this wall well. Again my horse is focused on the following fence.

Fig. 235   He's figuring out the exercise well, setting *himself* up in the tight, thirty-four-feet, two strides. The only help I'm giving is my seat and balance—my reins are quite light.

Something else this exercise teaches is the idea of "riding against the jump": rather than taking back, for the most part you're letting the jump back your horse off, so that he sets himself up for it in that ground-patting stride and meets the jump with plenty of impulsion. Still, you probably will have to help him steady a little with your hands: follow with your arms when you lengthen; then close your fingers a little on stride three and more on stride four to tell him to shorten and help him change his balance. *(When* to take back will be a matter of *feel*—some horses just about back themselves up, while others will run through the vertical if you don't strongly suggest otherwise. In general, though, the more careful your horse is, the less assistance he'll need from you.)

What you *don't* want to do—but what you'll see a lot of riders do—is jump the triple bar and take the mouth to get two normal strides, then suddenly push to make the vertical in four. That's backward, because it makes the horse's job harder—and they usually wind up either knocking down the first vertical because they've stood so far back from it and the horse has been looking ahead to the second, or they jump the first so big that they land way into the distance, get very deep to the second, and take it out.

The bottom line of all this work is that you, the rider, need to know the distances between the fences so you can make smart choices for your horse and level of competition. For me, a lot of the fun of competing is figuring out the course designer's questions and coming up with the right answers. In doing these and similar exercises you learn what is easy and what is difficult for your horse—long to short or short to long, or whatever. Then at the shows you can analyze the courses and find the best method of riding them.

EXERCISE 18:
SHORT TO LONG AND
LONG TO SHORT

In this vertical-oxer-oxer exercise, there are two lines: a bending fifty-four feet from the vertical to the first oxer, and a direct fifty-two feet from the first to the second oxer. The fifty-four-foot distance is six feet short of a normal four strides, and fifty-two feet is four feet longer than a normal three—and because the long three follows a very steady distance, it will ride even longer.

Once again, begin by analyzing. How can you ride this line in a way that both looks and is smooth—and so that your horse will jump his best? You know that the key to smoothness is not interfering with your horse; if you get your pace set up early enough, you won't need to make any adjustments—at least none that take your horse's

Fig. 236

eye off the fence in front of him and disrupt the flow of your ride. So, once again, the secret to riding this line is being organized correctly in the turn before the first fence. The better you know your horse's stride and responsiveness, the earlier you'll manage this successfully.

If you set up the steady pace you'd need to make the distance from the first fence to the second in four *straight* strides, you'd be going so slowly that you'd never be able to gear up in time for the long three, so jump the vertical a little to the right and just a little slow.

Fig. 236 I landed a little shallow and headed out to the right. This gave me the bending. My eyes are judging how much to stay out as I count the four and smoothly lengthen to the first oxer. My eye will bring us to a pretty normal distance. (You don't want to get to the first oxer short and dead, because you won't have the stride you need to get the long three.)

Fig. 237 I've found my straight line, and as I jump the first oxer I'm thinking about the forward three strides that follow it. In the air, I'll keep my leg on, so that I'm already riding the long three; he should land well out from the oxer and moving forward, so that he can make the three strides.

Fig. 237

When you're comfortable in this direction, ride the line the other way: the long three to the quiet four. You want to gallop to what is now the first oxer, so that you can start the line with two long strides and get as deep as you can into the second oxer, in order that the jump will slow your horse down a little in preparation for the tight distance that follows (like the line with the triple bar to the in-and-out). In the air over the second oxer, say "Whoa" quietly, keep your leg still, and take your hands a little to the left and keep them there on landing, creating a bending line that gives you the room for four slow strides to the vertical.

Mixing up the distances in lines this way—short to long, long to short, or long to long to short—helps you understand your horse's length of stride and what you have to do to make different distances work for him. It also keeps him sharp. He has to be adjustable to your aids and pay attention to his own situation. The different distances improve his coordination, and because they make him try to help judge the distances to help himself out they make him a better athlete, cleverer, and a horse that jumps in better form. If he jumps poorly through these lines, you're probably riding him too fast, too slow, or roughly, so that his confidence isn't what it could be. Go back to the simpler jumping exercises—maybe all the way back to "Basic Jumping"—and make sure both of you are confident, comfortable, and jumping in good form there. Then work up through these more advanced exercises again.

EXERCISE 19:
SERPENTINE WITH
THREE JUMPS

This exercise helps you to put "eyes" and your sense of distance together. Set up three fences in a single line down the center of your work area, with plenty of space between them, and ride a serpentine course that crosses each one just at the point where you'd change leads. In the air over each fence, look ahead to the next one so that you get the proper line. As you become more confident, look to the next fence even *before* you've jumped the one in front of you.

Fig. 238 On top of the first fence I'm looking at the second fence to my left. My eyes stay on it—I don't look down or anywhere else—until . . .

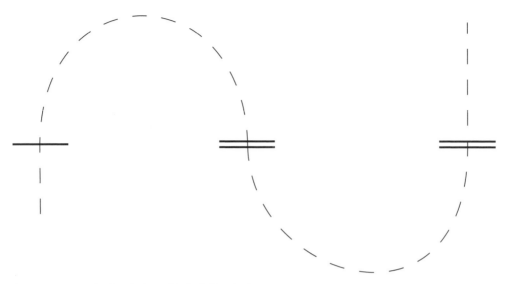

Three jumps on a serpentine (can be jumped in both directions)

Fig. 238

Fig. 239 . . . in front of the second fence, confident so I don't need to look at the jump, I look ahead to the third fence . . .

Fig. 240 . . . and will keep my eyes glued on it all the way around to meet it.

In this exercise you're constantly changing outside and inside rein and leg, so it's good for your horse's supple-

Fig. 239

Fig. 240

ness and responsiveness. If he's stiff turning one way, go back to riding him on a circle in that direction, meeting a single jump over and over, around and around, until he's bending correctly and following your eyes. Then go back to the serpentine.

EXERCISE 20:
THREE JUMPS, RIDDEN AS
A BENDING LINE AND A STRAIGHT LINE

This exercise, which is a variation of the serpentine, is one I frequently use in clinics held in small indoor rings where there isn't room for more than two or three strides between the elements. The three jumps—a vertical, a big crossrail, and a Swedish oxer (or use any combination you have available)—

are set in a straight line but at a bit of an angle to each other. Your job is to jump each one at the center, first on a bending line that lets you meet each one straight and then on a straight line that requires you to jump each at an angle.

As always, the secret to success is in the turn before the first fence, when you establish the pace and line you need. Your outside rein and leg are responsible for establishing the degree of bend you want, but you will need to coordinate reins and legs and eyes to pinpoint the center of each fence.

For the bending line, look over at the fences as you come through the turn to the first fence and establish the line you need for the first fence. Your seat must be secure so that it helps keep your

Fig. 241

horse straight and forward; if anything, stay a bit behind him. If you feel him drifting far-ther out than you want, correct him with a stronger outside rein and leg. If he cuts in, push him out again a little with your inside leg.

You may do the first two turns perfectly and then find your horse falling in on the third; in that case you've probably unconsciously pulled on one rein. Remember, right from that initial turn, that your hands work *together*, not against each other, moving in parallel so that you always have a direct rein and a neck rein.

Fig. 241 Over the first fence, I hold my horse straight but my eyes are left, on fence 2, to see how much to stay out and find a distance that brings us to the center.

Fig. 242 My horse is in the center of the crossrail on a perpendic-ular line. Again, my eyes are ahead, on fence 3, judging how much to stay out.

Fig. 243 I came out to meet this Swedish oxer right in the center. My eyes and hands work together to keep my horse on my line.

Fig. 242

Fig. 243

Fig. 244 Now in the turn I set my horse up for the straight track. Your reins should be like carriage shafts, keeping him straight so that he meets each jump in the center, on the angle that keeps him on your straight line. If your hands are a little left or right, he'll pop a shoulder and come to the jump on the wrong

Fig. 244

Fig. 245

Fig. 246

angle, or even run out if you keep changing his line, so sight your straight line through the three jumps and stick to it.

Fig. 245 We've jumped fence 2 right in the center. I'm right in the center of my horse, just holding my line.

Fig. 246 As we complete the exercise, you can see we're perfectly in line with the center of all three jumps.

To be a great rider, you have to be a feeler, a thinker, and a believer. To make my system work, you have to believe in the concepts I'm passing on to you—concepts that I've tested and proven to myself over and over again—and make your body perform in the way I describe, even if it doesn't seem to work at first. If you believe, you really try, and you keep trying, these techniques will work for you.

CHAPTER NINETEEN

CROSS-COUNTRY
NATURAL JUMPS

Jumping natural obstacles is good for horse and rider. It's a great way to break up monotony, and natural obstacles show up in a variety of surroundings, including the USET under-21 classes that work up to the finals at Team headquarters, in show jumping, and in eventing. But some of the obstacles, such as ditches and liverpools, can be intimidating to horses, so I like to introduce natural jumps in a slow, simple, confidence-building way.

I begin by making the obstacles I'm introducing as nonthreatening as I can, then ride more aggressively than normal. At this stage, it's better for my horse's confidence if I override him a little than if I underride him — I don't want him thinking tentatively. Once I'm sure that he's going forward and that he understands these new obstacles are just jumps, however, I ride each one as a normal jump. Toning down your ride is just as important as the initial aggressive ride; if I didn't, my horse would read my apparent defensiveness as a signal that he ought to be worried—and he'd never relax! (Occasionally you may encounter an older horse with a "liverpool problem" that just won't go away; it may be in his bloodlines, or it may stem from some early experience. With him, you may always have to attack liverpools, at least to some extent. But most horses will come to accept "scary" jumps eventually, provided that you go back to low versions of those jumps and ride in the same positive, confidence-building way every time you school over them.)

The following progression—ditches, grobs, liverpools, banks, water—is the one I use in training my horses.

Ditches

The scary thing about these obstacles is that the horse looks down into them—so in the beginning I camouflage the ditch with a flower box or small wall in front and a rail over the top so that the horse doesn't find out that he's jumping over a ditch until he's actually sailing over it.

Fig. 247 On the approach, ask for just a little more pace than normal—not a lot more, but enough to give him some extra heart. (After all, you wouldn't be asking for that much pace if you were worried, so you're telling him he doesn't need to worry either.)

Make sure your heels are down, and stay in a slightly deeper-than-normal seat, behind your horse so you can use your seat to drive him forward if he hesitates or spooks. Keeping the heel down is a key part of your position in *all* natural jumps. If your horse does something unexpected you don't want to lose your balance because your lower leg isn't secure. You want to keep him in front of your seat and legs, and sitting down lets you be ready to use your aids—leg and maybe even spur or stick—more strongly if necessary. I always begin with this override

Fig. 247

because it's important not to create a problem by being too weak the first time; that will scare your horse for certain. (Some very famous jumpers have habitually spooked at ditches, liverpools, and other natural obstacles. These horses were just chicken enough to

be careful—and their carefulness was what made them great jumpers!)

Fig. 248 Keep your horse's head up—lift your hands a little—and maintain your contact going to the jump. This is one place where you don't want to soften and drop your hands on the approach; if he drops his head and sees the ditch, he's likely to fall on his forehand and stop—or at least get fainthearted.

Fig. 249 This is an excellent time to use your stick behind your leg, in front of the fence, to give him heart.

Fig. 250 I like to jump ditches in both directions. This way is more open and spookier but, if practiced, not a big deal.

After you've jumped the ditch several times with your somewhat aggressive ride, try relaxing and softening your contact a little and

Fig. 248

Fig. 249

Fig. 250

see if he can manage to go over without your driving him. That's the goal you're working toward; you don't want him dependent on your forcefulness.

Grobs

A grob is similar to what eventers call a coffin jump, but the technique I'll give you works with any fence set in a dip. A grob is usually a combination fence with three elements: a jump-in over rails, one or two strides down to a ditch in the dip with a rail or rails over it, then up one or two strides and out over a third jump. It is very spooky for your horse the first time because it looks like a trap.

In this kind of jump, the two most important ingredients for success are your balance (neither ahead of your horse nor way behind) and your horse's responsiveness to your aids. When you close your leg, no matter what is in front of you—a ditch in the ground, a big combination, or open water—*he has to think "forward."* Even though he may want to look at the grob, especially the first few times he encounters one, his attention to you and your aids has to matter more. He has to respect, trust, and believe in you enough so that when you close your leg he *goes.* If he's not at that point yet, hold off introducing him to grobs until he is.

Eventually you'll ride a grob like any other jump, but during the introductory trips you'll again want to keep your weight back and your seat deep to communicate confidence. Maintaining contact with your hands will help your horse keep his balance; if you soften and he happens to be at an uncertain moment, you'll shove him onto his forehand.

As a rule I bring a first-timer to a grob with a bit more pace than necessary, to give him heart. You'll have to push your horse all the way through the grob. Coming down into it, he'll tend to back off, so you'll probably need to leg him—and maintain contact so that he has something to balance against. On the uphill, he'll need you pushing him to create impulsion that he can use to get out.

Fig. 251 I come into the grob with a deep seat and my hip angle open. I have a contact with my horse's mouth and his head up.

Fig. 251

Fig. 252

Fig. 253

Fig. 254

Fig. 252 As we jump the little fence, I stay behind him a little, in preparation for the ditch ahead.

Fig. 253 At the ditch, I maintain a full seat to drive him and my hands maintain a steady contact to give him support.

Fig. 254 At the take off I keep my legs on him for confidence. Then I'll follow for the two strides to the final vertical, which should ride "easy"—if anything a bit short after my strong ride at this ditch.

Liverpools

At these fences, like the ditches, keep your horse's head up so that he doesn't look down and become afraid. I school my green horses with rails or a brush box on the front side to help conceal the water.

Fig. 255   Give your horse a confident ride by keeping his head up with a steady contact and maintaining a deep seat and a strong back.

Fig. 256   This is what I call a backward liverpool (approached from the other side, it would be an open liverpool). Continue to ride forward in the air, across the water, because a green horse may peek down and lose heart.

Fig. 257   Keep riding across the entire jump—your horse will figure out the rails.

Fig. 258   Ride a bit stronger to an open liverpool than to a backward one, because horses tend to see the water and hang back. Again, keep the head up with contact and maintain a secure, driving seat and legs.

Fig. 255

Fig. 256

Fig. 257

Fig. 258

Fig. 259 Keep your legs on him as he takes off and stay slightly behind him (don't lean up the neck or look down) . . .

Fig. 260 . . . and ride him across the width. Many horses hang up and lose impulsion. This can scare them if you don't compensate with an aggressive ride all the way.

Fig. 259

Fig. 260

Banks

As with the liverpool, you want to stay deep in the saddle, behind your horse a little all the way through a bank jump to keep his engine running and to keep your seat secure. When a horse spooks, he drops down in front; you don't want to end up on his neck because you started out too forward. With your deep seat, your heel well down, and your hands maintaining a firm but not rigid contact, you'll tell him he's in your hands. That gives him confidence.

Fig. 261 In front of a bank is another time not to drop your hands; in fact, if anything, you want enough contact that he can jump up "out of your hand." By creating impulsion with your leg and giving him a firm place to get his balance with your hands you persuade him to jump up.

Fig. 262 Just try to stay with his center of balance so that you don't interfere.

Fig. 261

Fig. 262

Fig. 263 On top of the bank, stay a little behind him. He's trying to find his balance in a new situation, and he may peck or trip, so you're better off a little behind the motion to give him confidence.

Fig. 264 As he jumps down, follow him. Keep your eyes up for your balance, and your heels and legs down under

Fig. 263

Fig. 264

you so that you can't fall forward or back.

Fig. 265 You might need to let your reins slip through your fingers a little (something you see seasoned three-day-event riders do in this situation) to give his head more freedom. But don't overdo—you need to be ready for the following fences. Allow your entire arm to follow him, as I'm doing here, keeping your fingers firmly around the reins

Fig. 265

and your connection with his mouth all the way through the landing.

Open Water Jumps

Before heading to these, warm up over a few liverpools, first the easier, backward direction, then the open.

Start open water simply, with a small water jump about eight to ten feet across. Put a brush box or a little wall in front of it to help your horse get the idea that he's supposed to jump, and a rail or two over the water to encourage him to jump up and over, not down into it. Paint the landing edge of the water white as you'll find at a show. It is good to have a piece of PVC plastic pipe just above the white strips as you'll see in the photographs. You need always to ride across the tape. This is an important concept because your horse must learn to jump *over* the white strip.

It's generally a good idea to have more pace than you need when you introduce a horse to water jumps. (You never want him to learn to jump *into* the water, and your overriding diminishes the chances of that happening.)

Fig. 266 Ride the water jump as you would a triple bar. Gallop to the front rail or brush box. You want a close takeoff spot to be sure you get to the other side without stepping in the water; the farther back you stand off, the wider you make the water. "Riding the tape" is

most important. In the
Olympics, the water
jumps can be fifteen feet
across, so you really have
to get to the front of the
fence; even with the
much smaller jump
you're using, the closer
your takeoff, the better
chance you have of all
four feet coming down
on dry land. (Don't

Fig. 266

Fig. 267

Fig. 268

worry about hitting the takeoff box; it won't count against you the way hitting the water would.)

Fig. 267 I really attack the water. When I find the distance, I override with seat, legs, voice, even a stick if necessary. I'm especially strong when riding an inexperienced horse.

Fig. 268 In the air, I continue to "ride" my horse across the tape. Some riders ride strong to the water but never encourage the horse *across* it. Don't take it for granted.

Fig. 269 Look over the tape and ahead—not down at the tape—and keep thinking "Across."

Fig. 270 Follow him into his

Fig. 269

landing so that you don't hit him in the mouth or pull him up too quickly. He must think forward.

Practice the water just enough so that you and your horse are confident. Too much practice can teach him to be casual and jump into it. Once my horses have learned how to jump water, I rarely jump water at home—just at the shows.

Fig. 270

A Double of Liverpools

Fig. 271 Here's an example of a pair of liverpools: a short two strides between a square oxer and an open liverpool. I ride into this combination aggressively, because the two liverpools cause my horse to look and hesitate. On top of the oxer I'm looking at the second element and riding forward.

Fig. 272 I maintain

Fig. 271

Fig. 272

Fig. 273

contact with his mouth on landing to keep him straight and riding up into my hands.

Fig. 273 As he sees the open liverpool in front of him, I stay in him, especially with my seat, and use a cluck. I have to give him courage, what I call "heart," if he's losing his.

Fig. 274 Again, I ride him all the way across the liverpool, so he doesn't hang up and hit the back rail.

Fig. 274

A Double of Ditches

These two ditches are about the same size as the liverpools. Some horses may be braver at one than the other, some weaker. Ideally you ride both types the same way . . .

Fig. 275 . . . with a deep seat, secure legs, and keeping the head up a bit.

Fig. 275

Fig. 276

Fig. 276 Over the first element, I continue to ride forward as he sees the "out," holding him straight and sending him forward.

Fig. 277 In the landing, I'm already riding the second element . . .

Fig. 277

Fig. 278

Fig. 278 . . . so there is no hesitation when we get there.

As you can see, the progression of natural fences is very important in order for both you and your horse to consistently gain confidence and avoid unnecessary trouble. When you can jump a small, camouflaged ditch confidently, move on to a more open or bigger ditch. Follow the same principle with liverpools and then move on to the water jump.

If introduced and ridden properly, natural obstacles give a rider and horse courage and are not a big deal at all. However, because we don't jump them much in this country, they become a mental problem. So there is no substitute for experience. The more you and your horse practice over them, the less difficult they become. At Hunterdon, George Morris has all shapes and sizes of banks, ditches, liverpools, hedges, and water fences. My very young horses jump the small ones as part of their routine schools.

All over Europe there are natural obstacles in competitions. I love to ride there because I have encountered so many different kinds of fences and terrain—not just the rails, gates, planks, and walls that we see here so often. To be a great rider, you must know how to ride to a huge variety of fences, natural and otherwise.

HIGHER FENCES

The following two sequences will, I hope, help you to appreciate the importance of position over bigger fences.

Oxer-Oxer In-and-Out

Fig. 279 The distance is a forward one-stride so I'm galloping to it with my upper body slightly forward, seat close to the saddle, weight in my heels, and a straight line from my elbow to his mouth.

Fig. 279

Fig. 280

Fig. 280   As he jumps in, our balance is great.

Fig. 281   In the air, I allow him complete freedom and stay centered on top of him—I'm not interfering in any way.

Fig. 281

Fig. 282   I just follow him through the landing, as though my arms are a continuation of the reins, and . . .

Fig. 282

Fig. 283   . . . then send him forward to the second oxer.

Fig. 283

Fig. 284   Our balance is great in the takeoff—I am not ahead of or behind him, just staying out of his way to allow him to jump clean . . .

Fig. 284

Fig. 285   . . . and I stay *with* him into the air, centered and following the motion.

Fig. 285

Gate to
Oxer In-and-Out

Fig. 286   I'm coming to this forward two-stride in a secure *and* relaxed position: my seat "there" but light, upper body with the motion and arms elastic, a continuation of the reins.

Fig. 286

Fig. 287 At the takeoff we're in great mutual balance: my weight is down through my heels, my upper body neither way ahead nor way back, and my hands are light and following.

Fig. 287

Fig. 288 In the air, I keep a straight line from my elbow to his mouth to allow him complete freedom of his head and neck. My leg is under me and I'm looking directly ahead through his ears, not left or right.

Fig. 288

Fig. 289 In the landing I have independent hands (I don't fall on his neck for balance), so my arms can follow his head and neck. I'm centered on him, eyes up and ahead, weight down in my heels, keeping my leg secure and quiet.

Fig. 289

Fig. 290 As my seat sends him forward into the oxer, my back is relaxed and my contact extremely elastic so . . .

Fig. 290

Fig. 291 . . . in the takeoff he has freedom to express himself. I just stay in balance with him. I don't interfere with his job.

Fig. 291

Of course, there are many kinds of combinations you can build and school over. In training my horses, I continually mix up the questions: oxer-vertical-oxer, vertical-vertical-oxer, oxer-oxer-vertical, long to short, short to long, or any variety. Pay attention to the combinations you see at shows—the questions the course designer asks, and which rides best answer them. For the Olympic or World Equestrian Games, we know the course designer in advance. So we watch what he builds throughout the year leading up to the competition (generally designers try out different lines, fences, and combinations they are thinking of using in a Games course), and by so doing have a pretty good idea of what to prepare ourselves over.

I repeatedly school some horses over the very combinations that show up their weaknesses, until they figure the questions being asked and become confident. For example, in a wide-oxer-to-a-vertical combination with a tight distance, a horse may have trouble coming back and jumping up over the vertical after stretching over the oxer. Another horse might have trouble stretching to a wide oxer that immediately follows a very upright vertical. The answer is to know your horse and yourself, and to work on what is difficult until it no longer is.

And Finally, a Few Shots from Competition . . .

Fig. 292   This is a great shot of the galloping seat. In a jump-off, in a fast gallop, I'm leaning over to be in balance with my horse's center of gravity. My heel is down for *my* balance, my eyes are focused on the next jump, and my opening left hand is leading him lightly around.

Fig. 292

Fig. 293 Preparing for another left turn. This time, because I don't want to chance distracting my horse and pulling a rail, I've turned just my head to look at the next jump—not my upper body—and I'm leaving his mouth alone while he completes this fence.

Fig. 293

Fig. 294

Fig. 294 My galloping and turning position: eyes looking in, hip angle slightly forward with the motion, seat close to the saddle, heel down for balance and security, arms an elastic continuation of the reins.

Fig. 295 A jump-off turn: I'm really centered. My horse is slightly bent right to see the fence. My outside rein against the neck is supporting the turn.

Fig. 295

Fig. 296 In the next stride, I'm turning *and* moving forward to the jump. Again, outside rein, leg, and seat make the turn happen.

Fig. 296

Fig. 297 Now, on line to the jump, I continue to send him forward. I'm with the motion and have contact with his mouth; my hands, legs, and seat give him confidence to the fence.

Fig. 297

Fig. 298 In the descent, I really follow with my arms to allow my horse to use not only his head and neck but also his hind end. I always try to encourage my horses to express themselves by giving them freedom.

Fig. 298

Fig. 299   After our round, a well-deserved pat, and a relaxed and happy horse!

Fig. 299

V.
HORSEMANSHIP

CHAPTER TWENTY

Up to this point the principal focus of this book has been on your development as a secure, skilled, *feeling* rider on the flat and over fences. But as I pointed out in the opening pages, forming a successful "partnership" with your horse requires much more than just good flat and jumping work. It involves becoming aware of all the aspects of your horse's physical and mental well-being, and becoming so sensitive to changes that you can anticipate and correct problems almost before they begin— or at least before they can do serious harm. That level of awareness and understanding is what the great teachers and the great riders mean by "horsemanship."

Please don't think that "this horsemanship business" is nice stuff if you have the time for it but not really all that important if getting to the top is your aim. In fact, I can hardly think of anything *more* central. Years ago you might have been able to get away with having a horse a little bit sore, or a little too fat for the jumper ring, or in a bit that was a little too strong or mild; the courses weren't all that challenging and the fields weren't nearly as large. Today, though, the minute you let anything go, somebody else who has it all right will beat you. In the end, to be the very best you can be, whatever the level at which you compete, you need to concern yourself with the *whole* horse.

While teaching horsemanship in all its aspects is beyond the scope of this book, I do at least want to give you some basic awareness of this aspect of your riding regimen. Thus, these next few pages should serve as a sort of primer—a base from which you can go on to learn more from the horsemen around you.

KNOW YOUR HORSE

Besides knowing your horse as a performer, you need a clear, accurate "baseline" picture of the way he looks and behaves when he's happy and healthy: his normal eating and drinking and urinating habits; how his legs look and feel; the temperature, pulse, respiration, and weight that are normal for him. The clearer that picture is in your mind, the better able you'll be to spot a change—to notice when something is *not* normal.

When you first bought your horse, you probably had a vet examine him to identify any physical problems, you found out what "jewelry" (blemishes, lumps and bumps, scars, and so on) went with him, and you found out as much of his history as you could. As time goes on, however, you can miss changes to that first picture if they happen subtly and gradually, as most changes do, unless you make it part of your routine to "step back" from him once a day and try to see him clearly. Here's a quick rundown of basic things to do:

1. Run your hands down all four legs—any new bumps, unusually warm spots, or places where he seems more than normally touchy?

2. Check his expression; are his eyes as bright and alert as normal?

3. Look at and feel his groomed coat; is it smooth and gleaming? Or does it look dull and feel rough?

4. Is he cleaning up his feed in the usual time? Is he drinking well?

5. Check his pulse (behind the left elbow is usually a good place to feel it) and count his respirations by watching his flank move in and out.

6. If you want to be really sharp, check his temperature daily at the same time that you groom him (something George Morris's grooms at Hunterdon do for all their horses).

7. Once a week or so, use a weight tape (which you can get from your feed store) around his barrel where the girth lies to find out if he's gaining, losing, or staying steady.

Don't try to rely on memory to compare readings. Keep a notebook in which you record all your readings and note down a sentence or two on overall condition as well as anything new you observe about him, both at rest and in motion. Training your eyes and hands to observe detail will increase your awareness; and keeping records of your observations can help both you and your veterinarian in case your horse develops a problem.

Do I track my horses as closely as I'm suggesting you do yours? Yes and no. Like many other professional riders with a lot of horses in their barns, I don't have the time to track each one in this detail—but what I *do* have is a grooming staff whom I trust. *They* go over the horses just that closely, and they and I talk every day about what they're seeing and feeling and what I'm seeing and feeling.

If you're juggling the demands of horse care and a full-time job or school course load, you may be as short on opportunity to track your horse carefully as I am. If so, I urge you to look into boarding him at a reputable stable that offers full care. After all, your horse doesn't have any way to make up for what you don't have the time to do—or to do right—for him; if you can't provide adequately for him yourself, in fairness you need to make arrangements with someone who can.

Consider Condition

The regular work schedule I suggested at the start of Part II, "Basic Jumping," will go a long way toward keeping your horse fit. Still, be aware that some competitive situations take a lot more out of a horse than others. If you're planning to show on the big, galloping courses that some grand prix competitions feature, or if you're going to show in Europe, where the courses are generally more challenging, you need to fit in more galloping work than my schedule suggests.

This doesn't necessarily mean the kind of interval-training work that three-day-event riders do (unless you're aiming for three-day, of course—in which case, get advice from a top three-day rider in your area who consistently does well and whose horses are obviously conditioned well). Still, give yourself one day a week when you really gallop: I generally start with about ten minutes of relaxed trot, followed by a few minutes of walking, then I pick up a canter, get into two-point and gradually let my horse build into a good gallop for three minutes or so around our huge field. I walk for three more minutes and, depending on his fitness, repeat the "set" in the other direction.

Start with just one three-minute gallop. The next time out, try lengthening the gallop segment by a minute or so if you feel your horse handling three minutes easily. If that goes well, do two three-minute gallops the following week, one in each direction—always starting with the trot warmup, and interspersing the gallops with three minutes of active walking. Continue building your horse's fitness until you're doing three three-minute gallop sets with five-minute breathers in the walk between them. I find that a weekly "gallop day" like this does wonders for horse and rider: it gives you both a relaxing break from dressage, it's fun, it's good conditioning work, and it gets both of you comfortable with a fast pace for jump-offs.

I like to get older horses out at least twice a day for fitness. I usually turn them out early in the morning for thirty to forty minutes, then ride them on the flat. In the afternoon they go for a good brisk walk under saddle on the trails for forty-five to sixty minutes. When there isn't time for a second ride, at the very least they get out for a hand walk. The more they walk, the better. Before the 1988 Olympics, for example, I made sure of Starman's leg fitness by managing just this kind of twice-a-day outing: working on the flat for an hour in the morning, and then an energetic walk on the trails (no working) on a long rein for an hour in the afternoon. He seemed to enjoy it (and the silver medal we won suggests it did him some good).

While we're on the subject of conditioning, consider this: even the most superbly conditioned athlete in the world will have a harder time working in close, humid weather than in cool, dry air. If you ask him for a normal work load before he gets a chance to acclimatize, he could be in danger from hyperthermia. If you're going to be showing in Florida in the spring, for example, plan to arrive early enough so that he can get used to functioning in the heat and humidity. As a rule, my horses arrive at least two weeks before the first show, and some may wait another week or two before competing.

Be aware of whether he's sweating as much as he normally does in the heat (another place where your familiarity with him pays off!). In hot, humid weather, a horse can stop sweating. If he does, he can be in big trouble fast. Call your veterinarian immediately—and start cooling the horse out as much as you can by sponging him down with lukewarm water and walking him (if you can) until help arrives.

Besides conditioning before a major effort, your horse is likely to need some help in damage control afterward. Jumping stresses legs—and the bigger the jumps, the bigger the stress. Therefore, even after a light jumping school, my horses get their legs done up with witch hazel or some other mild astringent and wrapped in standing bandages. After a class where the ground was deep, or one where the jumps were big (a grand prix, for instance), poulticing the legs does an even better job of cooling and tightening. Your veterinarian can recommend whether your horse needs to be poulticed each competition day or whether he should have mineral ice or a whirlpool or just alcohol on his legs. Talk to someone with experience and knowledge.

The day after your horse has been in a big class, watch him jog out and see how sound he looks. Or give him a light trail ride and see if he feels as usual. Some horses always look a little stiff when they first come out the day after a class but improve with a few minutes of walking and jogging; others are fine right away. Once again, *it pays to know your horse—* and if he isn't recovering according to expectations, to have your veterinarian take a look. Even if the horse is fine, make the next couple of days' work load light; if he doesn't have to show again that week, just give him turnout (or hand-walking, if turnout isn't available) and quiet hacks for the rest of the week. Each horse is different. Some of mine are ridden six days a week, for fitness or physical reasons, some are ridden four days for the same reasons.

TEAM UP WITH VET AND FARRIER

You, your veterinarian, and your farrier (as well as your barn manager and/or professional, if you're working with either) form a critical team in keeping your horse in his best possible shape. Therefore you need to find a veterinarian and a farrier in whom you can feel confident.

Begin your search by asking for recommendations from horsemen in your area whom you respect. When you've identified a candidate (or two) who sounds promising, spend some time talking with him or her. You want to be sure the person you choose is someone you'll feel comfortable calling whenever something doesn't seem exactly right to you. The "chemistry" between you, your veterinarian, and your farrier has to be right for the team to really click.

Work with your veterinarian (and the barn manager, if you're boarding your horse) to set up a regular program for dental and medical checkups, worming, and so forth. In that same record book where you keep your own readings, note down when your horse is wormed, what shots he gets and when; when you're talking to your veterinarian, that notebook can be a great assist. If your horse is boarding, talk with the barn manager about the routine of regular visits you want to set up; if the veterinarian treats other horses at the same barn, your horse's visits and theirs can probably be coordinated.

In talking to the farrier, make sure to mention any foot problems you know about: any history of navicular, or a tendon or bone problem, including what's been done about it so far and which veterinarian is attending the horse. Tell the farrier how you plan to compete, on what kind of footing, and how often; he may have some ideas about shoeing to improve traction or pads for hard summer ground—using shoes that can take caulks, for instance, if you're showing a jumper, or if you're likely to be showing on slick grass. Don't press him to come up with something new just for the sake of something new, though—if it isn't broken . . . And, as with the veterinarian, investigate whether the farrier can see your horse on the same regular schedule as others in your barn.

ABSORB IDEAS — BUT SELECTIVELY

Horse care and training can be as subject to fads as anything else, so while I encourage you to watch other people and ask questions about what they do, I also encourage you to pick people you really respect as both performers and horsemen. When you ask a question, listen carefully to the answer; when you watch, focus on what you're seeing. Make sure you *learn* whenever you have the opportunity to do so.

Every horse and every situation is different in some ways, similar in others—so, while you need to keep an open mind, you also need to test every new suggestion against what you know (and what you know works). If some new bit comes along, or some new feed supplement, or some new wonder medication, don't feel you have to jump right onto the bandwagon. Stand back and watch a little; see what kind of acceptance the new item earns among those who are at the top of the sport.

While you're waiting for "the test of time" to deliver its verdict, stick with the solutions you can trust. I know, for instance, that, while somebody may seem to achieve terrific success with a new style of bit on some particular horse, I can achieve the same success on any horse—and have it "stick" longer—through steady, patient application of the simple, classical dressage that I've given you in Part I and Part III.

One of the things I really love about riding is that there's always more to learn—and that so many of the top trainers who truly combine a love of the sport with a concern for their horses are generous with their help if they know you're serious. Even when the advice somebody gives you isn't all that different from something you may have heard before, the words he or she chooses may be just the right ones to put the point across to *you*—so that you hear it more clearly and understand it better than you ever did before.

Keep Growing

"Reading" horses is a skill that comes with experience—as is everything else that goes to make up horsemanship. Sure, a lucky few people are born with a sixth sense about spotting problems and distinguishing genuine breakthroughs from fads, but those who aren't—and that's most of us, me included—can *learn* awareness by watching, listening, and asking questions. (I see things in my horses today that I never would have noticed ten years ago.)

For that reason, I urge you never to be embarrassed about asking questions. If it's a serious question, and you ask a true horseman, it will be treated with respect. If, for example, you *think* you're seeing something that isn't normal in your horse's way of going, but you're not quite sure, ask your veterinarian, your barn manager, or your professional to watch him as well. If you don't understand what you're told, keep asking; that's the way you learn. With all my questions, especially back in my days at Jimmy Williams's barn, I was something of a pest, but all that questioning—and listening to the answers, and finding out where they fit—made up a major part of my education in horsemanship.

VI.

SHOW PREPARATION

CHAPTER TWENTY-ONE

AT
HOME

*I*f you've been following my program through the first five sections of this book, by now you should be much more of a *feeling* rider (and a more secure and skillful one, too, of course) than you were before beginning. That goal may be enough for you; and if so, fine—it's certainly the one I most hope to enable you to reach, for both your sake and your horse's. But if, like me, you find the challenge of competition exciting, there's plenty more to learn. In the remaining pages of this book I'm going to help you apply the principles you've already absorbed to the intricacies of showing. In this chapter I'll spell out a methodical way of preparing for a hunter or jumper competition. In the next, I'll take you, step by step, around a hunter course, an equitation course, and a jumper course. Finally, I'll try to help you analyze your own riding goals, decide what overall goals are right for you, and help you break those big goals down into smaller ones that can keep you motivated and make your riding satisfying every day.

EQUIPMENT

Your show tack must be shining clean and in good repair, down to the smallest strap and keeper. Don't wait until you get to the show; take everything out for a thorough cleaning and check-over a couple of days before you leave. And don't stop with the leather: check your saddle pads, boots, wraps—anything your horse will be wearing in the ring.

To show, many riders switch to a slightly stronger bit than the one they use for normal schooling. For example, I generally school my horses in a plain snaffle, but I show several of them in a slow twisted snaffle; in the excitement of a jump-off they tend to get a little strong, and the slow twist gives me just a little extra measure of control. Using it, I don't have to take as strong a half-halt as I would in a plain snaffle, so I can get a horse's attention without disrupting his rhythm. Other horses may go better in a gag—that's what I used on Starman, for instance—while others go best in a snaffle. You'll need to do a little experimenting at a couple of shows to see what works best for your horse. (Don't make the show the place where you first try a new bit, though; make sure you've ridden him in it a few times before, so that he and you are comfortable with it, before you try it out in a show setting. Otherwise you won't get a true reading on its effect.)

Along with a slightly stronger bit, you may also need a slightly different spur—but here again, you've got to know your horse. Some horses (generally the hot, sensitive ones) go well at shows with a tiny spur. Others need a little more than usual if you're jumping them over bigger obstacles than they're used to at home. Your choice of stick may change, too: the sensitive horse may react better if you carry a very small stick in the show ring, while the horse that stopped at a liverpool in the last show may go forward better in the next one if he knows you're carrying a bigger bat than you were before.

Think about all these things before the show; the better you know your horse, the better the chance that you'll anticipate his needs correctly. You may still get surprised in the ring, of course, but you'll be better prepared for any eventuality if you think it all out beforehand in terms of what you know about him.

BEFORE YOU GO —
TO JUMP OR
NOT TO JUMP?

If you've been following the work schedule I suggested back in "Basic Jumping," your horse isn't going to need a great deal of additional work over fences before you go to a show. In fact, whether you'll be competing him in the hunter, the equitation, or the jumper division, it's entirely too easy to overdo your preparation. (Remember, he knows how to jump. While he does depend on you to establish pace and direction, what he needs you to do most is stay out of his way and let him do his job.) I'll give you a jumping school that you can do once at home, a day or two before you leave for the show. With a couple of minor adjustments, which I'll mention, it should do an adequate job of preparing your horse for any of the three divisions.

If your horse will be competing in the hunter divisions, all you really need to establish is that he's straight and confident and relaxed. Each horse requires his own specific preparation. Generally I prefer to do less with mine, so if he jumps ten or twelve fences correctly the day before I go, that's plenty; I quit while I'm ahead. But certainly there are some horses that need to jump lots of fences before a show — to take the edge off and make them concentrate.

With an equitation horse, whether you do the school one or two days before the show depends on your needs as well as his. If you're both fairly seasoned, and you just want to confirm such things as whether he's straight and his flying changes are smooth, two days ahead should be fine. But if you're a junior, or an amateur who's fairly new at this, or gets nervous, it's a good idea to give yourself a rehearsal the day before the show. That way, you'll feel more confident when you go into the ring — and your horse probably won't feel quite as fresh.

A jumper, of course, may benefit from being a little fresh. I usually don't jump any jumper much at home before a show (unless he's a young horse or coming off a long rest); most of what we do is flat work, keeping him supple and athletic so that he *can* jump when I ask him to. I normally give a jumper his pre-show school two days ahead; by the time he goes in the ring his freshness is restored but he remembers to respect the jumps. If I know there are natural jumps at the show I'll practice them. Or if he's weak on liverpools, I'll be sure to give him a little practice there, but I only do as much as he needs for confidence or sharpness. I mostly want to get his jumping muscles going and both of us tuned in to looking for the fences, turning, lengthening and shortening. But we don't jump big fences—I save those efforts for the ring.

A Routine Jumping School

The jumping school I'll give you consists of simple single fences and lines. They aren't challenging, but they should remind your horse of the job you'll be expecting him to do for you. In the show ring, he probably won't just meet "plain vanilla" fences, so make the obstacles you take him over now a little interesting: use some color, drag in a flower box or two, include a liverpool if you're on a jumper . . . The more varied the elements he meets now, the better off he'll be when you show him.

If you've been doing your flat work consistently and correctly, warming him up for this jumping school is really just a matter of making sure he's relaxed and loose and on the aids—it's suppling, not training, like the preliminary stretching a runner or swimmer does before getting down to work. It's also your opportunity to set the tone for the day, which should be "Today we're going out to jump; it's going to be fun!" No dressage, no drilling. If you were working through a difficult problem yesterday and didn't quite get it solved, let it alone for today. (If your horse is the hot, excitable type, though, be sure he gets turned out or give him ten minutes or so on the longe to get the bucks out and relax him before you start the school. If he's excited, you'll get excited—something I see all the time with riders who come to my clinics—and neither of you will pay enough attention to the school to benefit from it.)

Ten or twelve minutes is probably enough for your warmup (although you can certainly do a couple of minutes more if you're still feeling stiffness). Start with a couple of minutes at the walk. Then go on to the trot and do some lengthening, some shortening, a little lateral work—just enough to review basic skills, check responses, and loosen up any stiff spots; you're not asking for his best dressage—that can wait for your next flat session. (But if your horse tends to be stiff on the right, for example, do a little right shoulder-in.) Follow with a couple of minutes in the canter—just enough to get the edge off. Before you start jumping, you should feel him being round, light, "in your hand," "on the aids"—which won't take long now because of all the days you've put in on the flat.

(This school is for you as well as your horse, of course. From the warmup to the end, keep thinking "Eyes up, heels down," and work on keeping your position correct, supple, and relaxed. Don't let yourself get excited about the jumps—your horse knows how to do them, remember?—but focus on position, pace, and rhythm. If you're on a quick, hot horse, think "Slow, slow, slow"; your body language will carry the message to him. If your horse is the lazy, dead type, think a quicker, more active rhythm. Be sure *you* stay calm and relaxed.)

Begin the actual school by trotting a few very low obstacles—a pole on the ground, a brush box, a little cavalletti—focusing on keeping your horse *straight* and *forward*. Then make sure your turning aids are working: go over one or two of them again, this time turning to the left over the obstacle; then once more turning to the right. Be conscious of how you're using your eyes.

Now trot a couple of fences with a little more height (two feet to three feet three)—a crossrail, a low wall, or a low vertical—to make sure your horse is relaxed and smooth and maintaining an even rhythm. He should trot all the way to the bottom of the jump and stay very, very straight.

Canter those same low jumps now, concentrating on keeping a steady rhythm. Meet them straight first, then on a little angle; stay very relaxed—and maybe even relax your contact at the takeoff if your horse is confident enough. Stop once or twice on a line after the fence; then to encourage suppleness (if you're on either a hunter or a jumper) make a couple of turns following the landing, left and right—and try not to make a big issue out of it.

From single fences, go on to a few lines that pose questions, as the lines in my jumping exercises have done. Depending on the division in which you'll be competing (see the variations that follow for more specifics), ask the horse to lengthen, or shorten, or both (in a three-element line); use verticals and oxers, straight lines and bending lines; add strides, leave strides out; make an oxer-to-vertical into a vertical-to-oxer by circling around and riding the line in reverse. Make the fences just a little more challenging by raising the rails a couple of holes or widening the oxers a few inches—limited equipment doesn't have to mean lack of variety. You don't have to do much; you're just reminding the horse of what he knows how to do.

Basically you should remember from the earlier work you've done what your strong and weak areas are. Work on your weaknesses—if it's your eyes and turns, do more circles; if it's that generally you go too slow to your first fence, practice pace and soft hands. Know your horse and yourself so that you go to the warmup with a plan of what *you* need to do to produce your best effort in the ring.

Variations for Different Disciplines

For Hunter Classes: Set up lines similar to those you're likely to find at the show. Raise a few of the fences to the height he'll be meeting, be it three feet six or four feet, with distances between on a normal twelve-foot stride, especially if you're competing in junior or amateur hunter classes. On an older horse, or one being prepared for second-year or regular working classes, you may want to keep him sharp by lengthening a few distances a foot or two. Practice the lines over and over—not pulling up after each one, but just as you'd ride them at a show, continuing and maintaining a good rhythm.

For Equitation: Your horse will be meeting more challenges than the hunter will, so do more with adding and leaving out strides, riding different options to the same fence, approaching on turns, and landing and turning. Run down your list of skills—eyes, hands, seat, lengthening, shortening. jumping off turns.

For Jumper Classes: While I would make the jumps a bit bigger and tougher if I were preparing a horse for a big, important competition—a championship, a finals, the Olympics—for regular jumper classes at regular shows I keep the school simple and relaxed and the fences not too big. I might include a liverpool, a square oxer, a distance or two as much as six feet off normal, and some fairly gymnastic combinations, but I'd be careful not to overtrain or overface the horse.

No matter what the discipline or the level, the overall feel of your jumping school should be very relaxed. Certainly the more advanced you and your horse are, the more challenging your practice can be. But be smart. You want to remind your horse of how to do what he knows how to do correctly, not challenge him or yourself to do something new or different. Generally, any time you're going to a competition, a positive feeling is very important.

FINAL THOUGHTS BEFORE SHOW DAY

Between your final jumping school and the morning of the show, do what you can to keep your horse and yourself in the best possible shape: plenty of rest, the right amount of the right food—and, for you, methodical assembling of all the things you'll need at the show well before it's time to lead him up the ramp. If you're hauling to the show the night before your class, start packing early enough to get there, stable your horse, and still get to bed at a reasonable hour; if you're trailering over in the morning, still more reason to pack and get to bed early—if you're dragging the next day, you won't show your best. All this is being smart and anticipating what lies ahead, so you're not caught in a mess.

CHAPTER TWENTY-TWO

SHOW DAY:
EARLY PREPARATIONS

When you find out the time of your class, use that information and your knowledge of your horse to decide whether you should take him out for a bit of flat work early in the morning or perhaps just get on him an extra thirty minutes before your class. Some horses at a show are better just longeing and not riding in the morning before they show.

On the other hand, by the last day of a week-long show, even the keenest horse may not need to be flatted; just a quiet hand walk will be plenty. He might even need more grain to restore a little energy. As always, the key is to know your horse and do what will work for him. And the way to figure that out is to experiment to find what works best for him.

Whenever you do your early flat work, tailor it to your horse's needs. Give him fifteen to thirty minutes of simple walk, trot, and canter, a few transitions, a little lateral work, and a quick once-over of correctives for any problems (some leg-yielding to the left if he tends to drift right over his fences, for example). If he tends to be a bit chicken, do some lengthening work to remind him to stay in front of your legs; if he's a bit of a bully, spend more time on downward transitions.

Ride him up near the ring, if you can (especially on the first day of the show), so that he can look at and get comfortable with the surroundings. Some shows let the hunters into the ring early in the day to school on the flat. If yours does, take advantage of it. Even if they only let you lead your horse in to look at the jumps, the early acquaintance with the setup is worth it. It certainly won't hurt and most likely will help.

Use your look at the ring to begin sizing up the class in terms of your horse's needs. Is the footing damp or slick, so that you should put caulks in his shoes? How big? Is there anything distracting near the rail that may make keeping his attention on you harder and a stronger bit even more of a requirement? Are the fences bright and spooky? Is there a liverpool? Do you need more or less spur?

Learning the Course

Find the course diagram, which will be posted near the in-gate. Study it, and compare what you see on the diagram with what you've found out by looking at and/or being in the ring. Ring size, footing, grade, the direction and placement of the lines, the shape of the jumps—all these things affect how the course rides. When I take you around three courses in the next chapter, you'll see how these variables come into play. For now, though, let me just make you aware of them:

* Ring size:

The same line rides more forward (feels longer) in a small arena—indoors, for example—than in a big, open one, because the horses tend to back off the ends of the ring. Remember that and also take into account a naturally long or short stride if your horse has either.

* Footing:

Sloppy or deep footing effectively shortens your horse's stride: because he has to work harder to bring his foot clear of the ground, he won't move it as far forward before setting it down again. On a hard surface, with no give to stabilize his foot, he's also apt to be short—and quick as well.

* Grade:

An uphill line (even one with a very mild slope) rides more forward than one on level ground. On a downhill line, your horse tends to cover more ground, getting down the lines easier. You might tend to lean more forward and get into trouble.

* Direction:

Just as your horse is probably slower at home when you ride him away from the barn than when he's heading home, he'll need more pace up the first line, away from the in-gate, than he will coming back toward the gate, and the line will feel longer than it measures.

* Position:

Another reason that first line feels so long is that it *is* the first one: horses naturally pick up more pace and confidence as they advance around a course and get more into their stride. That normally means you won't have to work as hard to get down the last line—but not always. A good course designer may take this tendency into account and make the last line longer, so that you still have to ride to make it work. (Check for that on the footage of the diagram and by watching.)

* Familiarity:

This has much the same effect as position. Ride the same course later in the day, or even later in the week, and you'll find it riding much more easily.

* Fences:

The same line will ride more forward vertical-to-oxer than it does as oxer-to-vertical—because the horse lands farther into the distance over the oxer than he does over the vertical. And any odd-looking fence that makes a horse look will ride more forward than one with a familiar shape.

The course diagram usually has the footage of each line marked. In planning your ride, interpret that information in light of the variables just mentioned. And check the diagram for a "dotted line," which may or may not be marked by a line of small bushes on the course; if you cross that line in making your opening circle, you'll be eliminated.

Along with studying the course diagram, check for a starting order. If one is published (as is the case in many of the bigger shows), take it into consideration in figuring out when you'll need to be ready. If the class is on the "put in your number when you're ready" system, figure out where in the order you'd like to go.

In most cases, especially if you haven't already ridden in earlier classes in the ring, you're better off sitting down and watching several trips to see how what actually happens to riders compares with your expectations. Look for horses with stride lengths similar to your horse's (the more you show, the better you'll come to know the competition, since you'll probably be riding against the same horses and riders at a number of different shows), and see how the lines ride for them. Look, too, for corners where horses tend to spook, and plan to ride more positively there.

If you're watching either an equitation or a hunter class, look for places on course where you can show off your strong points—be a little more brilliant. Maybe there's a place to cut a turn smoothly, or somewhere that you can really gallop. Try to figure out all the options the designer has given you at each fence—the showy route, the conservative route—and figure out which one will best suit your horse and you.

In hunter classes, your aim is a smooth, relaxed trip. If you have options—riding a distance as a straight five or a bending six, for example—take the course, your horse, and your own skill into account as you ask yourself which option will give you a smoother ride.

An equitation trip should be smooth, too, but also show your strong points. The course may give you the option of leaving out a stride, but that's the wrong option to take if you're on a little, short-moving horse. Instead, you have to go in and show your brilliance with a ride like clockwork—and maybe, somewhere else on course, take an option to do a short, neat turn and show off *that* way. (I don't mean, by the way, that you shouldn't take a chance on something you feel you have a good shot at achieving. If you're on a horse with a reasonably big stride, you've practiced leaving out strides enough at home that you feel pretty sure he can manage it, but you've just never done it in a class before, this may be the moment to try raising your standards. I can't tell you "Do it" or "Don't do it"; that's up to you. But if you know for sure you can do it the easy way but you don't see an impossibility in doing it the challenging way, I sort of hope you'll raise your sights and go with the challenging way.)

In a jumper class, is the liverpool (which is potentially spooky) on a line away from the in-gate, so that you'll have to ride it more forward, or is it on a line coming back, so you won't have to work as hard on basic pace? What's the time allowance? What's the best track for making that allowance? If there's an option that half the riders are doing in four and half in five, and you know your horse has a knockdown every time you leave out a stride, you need to be smart enough to do it in five and find some other way to make up the time. But if leaving out the stride seems to be the winning way and you've been going well otherwise, maybe you need to figure out a way you can do the line in four without a knockdown—maybe ride him forward very positively, and add a cluck and your stick to send him still more forward at the crucial moment. If you're working with a professional and you're not sure about the course he or she suggests, don't just accept it—*ask* about it. You never do as well just "following orders" as following a course you understand and believe in.

With your observations and your knowledge of the course in mind, plan your trip from start to finish; know what you're going to do every moment you're on course, and mentally see yourself doing it, as if you were watching a videotape. Plan your entrance as well as your trip: in hunters or equitation, if you have a good mover that you want to show off, trotting in can look really nice; but if you know your horse gets high easily (or you know *you* are likely to take off too fast), walking in may be the wiser course.

On a jumper, you may be better off cantering into the ring—because the canter will let you show him a little more of the ring in less time. You'll make sure not only that he can get a look at any potentially spooky fences, but also that he's awake and in front of your leg.

Make sure your plan takes into account any consistent problems you've had in the past. Maybe you have a tendency to go too slowly down the first line; okay, make it part of your plan to start with more pace in your circle. If you tend to race at the first jump, plan to establish a quiet pace and *maintain* it to the first jump and down the line. Put all this in positive terms: instead of saying "I'm not going to do X or Y" (what you shouldn't do), tell yourself, "I'm *going* to do Z" (the thing you need to do). You know what your weakness is; focus on the positive response to that weakness—and go over it and over it and over it before you head through the in-gate.

MENTAL PREPARATION

I've talked a little before about the effect your thinking can have on your riding. Nowhere else, I would say, is that effect as strong as when you're showing—so the way you "warm up" mentally is at least as important to your success as the way you warm up your horse.

The first step is to recognize *how* you think about showing. Do you ride better under pressure? When you're at the big show and in the big class, does something inside you just blossom, so that you ride way beyond your expectations and surprise yourself with how well you place, yet you're never all that good at the local shows? Or do you go the other way: do you take ribbons consistently at the smaller shows, or in the beginning of the week at the big shows, but fall apart—or at least worry like crazy that you're going to—when you go in the big ring, in front of the big stands?

I work on thinking of the class ahead, no matter how big and important, as just another class, and on relaxing—being one with my horse. Another rider might have to figure a way to get "up" more for the smaller classes, maybe by reminding herself that, without paying enough attention in them, she might not qualify for the big ones. The point is, of course, that you need to analyze yourself, figure out what's going to work for you, and then do it.

To show you what I mean, let me describe my routine to you. I used to do it all the way through my warmup; now it's just a habit and happens automatically. George Morris really got me started on it. After watching me trying too hard and becoming stiff through my arms as I went through my warmup, he would say to me, "Let go, let go, and stay loose." Mentally, I made a very conscious effort to give with my arms and hands every time he (and then I) said, "Let go." For years, before a big event, I'd spend those last few minutes before my trip telling myself, "Relax; let go; relax; let go"—and it really did help me stay loose and able to focus. Today, this sensation is simply reflex; unconsciously my body stays loose. But if I feel any tension I tell myself, "Let go"—back to basics.

Besides taking control of your general feeling about showing, you need to be sure no outside concerns intrude while you should be concentrating on your round. You've formulated a riding plan. Now, as you run through it in mental rehearsal and when you follow it on course, concentrate on going through it step by step—no looking back to a mistake at the first fence or forward to what might happen six fences ahead. Consciously put aside any worries from the rest of your life, too—no matter how serious—for the few minutes you're in the show ring, and the twenty you spend warming up. You won't do either your ride or your other concerns any good by going around with your attention in two places at once.

I've worked with a lot of young people just breaking into the jumper ranks, or just getting into grand prix, and I can't tell you how frequently I've seen students beat themselves. Maybe you do it too: one tough round and you tell yourself you can't ride at this level, or you're not mounted well enough; or you let yourself get discouraged by comparing yourself with some other rider you started with back in juniors who's cleaning up in the division now. None of that has any relevance to *your* riding *your* best—and that's the thing every rider needs to focus on every time out. If you keep working patiently, persistently, intelligently, you will make progress—but none of us ever has it all made. You don't look for excuses for failure, but you don't blame yourself for the things you can't control, either.

And you *do* make yourself do the best you can with what you have. If you do that consistently, you can achieve honest satisfaction and make real progress, knowing that the great riders are the ones who have stuck with it and done the best with what *they* have, too.

WARMING UP
FOR YOUR CLASS

I normally start warming a horse up over fences about five horses before we're scheduled to go, because it doesn't take me long to get a horse to where I want him, but you may want to start eight or ten horses out. As with everything else, experiment and see what works best for you; you don't want your horse wound up too much, or worn out, but you also don't want him still getting the stiffness out over his first couple of fences on course. Do your six, ten, or twelve fences, whatever it takes to get the two of you feeling relaxed and confident—and finish up with enough time to have a helper give your horse and you a final polish before your round.

Before you head for the first jump in the warmup area, make sure you're in the right frame of mind—you don't want to waste any of your horse's physical energy going over fences before you're thinking positively. You've watched other people ride the course, you know the questions it asks—and because you also know the good and weak points of both your horse and you, you know the questions to ask yourself. Should you be practicing a bigger or wider oxer, to open your horse up more? Should you be jumping a big vertical and hoping for a little rub, so that you make him more careful, because it's a very careful course? Should you jump a liverpool, because the one on course is causing a lot of problems? Do you need to be very soft on this course, because the jumps are easy to bring down, or do you need to be very aggressive? If you're an overrider, as I tend to be, remind yourself to be moderate in your warmup; if you know you're sometimes not aggressive enough, tell yourself you've got to be stronger.

To warm up for a hunter class, start by trotting over a crossrail or low vertical. Keep your horse straight but relaxed; if he starts rushing, stop him and then go over the fence a few more times, until he settles down and trots it nicely. Then let him canter on, and take him over a three-foot or a three-by-three square oxer (an easier jump than a vertical, because it encourages him to round), doing it on both leads and in both directions, again working on keeping him straight. If he tends to jump to one side, turn him a little toward the other direction in the air so that you land straight. Concentrate on getting him into a good rhythm, maintaining the pace you're going to want in the ring, and taking him straight to the center of the fence. Once or twice you might stop him following the jump (with his head up if he tends to lug), so that you keep his attention after the jump.

From the square oxer, go on to a step oxer, the front rail a hole or two lower than the rear; the ramping will make a hunter jump confidently and round, encouraging the soft arc that you want in the ring. On an older horse that tends to be a little lazy, I like to finish with a step oxer that's slightly higher than the course—say, three feet nine if the course is three feet six—which might give him a "reminder" rub if he's lazy. (I wouldn't do that on a green horse, though; asking him to jump something higher than the fences on course might make him feel overfaced. Confidence is an extremely important thing, and I never want a young horse to feel he can't do something I ask him.) Jump a vertical too (with a ground line rolled out to get him using his front end), again keeping him straight, relaxed, and soft.

Do all the fences off both leads, concentrating on maintaining rhythm, using your eyes, and landing on a straight line. Then head for the friend you've asked to act as "groom for a day" (or your groom, if you're lucky enough to have one), who will give your boots and your horse's coat a last rub-over, paint the hooves, and check that all the straps are in their keepers while you mentally review your plan for the course you're about to ride. Review where you'll make your circle, how many strides you'll do down each line, what aids you'll have ready for the in-and-out, or the turn that's so close to the judging stand. . . . Play your plan out in your head like a videotape starring you and your horse, and keep your focus on it right to your final circle after the last fence and your exit through the out-gate. Your job now is to concentrate on riding your plan, not worrying about who's going to finish first or what anybody watching may think of you. The most you can do—and all that anyone can reasonably ask of you—is the best you can do on that particular day. That's all you need to be thinking about.

PERFORMANCE HINTS

As I promised earlier, in the next chapter I'll take you through three courses in detail. Now, though, while we're still talking about the way your mind influences your success, I want to pass on a few thoughts about what happens and what to do on course in any division.

No matter how well you've trained your horse and how well he goes at home, it's inevitable that he'll lose at least a little of his performance pitch at a show. Distractions—jumps he hasn't seen before, the P.A. system, concessions tents with flapping canvas—are everywhere, making it hard for him to keep his mind on his job. (And, to be fair, *you* may be having a hard time too, thanks to show-ring nerves.) Be aware that you're going to need to be extra sharp to compensate; but also be aware that everybody else in the ring will be losing pitch too.

In riding, there's a fine line between awareness and overreaction—between having a solution ready in case a problem arises and anticipating the problem so much that you may actually trigger it. Let's say, for example, that your horse has a past history of stopping at in-and-outs. You've worked on the problem at home, reinforcing your leg squeeze with a cluck and maybe a touch of your stick on the way to in-and-outs, and he's gotten much better, but you know that the improvement may not be grooved in deeply enough to withstand the show atmosphere. Don't ride him down to the in-and-out like gangbusters, whip flailing and spurs jabbing; instead, ride as if you expect him to go just fine (which he probably will), but be alert for subtle signs that he might be shutting off—and ready with your cluck, *tap* of the whip, and a little spur if you need them. You won't always call the situation right, but the more you show and the better you get to know your horse under showing conditions, the more dependably you'll be able to do *just enough.*

Being able to focus is extremely important for any athlete. If you catch your mind straying on course—you start worrying about whether you should do a straight five or a bending six to the vertical that's still four fences ahead, for example, or you start calculating your chances of winning the class—bring it back to the things you know make you ride successfully at home: position, pace, rhythm, line. Say, "Eyes up, heels down," over and over, count strides—do whatever you can to reach back to the simple techniques you've used in schooling to keep your mind in the present and on the job.

Wrap-up

You finish the course, make your final circle, and exit. What now? Wait for the results, sure—but right now, while your ride is as fresh in your mind as it will ever be, go back over it stride by stride: "I was too slow (or too fast) down the first line . . . my eyes were late . . . the turn to the oxer went just the way I wanted . . . too bad we hit that one fence; next time I'd better jump him bigger in the schooling ring. . . ." Compare what you actually did with the way you planned to ride; if there were differences, why did they happen and what was the result? If you work with a professional and he or she watched your round, compare what you saw and felt with what the professional saw. Just as you learn from what happens in the schooling ring at home, you need to learn from what happens in the show ring.

The most important question to ask yourself is this: Did you ride the best that you could on this day, on this horse? If you can honestly answer yes, the judge's decision is secondary. If you were on a short mover in a class full of beautiful, long-strided hunters, you shouldn't be surprised or resentful at not placing well. As long as you know you did the best you could with the horse you have—you didn't put him in impossible situations—you can be satisfied with your performance.

How about if you didn't ride as well as you think you could have? Maybe you had to go first, and you worried so much about not seeing anybody do the course before you that you ended up making a couple of dumb mistakes because you weren't concentrating. Be realistic; acknowledge where you went wrong and resolve not to let your attention stray that way again. Learn from what you did wrong, but don't rake yourself over the coals for it. As long as you do learn, the experience ends up in the plus column for you.

Once in a while, unfortunately, the way the judge places the class may just not sit right with you, try as you may; it happens to everybody who competes. If you went last in the class and you think the judge placed you fifth instead of first because he already had his card filled up, that's hard to live with, I agree—but it's the way the breaks fell today. That's show biz! One day you'll probably win when *you* don't deserve it as much as somebody else; for today, though, remind yourself that you *did* win on *your* terms because you rode the best you could.

VII.
COURSES

CHAPTER TWENTY-THREE

*I*n this section I'll be taking you around a hunter course, an equitation course, and a jumper course, showing you how to plan your ride and follow through on your plan. I'll also be giving you a few tips about the questions course designers ask through their courses, and the things judges are looking for in each of the divisions. By the time you finish, I hope you'll be able to approach any course with increased confidence in your ability to identify the questions and choose the answers that will be most suitable to your horse's performance.

HUNTER COURSES

The three key ingredients of a winning hunter trip are smoothness, straightness, and style: everything flows, and nothing requires any sudden surprise adjustments. By this stage, you have all the tools for a winning hunter round. As a thinking, feeling, responsive rider, you can manage just such a flawless-looking ride as long as you prepare intelligently. That means practicing a lot of different lines, so that you become confident in your ability to recognize and adjust invisibly to create a smoother trip. It also means carefully analyzing the course you'll be riding and developing a well-thought-out plan with provisions for all contingencies.

*Analyzing
the Course*

As early as you can, check the course diagram—and make sure you're looking at the right one; if two hunter classes are running back to back, there may be one course for the first class and another for the second. Check the footage on the chart, too. Normally, the distances in first-year-green and amateur-owner hunter classes are set on a twelve- or thirteen-foot stride; in second-year-green and the regular working and conformation hunters, the striding may be a little longer. In the pony divisions, too, the striding will be shorter for the small-pony classes than for the medium- and large-pony classes.

If you're going to be competing in the amateur-owner division and you're watching the regular working hunters, find out if the distances are going to be changed for your class; if that information isn't posted, don't hesitate to ask the in-gate steward or the course designer. If the distance *will* be changing, make that mental adjustment as you watch, looking for whether horses are having to hustle down the lines now or are getting the distances easily. Look particularly for horses you know to have striding similar to your horse's; the more you show, the more familiar you'll become with your fellow competitors.

Check whether the diagram for your class shows a dotted line: a line beyond which you may not go in making your opening circle. If there is one, it has to be marked on the diagram—but it *doesn't* have to be marked on the course itself. Many courses do have a line or bushes or some other marker to indicate the dotted line, but a lot of them don't. It would be a shame to be eliminated for crossing a line you weren't aware of. And don't assume that because one class doesn't have a dotted line none of them will; some shows allow you to go around the entire ring the first day but restrict your opening circle after that. Check the diagram or ask an official; don't depend on what other riders say.

As you watch, look for places where horses spook—a corner close to a billowing tent flap, a trash can—and anticipate what you can do to avoid the problem. Maybe you can shave a turn so that you don't get too close to it. If the dotted line permits, maybe you can ride by the "goblin" and show it to your horse before you start your trip. If it doesn't, maybe you can take him around the outside of the ring before your class starts and let him watch the flap flutter until he satisfies himself that it isn't coming to get him. Or maybe you'll just have to keep your antennae out and be ready to send him forward with a cluck and a tap at the first hint of hesitation.

Is your horse an experienced campaigner or on the lethargic or sloppy side? If either is the case, you may not want to take him to the hunter ring in the morning. A horse that goes to a lot of shows and jumps a lot of fences can get a little "plain"—a little lackluster and underimpressed about the whole business of jumping. To give him as little excuse as possible, I'd suggest that you not show him the course ahead of time at all; that way, he may pay more attention when he actually competes. If *you* need to walk around and see the jumps, go right ahead; just don't take him along.

Check the footing. If it's hard or deep, or it's mud or slick grass, you may want to put in studs. (My hunters are all shod for studs behind; that's just a personal preference of mine, but I think it makes a difference.) Think about what you know about your horse's way of going on whatever footing you're seeing. Does he go well on grass or not so well? Do you have to ride him a little stronger in deep footing?

Look for the details as you go around the course. If a jump rail has been set on the cups so that it bows up, it's easier for your horse to hit. Ask the paddock master or somebody on the ring crew to turn the rail and put the bow down; you'll do yourself and everybody else a favor.

The first several times you show, you'll have to *tell* yourself to look at all these details and think about all these questions—and it'll feel as if you always find out too late that you missed something. The more you show, though, the more this kind of thinking will become a reflex, and the more naturally you'll incorporate the adjustments it dictates into your riding plan.

Hunter Turnout

Appearance is a reflection of the rider, no matter what division you compete in. In hunter classes, your horse should be turned out beautifully, with coat shining, mane braided neatly and evenly, tail braided (unless he switches his tail when it's braided), hooves painted, and ears, nose, and muzzle trimmed. (The top stables turn their horses out this way every day!)

Look critically at your tack and compare it with what you're seeing on other horses in the show ring. Does it fit neatly? Does it gleam? Does the inch-and-a-quarter-wide leather of your bridle look old-fashioned and dowdy beside the finely stitched bridles on other horses (particularly the ones that win a lot)?

Your outfit counts too. Does your coat fit well? Are your boots high enough, close-fitting, and polished like mirrors? Is your hat dust-free? Do your breeches conform to current fashion in cut and color?

Looking the part is important: when you look good, you feel good about yourself; when you feel good about yourself, you generally perform better. Even if your trip isn't so great, you'll earn some approval from the judge and your fellow competitors for taking the effort to present a serious picture. And if you ride well enough to be in top contention with another rider, a bad mark for dusty boots or falling-out braids could be the tiebreaker.

A Little Last-Minute Coaching

If we were at a show together, in the minutes before you went through the in-gate I'd give you a last couple of strategic reminders, tailored to your riding needs. Since I can't do that for you individually here, I'm going to present a whole range of such tips; pick a couple that you know speak to your needs and tuck them into your thinking for the round you're going to ride.

As I mentioned right at the beginning of this section, smoothness is key, so you want to keep your aids invisible. The half-halt after you land, for example, is a way to test your brakes unobtrusively; as long as your horse isn't gaining on you or dropping behind your leg, make it the barest of aids and then just keep going, the way the great riders always seem to. If you have to make a change—a line rides a little more forward than you expected, or you're worried that your horse is going to spook at the in-and-out—pick up the pace and change your balance after the last jump of the line and into the beginning of the turn to the next, so that it's all done by the time you're approaching the next jump—no jerking on the mouth or sudden spurring to ruin the picture. A late pace or steering adjustment interrupts everything, so focus on getting all your homework done before you come out of the turn. The judge normally marks his card while you're in the corners, so this is the point where you may be able to pick up the pace over four or five strides or give a couple of additional *subtle* half-halts without attracting a lot of attention.

If you happen to catch a jump a little short because of an unexpected spook or some other reason, you know that you have to compensate right away by making up that little bit of distance again. Or if you suddenly find yourself with an unexpectedly big distance, you know you have to start slowing down just as promptly. You *can* do it, of course—we've done all the adding and the leaving out and the bending lines you need to have the technique down pat—so you just have to recognize the need (which all your counting will enable you to do) and adjust for it.

When you find a perfect distance, don't do anything. If your horse gains on you or takes a very big jump, react: "Whoa" him quietly but repeatedly; close your leg in the air and pick the pace back up as you land—whatever you need to do. Like the difference between a made horse and a green one, the difference between a great rider and a novice is experience. The more you work with your horse and learn to *feel*, the more the subtle adjustments you need—and their timing—will become automatic. You won't have to push or slow down in the next line because you'll have the pace and rhythm thoroughly organized by the time you begin it.

Step by Step Around the Course

Fig. 300   This course is designed around the typical twelve-foot hunter stride. The first line is a four-stride, the second is a three to an in-and-out, the third is a six, and the course ends with a single fence.

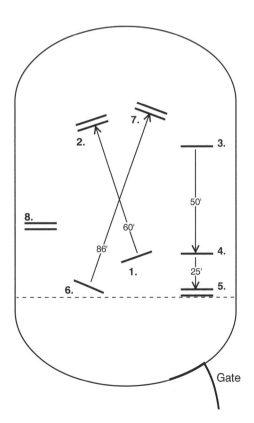

Fig. 300 Hunter course

As I mentioned earlier, I like to see a nice relaxed trot into the ring—but not if the horse is a bad mover at the trot. If he has a lot of knee action, just walk in; if he's likely to jig, take two walk steps in and quietly pick up your canter. Once again, knowing your horse is key; what you want is an entrance that will tell the judge, "Here we are, and we're well worth judging."

The dotted line gives you plenty of room, so use the whole end of the ring for your opening circle. This will give you a chance to get your pace organized, avoiding the mistake so many people make of starting to build only after turning for the first jump. It also ensures that the judge will have time to finish making his notes from the last go before you meet the first fence. If you make a tiny circle, you might be on your way to the second by the time the judge looks up.

What you want is a nice hunter pace. As you make your big circle, focus on being loose or on being strong (whatever you've decided *you* need to be to ride well), and think of just a few simple things. Stay relaxed, stay straight, keep your pace, and stay out to the rail. Don't cut corners—and on this course, which starts across the diagonal, don't rush your turn. You're going to want to come deep enough into the turn that you get a straight line from fence 1 to fence 2, staying out on the turn until you *see* the line through both fences. (With this kind of line, in many cases either the horse cuts in from habit or the rider hangs anxiously on the inside rein and *makes* the horse cut in; whatever the cause, the result is a line that isn't straight from 1 to 2. I've chosen this kind of opening line because of all the times I've seen it catch riders out.)

You've established your rhythm and pace on your circle, so now your job is to *look* for a line over both jumps. By at least the time you're halfway through the end of the ring, be looking up, with your eyes glued to fence 1. Then, as you begin coming through the turn, start looking over 1 at the center of 2, so that you come off your turn on a straight line to the center of both 1 and 2.

Don't start turning early; if you do, you'll have to jump 1 on a bit of an angle. Equally important, though, *don't overshoot;* the hazard there is that your horse might focus on fence 6. Do your homework in the corner, way back, so that he knows exactly where he's going and you don't end up steering him a little this way and a little that way.

Remember, if your pace, rhythm, and line are correct, you don't have to worry about the distance; just maintain your canter and head for the middle of both fences. If you're on a horse that looks every time he goes in the ring—and especially if you weren't able to school him in the ring and show him the fences—you may need a little cluck and more leg, particularly in his first class of the show. On an older, made horse, there should be nothing to it.

The sixty-foot distance from 1 to 2 is a perfect four-stride line, but because it is your very first line, it could get long. For that reason, and because it's going away from the in-gate, your horse may need a little more leg to keep going; in some cases, horses stare down the first line and decide they don't want to go all that way to the other end of the ring.

How the distance rides will also depend on your horse's reaction to the size of the ring. If it's big and roomy, he may be much easier to get down the line than he would be in a cramped indoor ring, or one with bleachers towering along the rail on all sides. It may be, too, that you have to ride him a little down the first line but can ease off on the second or third as his confidence improves. Different horses have differing degrees of reaction to their surroundings, of course; if yours surprises you now, store the information away for use next time.

As you land from fence 2, sink into the saddle so that your seat touches it—no perching!—and take a half-halt. This should be invisible; just enough to ask your horse, "Are you paying attention?" Canter right to the end of the ring—don't lean in or grab the inside rein—and as you come to the fence line, look toward fence 3 and gently think a turn by bringing both hands to the inside. Your horse will automatically turn that way.

(The only time you'd want to turn earlier would be if you'd seen that something at the end of the ring was spooking the horses you watched earlier. In that case you'd be smart not to canter all the way to the end of the ring—and if I were judging, I'd think the more of you for figuring it out!)

If you met both fences in the first line where you wanted to, maintain that pace through your turn and on to the third fence. If you got to 2 long, your pace was a little under; pick it up as you canter away from fence 2, heading for the fence line and through the turn. If you got there deep, it was a little over; you can "Whoa" your horse a bit—but keep a good rhythm as you continue through the turn, looking around and in to sight fence 3. The line from 3 to 4 is a little longer three strides (fifty feet) into an in-and-out; although your horse may pick up the pace because it's a line toward the in-gate, it's equally likely (especially his first time in the ring) that the in-and-out will back him off.

Go deep into the corner again and find a very straight line through 3 and 4. Carry your pace to 3 and make a very straight jump; don't angle over it. Land from 3 and keep your horse galloping to 4. It's a forward distance, and the more pace you have, the less chance that the in-and-out will back him off. (An older, experienced horse will just march right down there.) The in-and-out itself, set at twenty-five feet, could ride a little long—but it faces the in-gate, and your horse will be seeing all his friends down there behind it, so you may have to say "Whoa" quietly. Whether you need a cluck or a "Whoa"—or both!—on this line is going to depend on your horse; the better your relationship with him, the better the chance you'll figure out which one.

When you land from 5, take another "Are you listening?" half-halt. Depending on the pull of the in-gate, you may need another "Whoa" to let your horse know that he doesn't get to leave now—or you may need to cluck to keep him from hanging back by the in-gate where his buddies are and slowing around the turn. Make sure you maintain that same rhythm as you go through the turn—*smoothly*; in the hunter ring, a cluck or a "Whoa" is usually better than a kick or a pull. The little pace clock in your head should be ticking away, telling you how you were through the last line and what adjustments, if any, you need for the next one: to close your leg if he's slowing, and to "Whoa" around the turn if he gained on you through the in-and-out and is starting to pull your arms out.

The distance from 6 to 7 is eighty-six feet, two feet longer than a perfect six twelve-foot-stride distance. Make sure you come deep enough in the turn to 6 that you find a straight line to both jumps, and use the whole turn, staying out to the edge of the ring to make the turn correctly. This is another line going away from the in-gate, so you'll probably need to keep your horse coming again. You'll have seen from the previous horses just how the line really rides, however: do the two extra feet make it long or not?

Even though the diagram gives the measurements, it's quite likely that one line will ride a little longer or a little shorter than another owing to spooky jumps or an uphill or downhill grade. Generally, the farther along in the course you are, the more open the horse's stride becomes, so you may not need to "go" as much between 6 and 7 as between 1 and 2. Beware, however, as I mentioned when I was first talking about course chemistry, that some course designers take that open stride into account and make the striding longer on the later lines, so that you have to keep going just as actively as before.

Take another half-halt after fence 7. Ideally you'll keep the same even pace and rhythm to 8, the single jump at the end of the course—think of what you did in the counting exercises and the "jump without looking" exercise. Of course, if your horse is gaining as he heads for the in-gate, you will need to say "Whoa," so listen to the clock in your head and ask yourself whether he's speeding up, slowing down, running away, staying steady. . . . Be aware, though, that it's a very common fault in this sort of situation for people to think the horse is going to run away—so they slow down too much and then have to add, add, add to that final single oxer, or slow it down and then run again. Either way, of course, it's unmistakably a pace change—a major fault.

After the last jump, say "Whoa," sink into your saddle, and try to keep your horse calm as you finish out your trip. He may get a little fresh after the last fence when he hears a spattering of applause from your friends, or the voice of the announcer on the loudspeaker. Guide him onto a circle and pull up gradually, as invisibly as you can.

Your exit is another good place to show off a lovely trot if your horse has one, or a relaxed walk—it's your call. If he's being a little silly and you have to take his mouth, do it as invisibly as possible; don't stage a battle of wills. Try to sneak out. Judges remember from one day to the next which riders try to tear their horses' heads off and which ones spur aggressively, so keep whatever you do low-key. And remember there's a good chance that, even if your horse speeds up toward the gate as you start to make your circle, he'll quickly figure out that he's finished and let you pull him up quietly.

CHAPTER TWENTY-FOUR

EQUITATION
COURSES

A tremendous number of riders—and, worse, coaches—have somehow picked up the idea that the main way to win in equitation classes is to be "beautiful." Sure, a beautiful turnout, a beautiful horse, and a beautiful position make a favorable first impression on the judge. But if that was all that equitation involved, we could judge it from snapshots. I've seen riders who were turned out like advertisements for the finest saddler and bootmaker and tailor, but who told me by the way they picked up the canter that they wouldn't make it around the course. They weren't thinking, weren't using their eyes, weren't using those few moments around the end of the ring to prepare their pace.

The reason that all the books on riding—the German books, the British books, Bertalan de Némethy's book, George Morris's books, and so on—say "eyes up," "heels down," "hands in front of the withers" isn't because this position is beautiful, but because it's *effective*. It has become the classical position because it's the one that works best. As in any great design, form follows function. Having your heel down, for example, helps you anchor your lower leg so that it doesn't pivot back and pitch your upper body forward onto your horse's neck; keeping your reins short and your hands just in front of you lets you adjust the reins quickly when the situation requires. As the old saying puts it, "Pretty is as pretty does."

In designing the course for the 1989 Maclay Finals (which I also judged), the biggest thing I hoped competitors and their trainers would learn from it was that riders need to be *effective* as well as beautiful. For that reason, I made just about every line an option. I wanted to see *horsemanship*—to see people thinking and reacting, riding the course and showing with regard not just for their own ability but also for how they were mounted. I've chosen this course to go through with you step by step, and I'll explain to you the kind of thinking you'd need for a successful trip.

As you'll see on our "course walk," I don't agree at all with the equitation trainers who teach their students that "When in doubt, leave it out" is the winner's rule of thumb—that leaving out a stride whenever you have the option is the surefire way to a brilliant ride. I firmly believe that you should do what you *can* do; if you're on a 15.2 horse that can't do the long distances, you'll make a much better impression by adding the stride and showing the judge you know your horse and his capabilities. I grew up learning to ride a lot of tough sale horses. That taught me adaptability and effectiveness, and I feel that my developing those qualities gave me the best possible foundation for equitation work. I don't think it's fair to riders for their teachers to stress "beauty, beauty, beauty" at the expense of teaching them to feel, think, and react accordingly. So I want to see courses reward rides that are not just beautiful but also well thought out.

*Equipping
Yourself for Equitation*

On the whole, the points I made earlier about hunter turnout hold true for equitation too. Your equipment and clothes must fit well, shine with cleanliness, and be in good repair. If you're on the short side, a coat right off the rack may be too long and make you look shorter still; the extra money you spend going to a tailor for professional alterations (or maybe for a custom-made coat) will pay off. And don't carry any more weight than you should for your height, whatever that may be; slim legs wrap around your horse much more effectively than round ones do.

If you're in the market for a new horse, think about how any candidate you're considering suits you physically and temperamentally. For example, if you're short-legged, a great big warmblood will make you look even shorter; choose a narrower horse whose barrel is more in proportion with your legs. If you're a weak or hesitant rider, a bolder horse may be able to supply the extra "gutsiness" you need to get you through a difficult option. If you're an aggressive rider, a quieter horse that doesn't respond to your fireworks with some of his own may help your performance come closer to a happy medium.

There are lots of different types among quality equitation horses—big warmblood, small but scopey thoroughbred, and everything in between. What they have in common—and what makes them different from most hunters—is *range:* they're able to lengthen, to shorten, to do flying changes, to turn easily, and to stay rather unflappable. Because they are so capable, of course, they tend to be expensive. If you can't afford a horse with that capability, recognize that you won't really be "in the hunt" at the bigger shows; kidding yourself that you have a chance at a ribbon will only invite frustration.

Still, with a healthy attitude the experience of competing can have great value—if you recognize that there is a ceiling on what you can attain and you focus on helping your horse produce the best ride he's capable of giving. Or, if this is your first year in equitation and you're on a school horse, remind yourself that you're there for the experience—to observe and learn all you can. That's valuable too.

As for equipment, use whatever makes your horse go his best—a snaffle or a pelham, a standing martingale, boots, if he needs them. Certain judges may prefer certain details, but you shouldn't spend a lot of time worrying about that. Your job is to show yourself off and ride your horse as well as you possibly can. Concern yourself with that, do the very best you know how, and you'll be a winner on your terms.

Walking the Course

I'll walk you around this course as I would have walked a student around it. In that context, my first advice to you is this: keep an open mind. As you look at each fence, try to think of it as part of the whole line—think of what went before, what's coming after. You won't fully comprehend the line until you finish walking it, of course, but keep your "antennae" out and functioning, constantly receptive to new information from all directions.

Get yourself to the ring early enough so that you can study the course diagram and get a sense of its flow and its overall characteristics before the gate opens for course-walking; that way, you'll be able to go back and rewalk a line if you need to. Don't let yourself get intimidated by what you see on a piece of paper, though. If you think, "I can't jump eleven

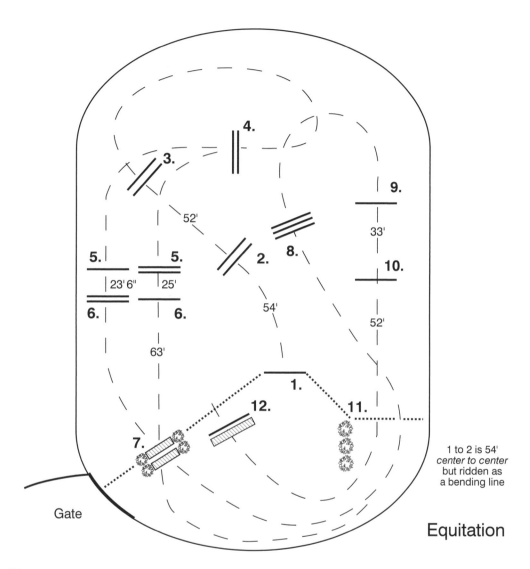

Fig. 301

jumps," you'll probably be right—but only because your negative thinking keeps you from making an honest try. Recognize challenge, but try to meet it positively; this course, for example, is a very technical one, but you have all the tools to ride it (or any equitation course) successfully.

Plan ahead so that you'll have enough time to walk the course. If the only way you can fit in a course walk for a big, important class is to skip an earlier class that's less crucial to whatever goal you're working for, decide what your priorities are and act accordingly. You do yourself no favors going into a class for which you haven't properly prepared.

Let's say you've read the diagram and had a chance to think it over. The gate swings open, and you're on your course walk. You know that the dotted line will keep you from doing much to show your horse the fences, so you're going to have to be alert for things that will be problems to *him* as well as problems to *you*.

Fig. 301   On the first line, fence 1 is pretty straightforward. Fence 2, a Swedish oxer, is set at an angle to 1, with a straight line from 2 to 3. To begin, walk the distance from 1 to 2 as a straight line from center to center. Starting with your back to the center of fence 1, take two three-foot strides straight ahead for your landing; then continue, counting four of your strides for one of your horse's (count "One-two-three-four, two-two-three-four, three-two-three-four . . .") and allowing two of your strides for the takeoff to 2.

You'll find that the distance is six feet short of a normal four, and from the work you did in "Basic Jumping" you know you can open up the distance by riding a bending line from 1 to 2. To plan your route, begin walking on a track perpendicular to fence 1, keeping your eyes focused on fences 2 and 3 until you see them in a straight line; that's where you'll make your bend. Keep counting to fence 2 (allowing two of your strides for the takeoff distance); you'll find that the distance is now just a bit snug for four normal strides.

The line from 2 to 3 walks long—at fifty-two feet, it's four feet longer than a normal three. (At the Maclay, it rode even longer: as this was the competition's first time at the Meadowlands, many of the horses had never been in the ring before; and the ring was small and certainly overwhelming for some—they were staring up into the end a little more than usual.) Three strides isn't much room to make up distance, especially in an indoor arena, where horses naturally hang back a little more than they do outdoors.

Okay—the distance from 1 to 2 walks a little snug, even as a bending line, and the distance from 2 to 3 walks a little long. How do you ride it? For most horses, the best option is a very steady bending four to a forward three. Jump fence 1 slowly, land a little slow, make the bend, and wait to begin building pace for the forward three until the last stride. Ideally you'd like to get to 2 in a nice distance, not a short dead distance, and get right to the center of the Swedish; you don't want to risk hitting it. Keep some leg on in the air over fence 2—you want to keep building impulsion with seat and leg as you land, telling your horse "Come on, lengthen—this is a forward distance"—and really make sure you get into 3.

The option I just described should work for most horses. But if you're on a little mover—a limited horse with a short stride—asking for a very forward three is not such a great idea. Your better choice would be to jump 1 to 2 on a line with not quite so much bend to it in four steady strides, without building impulsion, and then add a stride in the distance from 2 to 3, doing it in four as well.

If you ride this option smoothly, not only will you not be penalized but you'll probably beat a lot of people who blow the forward 3 and knock the fence down, or chip in and get a short fourth stride that they weren't planning for. And if you plan for the forward three but find your horse sticking off the ground at fence 2—it happens—have the good sense to change your plan and immediately add the stride to 3.

Adding the stride is a perfectly legitimate option, and for a lot of horses it'll be the best one. This is one of those areas where I hoped I'd see the Maclay riders choosing their options on the basis of what would work best for them, instead of thinking, "My teacher told me I had to do so many strides, so I'm locked into the plan whether it'll work or not." Unfortunately, none of them planned this option. They all tried for the forward three, and half of them were so nervous about it that they went from 1 to 2 on too direct a line and overrode the distance, putting themselves short and deep to 2 instead of standing back a little and attacking it to get a good start on the forward three. Even some very fine riders did this, landed short, and then couldn't make the forward three work and ended up chipping in. If even one person had chosen to do the four deliberately, more riders might well have followed, but nobody was willing to do that kind of independent thinking and riding.

Fence 4 is a high crossrail, so you'll need to get right to the center of it. After that, you can either go around 3 to the outside and take the outside 5 and 6 (a short vertical-to-oxer) or cut inside 3 to either the inside 5 and 6 (a longer oxer-to-vertical) or the outside (an option I didn't anticipate, but which at least one rider chose successfully). Both the 5-6 combinations are skinny fences, made of seven-foot rails that fall easily.

Which route you choose should depend on your horse. If he's a very confident, bold type that turns well, the inside route can let you show off those qualities. If you're at all unsure of him or yourself—he's green, or he seemed a little shaky going up the first line, or you're a little nervous—play it safe and give yourself a bit more time by going around 3 to the outside 5 and 6.

And be ready to change plans if need be: if you jumped 4, the big X, straight, intending to take the inside route, but found your horse spooking or hesitating at this fence, gently guide him to the less challenging outside route. As a judge and a teacher, I want to see you responding to what your horse is telling you—to what you're *feeling* from him. That's why this course has options.

Whichever option you choose for 5 and 6, to make fence 4 work you need to go deep into the corner after 3, balancing your horse and collecting him on a slightly shorter stride. You've got a short turn coming up, just two or three strides after you come out of the corner; by collecting him, you'll be sure you have him "between your hands and legs," so that you can be very accurate in telling him where you want him to go.

(In the Maclay, some horses whose riders weren't accurate enough came across the top of the ring, saw fence 9, and thought that was what they'd be jumping next. When they suddenly found they were being headed toward 4, some of them spooked at the big cross-rail, failed to get right to the center, and knocked it down.)

Keep your horse a little collected through the turn to 4 as you look over your shoulder to find exactly the line you want, either a slightly right-to-left line over the center of the X for the inside route or deeper into the turn, past the center line, and slightly left-to-right for the outside route. You have the tools—you've done lots of exercises in which you looked in through turns and coordinated your leg and hand aids to make your horse go straight.

Over the top of 4, look where you're going next—either around 3 to outside 5-6 or inside 3 and toward the inside (or outside) option. In setting these fences, a smooth, clean ride that used the number of strides that worked for the individual horse was my priority. I didn't design them with specific distances from 4 to 5 in mind; what I wanted to do here was to test each rider's ability to analyze an option situation and figure out what would work for her horse.

To pass that test, you have to *find* the distance for whichever option you choose, so you'll need to walk each line on a bending track. To walk the inside option, for example, start with your back to 4 and walk forward, staying out as much as possible—don't run into fence 3!—and keep looking at 5 until you see a straight approach to the center. After you've walked the distance, think about what you've found out about it in terms of the horse you have: if the distance is long and your horse is short-strided, you're going to have to shave the bend a little; if the distance is short and he's a really big mover, you'll want to stay out as much as fence 3 allows. (In the Maclay finals, some people overrode the inside-3-to-inside-5 distance and ended up knocking 5 down.)

Not only were the approaches to the 5-6 options different, but so were the in-and-outs themselves: the outside option was a vertical to an oxer with a twenty-three-feet-six-inches short distance inside; the inside option was an oxer to a vertical with a twenty-five-feet-long distance. So in figuring out which option would work best for your horse, you also needed to consider how he'd handle the in-and-out distance itself. And one final point to factor in before making your decision: the fence that *followed* these in-and-outs, number 7.

Fence 7, which is half of a wall, just seven feet wide, with a bush on either side, is a rider fence. It's tricky because it's right by the in-gate, tempting your horse to duck out. The temptation is even greater if you're coming from the inside 6—you catch the wall at even more of an angle. The distance from inside 6 to 7, measured center to center, was sixty-three feet, a long, risky four (risky because of the angle and likelihood of getting a run-out).

The wise choice was to ride 6 to 7 as a bending line, smoothly opening up the distance into an organized five that placed the horse safely at the center of the wall. You *had* to pinpoint the center. You couldn't just sit pretty here. I designed this fence to make you *feel* and *ride.*

In a tricky situation like this, a short stride always gives you the best control, so start shortening as soon as you land from 6. If you're coming from the inside 6, you want to land, sit down in your saddle, collect, and bend your track out a little until you pinpoint the middle of 7, leaving your horse no option of running out. (You may have noticed on the diagram that you can ride by this fence in your opening circle; do that and you decrease the chances that you'll get a spook when he meets it on course.)

In the Maclay, one rider tried to be extra brilliant by not only taking the inside track but also leaving out a stride. That was a particularly bad decision; leaving out the stride practically *told* the horse to duck out! If you're a terrific pilot, and you have the perfect equitation horse—who's done the finals for the last five or ten years *and* is willing to jump through hoops of fire for you—you can do the brilliant option and leave out the stride. But if you have *any* question—if your horse tends to be sour to the in-gate, is a little green, or isn't the biggest mover, or if you know you're a little tense—take the option of adding. (My rule of thumb, then, is "When in doubt, *add*": put your horse together and pinpoint the line.) It's better to take a little bit of a short stride and show the judge you can hop over the wall without a problem. (A lot of the Maclay horses that ran by the wall came right back and jumped it perfectly well—as they would have done the first time if given a more conservative approach!)

Looking back over this section of the course, the safest option from 4 to 7 is "outside all the way": around the outside of 3 to the outside 5 and 6 and bending a little to the outside to meet 7 dead center. The number of strides you get isn't important; what I want to see is a smooth ride with you influencing your horse correctly. I'm always looking for the workmanlike rider who absolutely has the right pace and the right rhythm, who meets the center of every jump and shows a safe, secure, beautifully executed, deliberate ride. Even at—*especially* at—the Olympic level, "lucky" or "crazy" or "excited" won't do. The kind of rider everybody wants to see on the Team is the one who's going to jump each jump and look very secure and definite—no racing around and jumping off one hind leg in the rush and excitement of pressure.

After fence 7 comes a little bit of a breather (not much, but a little bit) to 8: a straightforward triple bar with no ground line—nothing complicated. The track from 7 to 8 is a long gallop around the end of the ring and around fence 11. If you're on a green horse that might spook at three rails and no ground line, you may want to go for a nice, conservative jump here. But what I'd like to see you do, if you can, is show yourself off by galloping down to 8 and being a little brilliant. After the wall, where you may have had to put your horse together to make sure he jumped the wall neatly, I'd like to see you relax, take a deep breath, let him gallop on, and find the distance to 8 out of stride (especially if your ride has been conservative to this point; if you started out aggressive, on the other hand, jumping this fence out of a normal pace would give you a chance to show the judge a different type of ride).

Following the triple bar, you'll want to begin gradually collecting your horse because the next line (fences 9, 10, and 11) begins with a very steady two strides—thirty-three feet, three feet short of a normal two—between a pair of verticals, followed by a long three strides (fifty-two feet) to 11. Coming to 9, I'll want to see you collecting your horse and putting him together before you come out of the turn, especially after the gallop to 8; you want to show the judge that you understand the distance is thirty-three feet, not thirty-six or thirty-eight. You want to jump in slowly, have an easy two strides to fence 10, and then pick up the pace to 11. If you jumped in with too much impulsion and chipped at 10, you'd make the distance longer and have to run to 11.

(A lot of people did that in the Maclay: they cantered up with too much pace from 9 to 10, leaving their horses to collect themselves, so the poor horses chipped in the two strides. Were they worrying about the long three from 10 to 11? Maybe—but fifty-two feet is only four feet longer than a normal three. If they'd remembered their course chemistry, they'd have realized that, this late in the course, all they'd have to do to get the three would be to relax.)

The route from 11 to 12, the final fence, is around a few bushes that obscure the view of 12, which is a rather startling yellow and black wall oxer (but which, like 8, you could let your horse take a look at on your opening circle). The biggest thing to remember about 12 is that it's on a track away from the in-gate, at the end of your course, and a lot of horses will have started thinking "Can we stop now?" after 11.

I put those bushes on course so that you couldn't get locked into a specific number of strides from 11 to 12. I wanted you to come farther down the ring before turning and jump 12 as a whole new jump, not part of a line. Riding to it, you know it's yellow and it could be spooky, so you should think a bit aggressively, keeping your horse in front of you through the turn. (I'd award Brownie points for using your stick on his neck through the turn and maybe even giving a little cluck to tell him he's not finished, that there's another jump coming.)

It's very important that you look in early—on top of 11 you should be looking at 12—and *keep* looking as you come by the bushes, maintaining the rhythm and keeping your horse in front of your seat and leg, using a cluck if needed. If he's on the aids and you're using your head, it shouldn't be a big production: *feel* the rhythm, *feel* for whether he's in front of your leg or spitting out the bit and coming behind. If he's spooking, add a stride and collect him, packaging him to make it work.

In the Maclay, a number of horses came around the turn and stopped dead at 12, then came back and jumped it fine. What that told me was that they wouldn't have stopped if they'd been presented properly. Some horses spooked and then jumped; their riders weren't awake enough to see ahead of time that this was a place for the outside rein against the neck, the outside leg, the cluck, the spur—that they'd need to ride aggressively early to prevent the spook. Some horses were obviously afraid of the wall—but I think that, in a championship, riders should be able to get their horses to jump a spooky obstacle.

Summing Up

The course I've just taken you through asks many, many questions—but they're all questions we've answered somewhere earlier in this book: bending lines, forward lines, short lines, turns, a high crossrail, a simple triple bar, narrow jumps, short to long distances, long to short, options such as choosing a more direct or a more bending line . . . Being able to answer those questions is what effective horsemanship is all about.

In the Maclay, most of the riders who made mistakes on this course had weak basics. Some riders came in and looked beautiful on the circle but went over the first fence with their hands buried in the neck and their lower legs swinging, looking at their horses' ears instead of the next fence. They told me right away that they didn't have the basic skills to get around the course. One girl looked beautiful most of the way, but her heels were weak and not deep; she chipped up the neck at one jump because she had no leg and her horse wasn't out in front of her. A lot of riders' weaknesses showed up in the turning lines—to the big crossrail (fence 4), to the inside or outside narrow fences (5 and 6), to the angled wall near the in-gate (7), to the brightly colored final fence (12). Weak, ineffective position was one problem on the turns; for example, a rider might jump fence 11 with no leg, and with hands jammed into the neck instead of lifting the horse, need two to four strides to recover balance on landing, and miss the turn to 12.

Weak eyes were another: riders who didn't look in early enough didn't get the right line. Overdependence on the crest release caused a lot of problems: some people had trouble riding and guiding because they couldn't get their hands off their horses' necks; others got around the course but were so shakily balanced that they kept hitting their horses in the mouth. I saw a number of horses jump hollow through the short 9-to-10 distance because their riders hadn't slowed and balanced them through the preceding turn and now were pulling on their mouths on top of the fences.

If you have trouble with this course, *your* basics are the first thing to check. The most basic is mental readiness: are you going at the course with a positive, "can do" attitude, or is it more like "What if I can't"? Next, make sure your position isn't weak. Your body won't be able to do what your head tells it to if your legs are swinging or your hands are jammed in your horse's neck; if you can't control your body, you can't control your horse. Go back and work through the exercises that strengthen the places where you're finding problems; take your time, and don't push yourself ahead until you feel ready to move ahead.

Equitation at its best is a combination of effectiveness and style—no cowboying, jerking and pulling, but no posing and perching, either. In judging equitation, I look for the smoothness that comes from thinking ahead. If your basics are secure and you've worked out a mental blueprint of your ride—you come through the in-gate knowing not only what you want to do but why you want to do it—you'll be able to stick to your plan successfully or make smart changes when needed. *That's* equitation.

CHAPTER TWENTY-FIVE

JUMPER COURSES

A jumper course is similar to an equitation course in that the course design asks questions, but the questions are more challenging because the fences are. From the horse, a jumper course demands bravery, carefulness, scopiness, speed, and adjustability; from the rider, it demands skillful analysis, strategic thinking, quick responses, and effective riding.

Responding well to this level of challenge requires advance thinking and preparation. First of all, of course, you have to have a horse that's physically and mentally equal to the demands jumper courses are going to place on him. Second, you need to identify far enough ahead whether a particular competition toward which you're aiming will need an extra level of preparation. If you're going to have to gallop on big, big courses—at Spruce Meadows in Calgary, for example, or in Europe—you may need to spend several weeks building your horse's fitness so that he'll be equal to his work. If the weather has been consistently cold and windy, making your horse very fresh, you may need to cut back on his grain for a week or so or, if the weather is hot and humid, perhaps feed him more grain and vitamins, before taking him to an indoor show. Third—as always—you need to know your horse so well that if anything starts to feel not right on course you can instantly assess what's different about him and/or about your surroundings—you're indoors, he's not all that fit, the weather's hot and muggy, et cetera—and try to do something to bring his performance back to where you know it can be.

The points we've just talked about are the underpinning for your success in jumpers, of course. They have to be attended to well in advance of any competition—and if you're working conscientiously through my program and becoming the kind of *feeling* rider I look for, they will be. For the moment, then, let's say that they are and go on to getting you ready to do a jumper course.

Know What's Involved

Unlike equitation, the jumper division has classes run according to several different procedures, so besides finding out what the time allowed is and whether it's tight, for both the first round and the jump-off, be sure you know which kind of class you're entering. Is it a power and speed class, where you jump six or eight fences and then go right on to the speed portion? Is it a Table II-2B, where you do one round and then stay in the ring and jump off if you're clean? If it's a speed class, is it judged by faults converted into seconds or by fastest clear round? If it's a pair relay, is there a baton you have to pass? If it's an FEI class, are you permitted to get back on if you fall off? Part of being a competitive rider is making sure you know the rules of the game.

Analyze the course chemistry, taking into account all those factors that I talked about back in Part VI, "Show Preparation." The chemistry is even more important in jumpers than in hunters or equitation because the whole course is more challenging—and course chemistry is one of the ingredients the course designer uses to ask the questions. If the course is in a little ring, any line that walks long is going to *be* long, and some that walk normal may turn out to ride long because your horse can't get as good a running start or he feels cramped in the turns and gets backed off his fences. But in a big, open field a line that walks a little long may turn out to ride as a normal distance because the horse feels safe opening up his stride more.

Look at the placement of the jumps, and also at their composition: liverpools are spooky fences to a lot of horses; Swedish oxers require precise positioning of your horse; flat jump cups, flimsy gates, and light rails pose the threat of easy knockdowns and may require you to take a little more contact and a little more time to jump them carefully. Look at the footing, and find out how it's been holding up. While you'll do best using small studs on your horse's shoes in a sandy ring, like the one in the Dixon Oval at Devon, you'll do better with medium to large studs that are a bit pointed on a slick grassy or muddy course. On good grass footing, small studs in front and medium behind usually work well.

Think about the problems the time of day may pose—your horse may not see the fences as well in the long shadows of early morning or late afternoon, or under artificial lights at night. Look for places that are likely to provoke a spook, and look as well for places where you can really gallop or shave off a turn to make up time if the time allowed is tight. (You'll keep these considerations in mind as you watch other horses' trips before yours, of course, and factor in what you see happening along with what you expected to happen.)

By going to a variety of shows, you'll get to know the characteristics of different designers' courses—who uses a lot of liverpools, who favors a tight "time-allowed" and who's more generous, and so on. Eventually you'll reach the point where you have a pretty good idea of the kind of course you'll be facing as soon as you see the designer's name on the prize list, and that may influence your decision about whether to fill in an entry blank.

Personally, I like designers whose courses flow, so that I can gallop and jump instead of constantly jumping and turning and turning. That's the kind of course I try to design, and it's the kind I prefer to compete over. In a week-long show, I also like to see the horses jumping better, not worse, toward the end of the week; a designer who builds courses so that this happens consistently is tops in my book.

Walking the Course

The course I've given you here is fairly simple and straightforward; depending on the height of the fences, it could be at any level. While there's nothing extraordinary about it, I think it provides a useful vehicle for letting you see how I think as I walk and then ride a jumper course.

Even before you walk into the ring you can begin assessing the course. It's in a medium-sized field, neither huge and galloping nor cramped, so the lines should ride pretty much as they walk. The ground is reasonably level and the footing is grass, so you'll add small studs in front and medium behind to your horse's shoes. I always advise riders to walk the jump-off course after walking the first round, because you won't get another chance. You can see the angles, places to turn or leave out a stride, where the timers are, and figure out how to deal with all these things *now*.

Fig. 302   When you enter the ring, start off by absorbing the general layout, looking for where the more challenging fences are set and whether the jump cups are flat, and keeping an eye out for anything spooky that you'll want to show your horse before you start. You see that there's a triple combination (9A, B, and C), a two-element combination of planks on flat cups (6A and B), and a liverpool (8). Be sure you know where the start and finish markers are.

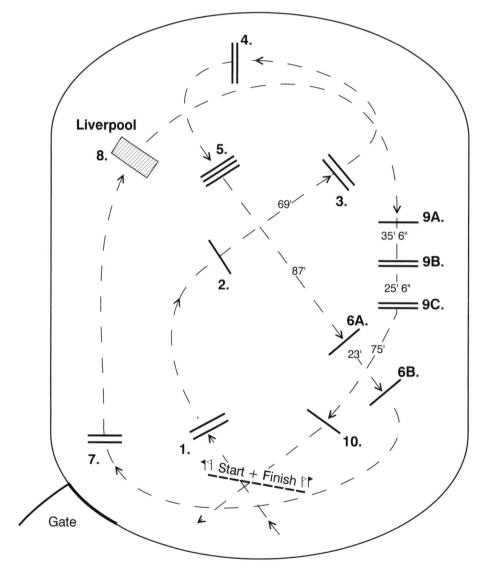

Fig. 302

You're allowed sixty seconds from the time the start whistle blows to ride through the start markers, and I like to use that time to show my horse the ring a little. (Jumper courses don't have dotted lines, so the limits are time and not crossing the start marker until you really mean to.) In this class, I'd canter right up between 7 and 1 to let him see the liverpool, then show him both combinations by coming down alongside 9A-B-C and cutting through between 6A and 6B. That gives him a chance to see the things that might spook him and gives me a look at them from his back, so we'll both be more comfortable in the ring.

From there I'd start for the first fence on whichever lead my horse was most comfortable; from the looks of this course, I'd start off the left lead—unless he happened to be a little sour about going past the in-gate. In that case, since the in-gate is at the bottom left, I'd avoid taking him past it by going the other way on the right lead.

Fence 1 is an oxer, and you'll be meeting it going away from the in-gate. I like to gallop loosely to my first fence in a nice bold rhythm to start off on a positive note. If you're too soft and sleepy to the first fence, you could cut down and hit the back rail. Some riders may not walk the distance from 1 to 2, since it involves a pretty big turn, but you'll probably feel better if you walk it *twice*—once for the first round, and once for the jump-off, where you'll be going from 2 to 4. (When walking these two fences for the jump-off, walk a straight line center to center—it's seventy-four feet, so it is two feet longer than a normal five strides.)

Your main objective between 1 and 2 is getting a straight line to 2—and the reason to be concerned about *that* is the sixty-nine-foot distance from 2 to 3, which is three feet short of a normal five strides. If you fly in over 2, you're going to have a problem bringing your horse back for 3—which you obviously don't want. Instead, gallop to 1 so that you have enough scope for the oxer, but then begin balancing your horse as you land from 1 so that you shorten his stride just a little, without any snatch-and-grab, as you ride straight from 1 and look in toward 2, waiting until you see a straight line from 2 to 3 to make your turn. Keep your slightly shortened stride to 2, meeting it at a fairly short distance—because it is a vertical, the slow short distance will not be a problem—and jump 2 a little slowly, land the same way, and maintain your shorter stride to 3.

Fence 3 is a Swedish oxer, so you want to be sure to get to the middle of it (and your horse may look at it a little, which could help you in maintaining the short stride). The left side is the high side; since the turn to 4 is a left turn, you'll pull a rail if you turn early or drift left before you complete the jump. By jumping 2 quietly, you'll be able to wait and even "ride" the Swedish a little, despite the tight distance: you can wait for the first couple of strides and then build a little in the last two. That way, you won't get to 3 backward and dead, and you'll be able to jump out with enough scope for the next fence.

Look toward fence 4 in the air over 3. Fence 4 is a narrow oxer, pushed in so that it's only about two and a half feet across—very tall and skinny, like a vertical—and at the end of the ring, where your horse may be a little distracted. When you land from 3, head over toward 4; then collect him and ride very, very straight to 4 off a short, active stride—but don't meet it dead, or your horse may cut down with his hind end and catch the back rail. (You may want to jump an oxer set up this way in the warmup ring, so that the fence doesn't catch him sleeping on course.)

From 4 to 5 is a neat, shortish turn to a triple bar—a wide jump—followed by a long distance from 5 to 6. After your quiet jump over 4, look at 5 and start picking up your pace right away. As you ride to 5, be sure to head for the center and find a line to 6A and B. You don't want to go way past your center line, but you also don't want to cut in—and you *do* want to pick up your pace because that triple bar is a little wide; you want to be able to gallop right to the bottom of it. (For the jump-off, though, you'll be jumping 5 and then turning left around the outside of 2 to fence 8—so when you walk the course, also get a number of strides for as direct a track from 4 to 5 as you think your horse can manage.)

The distance from 5 to 6 is eighty-seven feet, three feet longer than a normal six. If your horse is short-strided, or if you happen to catch the triple bar very dead, you may be better off adding a stride and doing the line in seven. In most cases, though, if you've galloped the triple bar, you probably won't have trouble making the six—just land and keep galloping, and let your horse get into 6A, to a tight distance.

Fences 6A and 6B are a pair of verticals, twenty-three feet apart (a tight one), made of planks on flat cups—so this is not a place where you want a long, flat jump in. Instead, you want to get in deep and snug to 6A at the end of the six and feel his mouth to get him coming back on his hocks and really curling around the first and second verticals. You want almost no leg and just enough contact. Too much leg and he'll jump through the planks instead of around them; you may even want to say "Whoa" inside the one-stride so that he waits.

You'll want to pick up the pace again after the planks. The long right-hand turn to 7 would be a very good place to make up time by shaving off the end of the ring, especially if the time allowed is tight. You'll need plenty of pace for 7, a big wide oxer, and you'll want to "keep going" because you're heading away from the in-gate, so gallop to and over 7.

From 7 to 8 (the liverpool), you have two options: you can go past the center line to 7 and ride a direct line to 8 (seven strides), or you can jump 7 straight and make a bending line to 8 (eight strides). If the time is tight, galloping the direct line is preferable. But if you're on a horse that might be afraid of the liverpool and duck out, jump 7 straight, stay out so you get a good straight line to the open liverpool, and add the stride. (Most course designers put in some options like this, and in principle the way to make the time allowed and jump big jumps is to gallop and jump, not to add and add. The more pace you have, the easier it is for your horse to jump big jumps; the more you add, the harder it is.)

Fence 8 is an open liverpool, with the water in front of the vertical; in most cases that's spookier for a horse than water beneath an oxer. If there's a brush box in front of the water to camouflage it, he won't look down quite as much as he will if the water is really open, but he'll *always* look down some. In the last few strides into the liverpool, what *you* will want to do is sit up, cluck, and give a little bit of an override to counteract the spookiness, keeping his head up and legging him whether you do the direct line or the bending line.

From 8 to the combination 9A-B-C, you have another long gallop to the other side of the ring—another place where you can make up a little time. You can gallop away from the liverpool and then get organized for the combination, which is a vertical-oxer-oxer with distances of thirty-five feet six inches to twenty-five feet six inches. Generally an oxer-oxer combination is scopey; whether the distances are tight or long, you tend to have to ride two oxers in a row a little stronger. After the 9A vertical, you'll want to keep building to ride out. This is a very different question from the one posed by 6A and B, which had a short distance and rode even shorter because it was vertical to vertical.

The distance from the 9A vertical to the first oxer is a little tight for a two-stride. After the strong forward ride to the liverpool, you will want a short stride to this triple. You need to jump in a little steady so that you give yourself room to ride to 9B, the first oxer; if you jump in too big, you'll get to that first oxer on a short stride and land short. The distance coming out is a little long, but if you jumped in a little steady and were able to leg your horse to the first oxer, you can just keep your leg on to ride out in one forward stride.

After riding aggressively out over 9C, your final fence is 10, a tall vertical at the end of the course, headed for the in-gate. The distance to it, seventy-five feet, walks three feet longer than a normal five strides. Because your horse will have just come out strong over the oxers, the distance won't be a problem. But because he's probably a bit strung out and on his front end from those oxers, you're going to need to make sure he sets himself up properly to curl over the vertical. Help him by adding a stride to make 9C to 10 a bending line, enabling him to jump up and round over the fence. (In walking this 9C to 10 for the jump-off, however, plan to try to make the five forward strides—that is, if you want to win. This late in the course, heading for the in-gate, the distance will most likely be fine; just focus on keeping your horse as up and balanced as you can.)

From 10 let him gallop through the finish markers—turning him *away* from the in-gate and pulling up away from the gate. As you pull up, you can bend him, or stop and back him, for his training, before you leave the ring—or if he went very well, simply walk out on relaxed long reins.

The Jump-off

The course for the jump-off includes fences 1, 2, 4, 5, 8, 9C, and 10. That means a lot of turns, so one thing you want to be sure to do in the schooling ring before you go back in is give your horse some turning work. If he's hard to turn to one side, practice jumping and

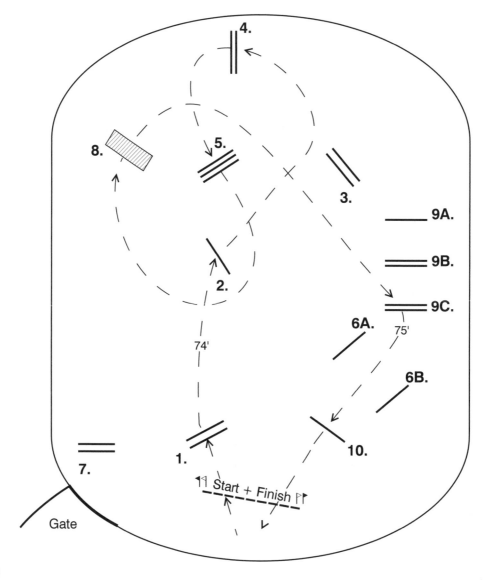

Fig. 303

turning to that side. You might also want to build a skinny oxer (like fence 4) and jump around and to the left a couple of times to get him sharp for that turn.

Fig. 303   Before you go in, be sure you know where the timers are, and be careful not to go between them in your entrance. As in the first round, when you ride in you'll want to take a little tour of the course before you start, so that you and your horse get some idea of where you're going. Canter up along the first line (1, 2, 4) and look at the turnback from 4 to 5; or go by 1, 2, and the liverpool, if you're concerned about that, and then turn back to 9C. Use your sixty seconds to look at your turns, find out how the footing is, and keep an eye out for rails bowed up or ready to fall off the edges of flat cups.

You'll want to break the timer beam for your start as late as possible; staying way to the left side as you go through the beam will give you the shortest distance from there to fence 1. Gallop past the timers and angle your jump over 1 to give yourself a straight line to 2 (although if you really gallop 1—the seventy-four feet is a nice five at a gallop—putting a bend in the line to 2 may not be an unreasonable option if you thought doing so would make 4 easier to get when you looked from 2 to 4 in your course walk; you don't want to approach 4 so sharply that you get a run-out). You also have to decide how much of a shot you want to take at 4, way up there in the end of the ring. You can make some time by galloping away from 2, looking for your line to 4, and not taking back; keep galloping and reorganize your horse only as much as you need to in front of 4.

On top of fence 4, think "very direct to 5" and look at it. If you have a horse that turns well in the air, you might ask him to begin his turn now—but remember that this is a skinny oxer and he might cut down too soon, so you may be safer to jump, land, and then turn. In any case, don't let him bulge way out—use your outside leg.

After 5 comes another stretch where you can gallop away, keeping your eyes on 8. Here again, it's up to you how much of a shot you think you can take turning back to 8. If your horse is a little chicken about liverpools, stay a bit wide; if he's likely to duck out, keep riding until you see the line that lets you aim him as squarely at 8 as you can. Keep galloping through the turn, your eyes glued on 8, your outside rein against his neck, and your leg on; look right to the center of 8 and ride it strong, keeping his head up a little bit, and land galloping.

Fences 9A and 9B will be gone, so you have the option of either cutting inside 3 for the fast track to 9C or going around it to the outside for the more conservative approach. Whichever route you choose, the distance is too great to worry about a number; just keep thinking "Forward"—and aim for the right side of 9C because you want the shortest possible distance from there to 10.

The distance from 9 to 10 is three feet long for a five-stride line. As I mentioned earlier, this late in a jump-off, after the long gallop from 8 to 9C, it probably won't even end up that long—unless you make the mistake of angling your jump at 9C from right to left too much and bulge out to the left on landing, in which case you'll have to add a stride to 10. The ideal, then, is to jump the right side of 9C and then go as straight as you can to 10, galloping from there to break the timer beam as soon as you can—which probably means going either straight or just a little to the left.

Even though you've raced through the timers, don't stop now. Turn your horse away from the in-gate, as always, and pull him up away from the gate. Then let him walk out of the ring on a long rein.

VIII.

GOALS

CHAPTER TWENTY-SIX

From the time I started riding, as a child, I wanted to compete in the Olympic Games. I didn't tell anybody, because back then I didn't think I could ever make that dream a reality, but I really wanted to do it nonetheless. I knew there were some obstacles in the way—I didn't have all the money in the world for horses and, growing up on the West Coast, I felt my chances of ever making a U.S. team were next to impossible. Only a couple of West Coast riders had ever gone to the Olympics. But I did have tremendous desire and willingness to work hard. Somehow those things helped me be in the right places at the right times, and with a lot of planning and hard work—and a lot of help from people who saw my desire—I ended up realizing my dream. That's why I honestly believe that if you want something badly enough, and you're willing to be patient, open-minded, and hard-working, you can find a way to achieve it.

MAKE SURE YOUR
GOALS MAKE SENSE

Having a goal to work toward gives you a sense of purpose; it helps get you going on that rainy Saturday morning when you'd really rather sleep in than go down to the indoor arena and practice your flat work. But before you adopt a goal, be sure it makes sense for you in terms of who you are, what you can reasonably expect to do, and what you're willing to do; otherwise, you'll just end up frustrated and miserable. Don't let anybody else tell you what your goal should be—not your mother, not your coach, not your friend, not your spouse. You can't achieve a goal that's somebody else's; only if it belongs to you, and you've committed to it, will you work for it the way you'll need to if it's anything meaningful.

Remember, too, that you can only do what you can afford to do in terms of both money and time. I was pretty single-minded about my aims from very early on: I knew riding was what I wanted to do with my life, so I tailored everything else around it—and recognized that the kind of self-discipline required to get me where I wanted to go would mean other parts of my life would have to take a back seat. I'm not the only kind of rider there is, though; you, for instance, may be a rider and also a student, and/or a spouse, and/or a parent, and/or someone with a career. That means budgeting your time (which requires its own kind of self-discipline!), so that you don't shortchange the rest of your responsibilities, and defining your riding goals so that you're not asking the impossible of yourself.

For example, if you can only spend an hour and a half a day on your horse, or if the horse you can afford reaches the pinnacle of his achievement over three-foot-six fences at local schooling shows, you know it's unreasonable to aim for the Amateur Owner title at the National Horse Show. What's not unreasonable, though, is to resolve to make the full ninety minutes quality time, every time—to clear your mind of all the distractions from the rest of your life and concentrate on the job you're doing. And what else is not unreasonable is to aim for the two of you to do well consistently in those three-foot-six classes. Whatever goal you set yourself is worthwhile if it gives you something to stretch a little for and to take pride in once you reach it.

Desire makes a terrific difference in whether people achieve their goals. The people you see competing for the United States Equestrian Team aren't there just because they had the money to buy the fabulous horses and fly all over to compete. Plenty of other people have those resources and don't go anywhere particular in their riding. The difference is the willingness to take those advantages and *work* with them. (Or, in the case of some of us, like me, to find ways to compensate for not having those advantages. I wasn't a naturally talented rider, and I had friends who were very talented and a lot wealthier, but they didn't have the same degree of desire.) Success depends on what you have inside you.

THINK BACKWARD
TO PLAN AHEAD

Although riding in the Olympics was my goal from pretty close to the beginning, that wasn't all I set my sights on. If it had been, I could have gotten discouraged and given up—because it took a pretty long time to see real progress toward that goal. Most of us need not just long-term goals but also intermediate ones that build toward the final goal—and that let us have a sense of achievement when we reach them and can move on to the next step in the process.

Finding the right intermediate goals is to some extent a process of working backward: what do you have to do to be able to reach that big goal? In my situation, for example, I had to figure out the kind of horse I needed—I was lucky to find a great one, and owners who were willing to buy and keep him for me; then I had to figure where and when to compete him, when not to, when to go to Europe, when not to go to Europe, all the way up to the Olympic trials. To succeed at the trials, I needed luck, too—and I'm thankful that I had enough to be picked. From there, the big goal of the Olympics was in plain sight—but even then I had little goals along the way: making my horse fit enough, keeping him sound, and so on.

Long before trying for the Olympics was anything like a reality for me, of course, there were other goals that could lead me that way if everything worked out well. First I had the goal of doing well in the hunters and equitation as a junior. When I'd established my basics and was doing well there—so that I knew I was good enough to go on—my next goal was to ride the jumpers. As a junior jumper rider, I really idolized the riders competing in the open-jumper and grand prix divisions; that was the next goal. And there again I was lucky; people saw my desire, and that I had developed ability to back my desire—and so, while I was still a junior in California, I was given the chance to start riding open jumpers.

(As for equitation, I didn't like it at first when I was a junior, but the better I became, the more I enjoyed it. And once I really could do it, I formed a goal of riding at the AHSA Medal finals in Harrisburg—which, fortunately, was only twenty minutes away from my grandmother's home in York; she helped with the trip and I stayed with her. Coming from California, I knew it was unrealistic to think of winning the equitation, but I figured getting a ribbon *was* a realistic goal. And that's what I did, taking ribbons both at the Medal finals and at the ASPCA Maclay finals in New York. Jimmy Williams, my trainer in California, found a horse for me to lease on the East Coast the first year. Once my parents saw that I was dedicated enough and that, yes, I did have a chance, they paid to send my own horse the next year.)

STEPPING-STONE
GOALS

Set your goals in relationship to your level of riding; as your expertise increases, your goals can become more ambitious.

It's important to start with small, achievable goals: to go in the ring and get the numbers (do the right number of strides in every line); to be able to come out after you complete your course and tell your teacher what happened (a lot of riders end up so out of breath that they don't even remember!). Once you have the number of strides correct, aim to do the course smoothly, keeping your heels down and getting your lead changes. The goals can be that simple.

When you can get around nicely, you may find yourself saying, "I ride pretty well, but my horse isn't good enough for the next step." (Don't sell him short, though; most of us need a safe, sensible school horse to start. You shouldn't be trying to drive a Porsche when you're only ready for a Volkswagen.) Now, if your goals and your finances permit, you can look for a nicer horse that can be competitive at the A-rated shows (and that you might have ruined if you'd bought him a year ago). And maybe at this point you should consider whether to move on to a new teacher—a terrific kindergarten teacher may not be a good sixth-grade teacher, and almost certainly won't be as effective a college teacher as somebody who's experienced in teaching at college level. For a different range of goals, you may need a different teacher.

Are you laying down consistent, beautiful hunter trips now? If you have the time and the resources, maybe your goal is to go to the National Horse Show. Don't just commit to that, though; think it out: can your career, your home life, your education take the stress of a year getting ready for New York? Talk over with your trainer how many shows you'll need to go to to qualify; then, if this goal is really important enough to you, tell your spouse or parents and/or college adviser and/or boss what you're going to need to do. Plan *way* ahead. (Make sure everybody understands and agrees up front; otherwise, you're in for misery and frustration instead of support and encouragement.) Keep being realistic: If this is your goal, you're going to need more lessons; you're probably also going to need a professional to show your horse for you to keep him tuned. Make sure you can swing it, in terms of time and money, before you get in.

Switching the scene a little, maybe you're a junior rider who wants to make the junior-jumper team from your region that goes to Harrisburg. Well, then, you have to be as good as or better than everyone else in your AHSA zone. That means being seen by the selectors—and where are the selectors going to be? Which horse shows count? And is your horse really good enough? He is? Good. Now, do you have the desire to go and outride everybody? Or if he isn't—maybe he's a little junior jumper—can you afford to buy a better horse, or can you lease one to compete this year?

If you think about where you want to go and how you can get there, and if you want to get there enough to plan your steps logically and follow out your plan, there's a good chance that you'll get there. If you don't, you probably won't.

GOALS TO KEEP YOU GOING

What I've just been talking about are sort of medium-range goals—and underlying them are the small, simple, everyday goals you can use to achieve some success almost every day. Identify the elements you need to solidify to make yourself a better rider and your horse a more dependable performer, and work on them one at a time.

For example, if you have a made horse, you can focus mainly on yourself. In the early stages of your partnership (the stages we talked about in Part I, "Basic Flat Work"), your goal for a particular day might be something as simple as keeping your eyes up or your heels down. When you've turned the basics of position into good habits, you might tell yourself, "Today I'm going to work for an hour without stirrups." Or, if you worked really hard yesterday, "The two of us could use a break, so today we're going to go on a trail ride that we can both enjoy." (Having fun with your riding should *always* be a goal; if all you do is work, work, work, neither you nor your horse will enjoy it. If you qualify for the National Horse Show but end up as a burned-out rider on a burned-out horse—which, sadly, I've seen happen—what good is that? I've always said that if riding ever stops being fun I'll stop doing it.)

If you're having a jumping school today, start out by working on whatever it is you learned in your last lesson; aim to do it better. When you've achieved that, go on to something else. Maybe you've been working on getting the numbers; today you're dependably getting six strides down the six-stride line and five down the five-stride, so you say, "Okay, now I'll work on my release and numbers." Set your goals in doable increments.

How about if you're the more experienced one and your horse is the greenie? Your goal for today could be to get him light and listening. Once you have him soft and responsive, you'll have achieved your goal for the day—and you can wind up your work session on a relaxed note. If I'm riding a horse that's never really been collected before and he manages a big improvement in thirty minutes, that's great—and if he doesn't, but I can feel he's a little less on his forehand by the end of the session, that's okay too: at least he's a little closer to the goal of collection.

How about a day when you *don't* progress? (It happens to everybody.) You can still be learning; so can your horse. And every day, but especially on a day when you haven't made progress, find a good note to finish on—something you know you can do. Maybe you've been trying to get your horse a little lighter, but he's still pretty heavy; finish up with some-thing like lengthening and shortening, or galloping and then collecting, that gives him a real change and lets the two of you end up feeling good about each other. Even if it wasn't the best day, don't walk away thinking, "Oh, he was horrible today." Tell yourself, "It'll be better tomorrow." And if you approach tomorrow's work with that positive attitude, it will.

Staying upbeat on down days is easier for a professional like me, with lots of horses to ride, than for somebody who just has one. Maybe I have ten rides in one day at a show; I have one winning round, five really good ones, and one really bad one. I could choose to take the bad one "home" with me, but I don't; I analyze what went wrong and learn from it, and then I put it away. It's just another day at the office.

That's harder to do when your only ride goes badly, but you need to. If the horse you have now (because he's the one you can afford now) is a limited fellow that always has four faults or rubs a couple of rails, don't let yourself fret about his doing what he always does. Look at your own riding instead—and if you find elements *there* that are improving, you have cause for encouragement. If you see something that needs working on, great—you have something you can make better for the next time.

All of us, the top pros included, actually lose more than we win; statistically, we *have* to. But I don't dwell on that fact, and neither should you. Instead, when you ride through the in-gate, tell yourself, "I could win this one—and I'm sure going to give it my best effort!" If you do win, great. If you don't, but you can look back and say you rode the best you knew how, you've achieved a goal even without a ribbon. And if you can look back and see some-thing you could have done better, you have a head start on next time.

THINK BIG

If your desire to become a better rider has taken you all the way through my program—if you've had the patience and persistence to work on all the exercises I've given you—I hope that by now you're a good way further along toward that goal. "Becoming a better rider" is a funny kind of goal, of course: you can reach it every day, but it's always there for you the next day—because you can always be better than you are. (That's why I love this sport, and why I can't imagine ever getting tired of it.)

I hope, too, that you're clearer now about the rest of your riding goals—what it makes sense for *you* to work toward, and how to get there. Whether that's a Medal or Maclay ribbon, a grand prix trophy, or a consistently good amateur-owner round at the annual charity show for your local hospital, I wish you desire and persistence in sufficient measure to take you there—because I truly believe that if you have the desire you'll attain your goal, whatever it is.

INDEX

Warmup, 266–67, 275–76
   mental, 273–75
Weight (of horse), 26
Whip, 119
   avoiding, 58, 112
   in basic jumping, 58, 61
   in-and-out and, 277
"Whoa," 61, 104, 151
   in advanced jumping, 196

in showing, 285, 287, 288, 306
Williams, Jimmy, xii, 13, 188, 259, 316
   quotes from, xv, xvi, 53
Working canter, 149, 156
Working trot, 40
   transition from sitting trot to, 144–45
Working walk, 119
Wrists, 13